THE SHAPING VISION

Imagination in the English Novel
from Defoe to Dickens

THE SHAPING VISION

*Imagination in the English Novel
from Defoe to Dickens*

‡‡‡‡‡‡‡‡‡‡‡‡‡‡‡‡‡‡‡‡‡‡‡

ROBERT ALAN DONOVAN

Cornell University Press

ITHACA, NEW YORK

Copyright © 1966 by Cornell University

CORNELL UNIVERSITY PRESS

First published 1966
Second printing 1967

Library of Congress Catalog Card Number: 66-14021

PRINTED IN THE UNITED STATES OF AMERICA
BY VALLEY OFFSET, INC.
BOUND BY VAIL-BALLOU PRESS, INC.

To Hope

Acknowledgments

This book had its beginning in a course in the English novel which I taught at Cornell University several years ago, and some of my earliest obligations are to students who debated, and thus helped to shape, the ideas and interpretations offered here. During the five years that this book has been in preparation I have also incurred many deep obligations, both for professional assistance (most of which will necessarily remain anonymous) and for more casual criticism and advice from friends and colleagues.

To Mark Spilka of Brown University I am indebted for incisive and detailed criticisms of the entire manuscript. I am grateful to Ephim Fogel, William M. Sale, Jr., and Walter Slatoff, of Cornell University, and to William R. Keast, formerly of Cornell, now of Wayne State University, for help of various kinds. Among many associates at the State University of New York at Albany who took a friendly interest in my work and offered help or encouragement I wish to thank especially Walter Knotts, Audrey and James Kouvel, Thomson Littlefield, and Judith Horton Campbell (now of Sweet Briar College). To my wife I owe the greatest debt of all, for never-failing support that I cannot adequately acknowledge or even specify.

I am grateful to the Research Foundation of State University of New York for timely assistance in the form of a summer research fellowship.

Two chapters have appeared previously in slightly different form. I wish to thank *Studies in English Literature* and the Rice University Press for permission to reprint "The Problem of Pamela, or, Virtue Unrewarded," and *ELH* and the Johns Hopkins Press for permission to reprint "Structure and Idea in *Bleak House*."

R. A. D.

Albany, New York
September 1965

Contents

THE SHAPING VISION

Imagination in the English Novel
from Defoe to Dickens

‡ CHAPTER I ‡

Vision and Form

. . . 02946 85697 26734 47829 76603 47526
70100 . . .

—H. Burke Horton, *Random
Decimal Digits*

Formal analysis is a characteristically modern approach
to the criticism of the novel. It differs as much from the
leisurely and urbane commentary, with its catalogue of memorable scenes and characters, that we associate at its best with
Saintsbury, as Joyce differs from Fielding. No doubt the fact
that the novel has grown more subtle, complex, and difficult,
that it often requires the sort of explication that analysis is so
well fitted to provide, adequately explains why the one critical
technique has yielded to the other. No one can get through
Ulysses without a key, but *Tom Jones* is immediately accessible to anyone who can read. On the other hand, the subtle
techniques of formal analysis can feed only on a work that
offers them scope, and this kind of criticism therefore demands
(and chiefly values) works of considerable technical sophistication, in which there is a more or less conscious adjustment of
means to ends. Understandably, then, modern critics have
tended toward an exclusive preoccupation with the contemporary novel, leaving more primitive works for the historical
scholar who is less interested in literary form than in social and
intellectual backgrounds.

The attitude of much, possibly most, modern criticism toward the English novel from its beginnings, early in the eighteenth century, to the middle of the nineteenth century— let us say from the earliest productions of Defoe to Dickens's arrival at maturity—has ranged from outright contempt to a kind of patronizing condescension. The critical stance of F. R. Leavis is too contentious and opinionated for him to be taken as perfectly typical; nevertheless, in spite of its truculent defiance of critical orthodoxy, *The Great Tradition*, in its denigration of the novels of the eighteenth century, in its assumption of the natural superiority of the novels of the nineteenth, and especially of the twentieth, centuries, and in its choice of novelists within "the great tradition" (Austen, Eliot, James, Conrad, and eventually Lawrence), may fairly be taken as representative, in substance at least, of mid-twentieth-century critical opinion. Jane Austen is the only novelist before 1850 to be considered worthy of serious critical attention, the only one to make an art of storytelling by bringing form and substance into meaningful relation to each other. The rest, from Defoe to Dickens, have chiefly "historical" importance, and can make few claims to artistic values which are not simple and obvious.[1]

Ironically, there are reasons to suggest that modern analytical criticism, for all its finesse, is really not very well equipped to deal with the novels of the eighteenth and early nineteenth centuries, if only because they do not necessarily, and certainly not overtly, share its presuppositions about form.[2] One cannot very well pretend that *Moll Flanders* is a work of the same kind as *The Portrait of a Lady*, and it would be absurd to bring the assumptions of Jamesian criticism to bear on a novel by Defoe. Criticism does not create its own values or determine a priori the questions that ought to be raised about a work; it derives both its values and its questions from an existent body of works, in the manner illustrated by Lubbock's building a critical edifice on the works of Henry James. But a serious problem arises when criticism turns its attention to works of a much earlier period. For the earliest stages of the English novel, perhaps even as late as 1850, no clear cut body of works can be defined, because the line of demarcation between novels and quasi-fictional literary forms like the rogue's biography or the periodical essay is still not clear. The critic apparently faces the impossible dilemma of taking books like *Moll Flanders* (or, for that matter, *Bleak House*) either as novels which aspire to the condition of Joyce or Henry James, or as something else altogether.[3] The criticisms of Smollett's *Humphry Clinker* illustrate some of the possible confusions. *Humphry Clinker* may be (and has been) read as a travel book, as an autobiography, as a collection of personal essays, as a nationalist polemic, as a comic romance, or as a parody.[4] If it is impossible to be sure whether a given work offers spurious history or real fiction, how is the critic to arrive at a rational judgment of it, or even to talk about it?

I think it is possible to approach the early novel without either contempt or condescension, but the approach of criticism, as distinct from historical scholarship, seems to me to require several assumptions which I should like to make explicit. I shall begin by stating these assumptions as simply and concisely as possible, and then proceed to discuss them:

1. Every novel is exactly what it is, not a shadowy and imperfect rendering of some unrealized ideal novel.

2. It is possible, and even desirable, to talk about a novel as a literary work.

3. The distinctive attribute of any literary work is form.

The first of these propositions is simply another way of saying that criticism must deal with the text that exists. It does not mean that every novel is perfect, or that we must abandon critical judgment for description. It does not even mean that we must be doctrinaire in our rejection of the intentional fallacy, for what the author intended may be a relevant consideration as long as we do not arbitrarily substitute the intention for the fact, or consider the aim instead of the result. The point is really a very simple one, so it ought to be unnecessary to insist on it except that critics persist in talking, not about the novel that editorial scholarship has provided them with, but about a novel that never existed at all—the one they assume the author was trying to write. Modern critics of earlier novels seem particularly disposed to fall into this error, no doubt because they often assume that their authors had very little idea of what they were doing. For more than a hundred years critics have commonly accepted the view, which seems to have been originated in the nineteenth century by Frederick Lawrence, that Fielding set out to write *Joseph Andrews* as a parody of *Pamela* but changed his mind in midstream and produced instead a quite different kind of novel. I cannot judge this statement as a description of the creative process by which Fielding produced *Joseph Andrews* (and I doubt whether Lawrence could either), but as a critical proposition it seems to me vicious. It sets up as a standard of judgment (in spite of Lawrence's readiness to forgive Fielding for what we are made to feel is a quite amiable inconsistency) a proposition about what the novel ought to have been, or aspired to be, that we have no means of verifying. David Cecil is guilty of a similar lapse, I believe, in assuming that the characters of *Mansfield Park* get out of hand and try to prevent Jane Austen from doing what she really wants to, and Wayne Booth verges on the same error when he attempts to deal, on internal evidence, with the question whether Sterne planned to write any more installments of *Tristram Shandy*.[5] To avoid guessing what the author might have done if he had taken more time, or revised more carefully, or not written so compellingly as to become a dupe of his own creative powers, I prefer to assume that every novel represents, as it stands, the full realization of its author's design, and I will surrender that assumption only when it leads me into contradiction or absurdity.

My second assumption is an attempt to distinguish between novels as imaginative constructs and as disguised autobiographies, histories, or travel books. I offer no rigorous theoretical definition of the term *novel* but am content, for the moment, so to call every work that has commonly been given that name. It ought to be fruitful, I believe, to assume that the novel is what I have called a literary work, meaning any work organized by a formal principle which is internal and self-generated, holding the reader inside, not carrying him beyond the work to something outside. I see no reason to exclude other, perhaps equally arbitrary, assumptions, and I am prepared to acknowledge that the works which I shall attempt to explicate in terms of their form might also be convincingly explicated in quite different terms. It would be both pointless and irrelevant, for example, to deny the utility or value of Martin Battestin's study of *Joseph Andrews* as a latitudinarian tract, or of John Butt's and Kathleen Tillotson's study of *Bleak House* as a topical portrait of a real society.[6] My own special concern, however, is with the novels qua novels, conceived as imaginative structures in which the subject matter does not give the form but fills it.

Both the foregoing assumptions are in a sense tautologies. The second proposition might have been stated, "A novel is a novel, not something else." The third assumption, however, goes beyond tautology and makes an assertion that though widely agreed upon, is hardly self-evident. "The distinctive attribute of any literary work is form." Before assenting to this proposition one must be clear about what it means, though the only term that it contains which is likely to prove at all ambiguous is *form*. In literary discussion the term usually occurs in one of two senses; either it refers to the *genre* or *kind* of a par-

ticular work, or it refers to the *structure* or *shape*. I should like
to give some attention to both these meanings of form, in order
to show that, though they are necessary to the concept of
literary form, they are not sufficient to it.

In the first meaning, form designates something which must
be located ontologically outside the work, and which I shall
hereafter refer to, for reasons of convenience, as *outer form*.
This conception clearly places form above and outside of
literature and is no less clearly a part of the assumption that
leads T. S. Eliot to declare that each new work of literature
not only joins but alters an existing tradition, as though *A
View from the Bridge* changed the nature of *Oedipus Tyrannus* by altering the form to which it belongs.[7] This is an in-
triguing notion to the literary historian or even to the synoptic
theorist, but to the practicing critic, whose concern is with
individual works, I am less sure of its utility. The concept of
outer form limits in peculiar ways the kinds of things it is
possible to say about literature and generally serves to redirect
attention from the concrete and specific to the abstract and
universal. Thus "*Macbeth* is a tragedy" is a statement that tells
us more about tragedy than it does about *Macbeth*. No doubt
it is useful to know that *Macbeth* is a tragedy, i.e., that it
belongs to the same tradition as *Oedipus Tyrannus* and *A
View from the Bridge*, but to deal fruitfully with *Macbeth*
it is much more important to be able to talk about the play
as though it were (as indeed it is) unique. It will be necessary,
in other words, to talk about the *inner form* of *Macbeth*.

Inner form would seem to be precisely what is specified by
the second meaning I have noted for the word "form," structure or shape, but these terms quickly reveal their inadequacy.
Some idea of structure is doubtless given by the notion of
outer form; to assert that *Macbeth* is a tragedy implies certain
aspects of its structure, as for example that it will end unhap-
pily, but to know its structure more intimately requires a close

look at the play itself. Such an act of inspection presupposes two things: some notion of form, to enable the seeker to recognize it, and a procedure for giving an account of it once it is found. One might begin by assuming that "form" here means the rationally explicable sequence of events or the intelligible pattern of ideas (*mythos* and *dianoia*).[8] The best way to describe such a sequence or pattern would obviously be to provide a synopsis of the plot of *Macbeth* sufficiently particularized to distinguish it from the plot of any other work, and sufficiently detailed to include all potentially significant ingredients. What emerges is not so much a synopsis as a paraphrase, or ultimately—and absurdly—an exact copy. There is nothing theoretically wrong with this procedure, except that it eventually goes back to the starting point, the play itself, and the goal of isolating the inner form of the work is no nearer than before.

Any further effort, obviously, must be directed toward giving the inner form without the content or matter being formed. The problem is a good deal easier to state than to solve; all that is necessary is to separate the form from the matter, or vice versa, for if matter can be isolated, what is left will be form. But what is theoretically simple proves in practice to be not simple at all. Is it possible to imagine a work without form? The existence of such a curiosity ought to demonstrate the feasibility of making a separation, and that it is at least conceivable seems to be supported by the existence of a theory of antiform. Yet I think it is readily apparent how difficult it would be to produce a work devoid of form—even more difficult, perhaps, than to produce a perfectly formed one. The most extreme example I can think of belongs, not to the world of art, but to that of mathematics. For various experimental purposes which all necessitate the selection of random samples, statisticians require a procedure of selection which will operate without any numerical, mechanical, or psychological bias. The simplest procedure in such cases is not to devise anew for each experiment elaborate techniques of ensuring random selection, but to make use of existing tables of random numbers of the kind illustrated by the epigraph to this chapter. These tables or "books" stand in an extreme relationship to the ordinary, literary kind of books in that they might be said to be devoid of form. It could even be argued, I suppose, that they are also without matter, on the grounds that numbers, being pure abstractions, are without substance, but the argument is specious, for numbers are real in much the same sense that the characters or events of a novel are real. They are equally, so to speak, adjectives without substantives. We merely suspend our disbelief and grant credence to "red" or "three" even when there is no reality so colored or quantified, in just the same way that we grant existence to the collection of attributes named "Uriah Heep" or "Mr. Micawber" without being convinced of the real existence of those people. The book of random numbers, then, does contain matter or substance in the same sense as *David Copperfield*.

The extraordinary difficulty of achieving formlessness is suggested by the fact that one cannot simply sit down and write out a list of numbers "at random." The ten digits of our number system are inevitably surrounded by connotations which unconsciously operate to bring about the selection of some and the avoidance of others, and so the effort to produce a random series is frustrated by an unconscious psychological bias which may also dispose of other claimants to formlessness: automatic writing, stream of consciousness, dreams, or just plain careless writing. Any numerical or arithmetical system made use of to defeat the psychological bias will of course introduce bias of another kind, and even a machine, such as a roulette wheel, is inadequate because the machine itself, as all roulette addicts know, has a bias in favor of certain numbers. The book of random numbers is actually a minor triumph of human ingenuity not unlike the platinum-iridium meter bar in the Bureau of Standards. The question that must still be dealt with, however, is whether, after all bias has been removed, the result may truly be said to be without form, and the answer, rather surprisingly, is No. Setting aside the point that books of random numbers constitute a genre and thus have what I have called outer form, it is readily apparent that we can describe the logic (which is only another way of saying the *dianoia* or thematic unity) of such a book in a number of ways, and surely only that which is without form and void defies description. For one thing, the book has a principle of exclusion; it does not contain 6⅞, or −2, or 23 (though these quantities could be derived), because it is arbitrarily limited to positive integers of one digit. Furthermore, the numbers are arranged in tabular fashion so that they are offered in order; one of them is first, another is last, and the rest are grouped in sequence from first to last. This arrangement is not quite what Aristotle meant by saying that a poem should have a beginning, middle, and end, but it does indicate an order that may not be arbitrarily altered without destroying the book's integrity and purpose. Finally, and I think most conclusively of all, the ideal of randomness is itself a structural principle which is as rigorous in its way as the rhyme scheme of a sonnet, perhaps even more so since as an ideal it is manifestly unrealizable.

The conclusion which seems to me irresistible is that a book without form is a practical impossibility and therefore also a theoretical impossibility, for I refuse to acknowledge a valid distinction between what is theoretically sound and what is practical. Since the time of Aristotle literary theory has contented itself with offering a schematized description of actual practice, and as such it cannot describe what does not exist. The further conclusion is not that the traditional distinction between form and content is meaningless or absurd, but that theoretical formulations might perhaps be modified to acknowledge the curiously intimate fashion in which they co-exist.[9] To do so, it will be helpful to discard some of the conventional metaphors for form and to substitute some new ones. "Structure" and "shape," the terms that at first sight seem to give the most exact ideas of inner form, are implied metaphors in the context of literary theory. "Structure" directs attention to the act of making or building, and thus likens an intellectual process to a physical one. Even a physical edifice may have an abstract structure, but the word generally brings to mind a framework of timbers or girders, and is thus in a second sense metaphoric, like various similar terms: skeleton, outline, framework, matrix. "Shape" is probably borrowed from plastic art, but even there it is metaphoric, for the shape of a vase or a statue is not the same thing as the form; the first is merely sensible, while the second is intelligible. Other terms or forms of expression are explicit or implicit metaphors, the most common, perhaps, being the metaphor of the container; the form of a literary work is the bag which holds the content. Now it is worse than useless, it is perverse, to object to the use of metaphor in critical discussion, and my purpose is to call attention to certain terms, not because they are metaphors, but because the analogies they suggest are inadequate to render the idea of inner form. All of the terms I have been discussing, in fact, give an idea of form as something perfectly separable, most often in a simple physical sense, from matter. These metaphors are useful, perhaps even unavoidable, in that they denote something which really exists, but their referent is still only halfway between outer and inner form. I shall designate this intermediate form by the most conveniently accessible term, "structure," in its most abstract sense, recognizing, however, that an adequate concept of what I have called inner form is still wanting.

To approach the notion of inner form requires some new metaphors. I begin from a point already, I hope, established—

that matter does not exist unformed. It follows that the inner form of any literary work is displayed in every part of it, but this still does not answer the two main questions: what is it? and what account of it can be given? The concept to be specified is that of an inner, cohesive force, not only holding together discrete particles of matter, but also determining the ways in which they can be combined to form what I have called structure. The metaphor that immediately suggests itself derives from the chemical concept of valence. What I am moving toward is an idea of the literary work as a kind of molecule, the overall structure of which is limited by the chemical properties of the particles or atoms it is composed of. But how, it may be asked, if the form is already inherent in the stuff, is form to be achieved? Obviously it will not do any longer to speak of the artist as imposing form on matter, as the sculptor imposes shape on the marble. The difficulty is a real one, for if matter, including the artist's matter, only exists formed, what is the artist's function? I should like to try to clear this difficulty away in one sweep by suggesting that the achievement of form, which is the heart of the artist's mystery, is inseparable from, and indeed identical with, the imaginative act of seeing which provides him with his subject matter in the first place; the artist's vision is itself the shaping instrument. As soon as the artist "sees" his subject, the form is in it, and also the potentiality of structure. Form, in fact, is if anything antecedent to matter, as singing is prior to songs and playing to plays. In this view form, that is, inner form, corresponds to vision, but not to intention. The inner form is the objective result, in the work itself, of the author's way of looking at experience, and it stands in the same relation to structure (or architectonics, which is the science of structure) as the imagination to fancy. Art is more than a craft; it is a way of seeing.

Something very like this concept of inner form seems to me to serve as the implied theoretical basis for Erich Auerbach's admirable *Mimesis,* a book which amply demonstrates what can be done with an analysis of literature in terms of its inner form, the kind of vision which shapes it. I think, however, that it might also be fruitful to explore the ways in which inner form is related to the other aspects of form, and particularly to structure. The kinds of form I have been talking about are not, after all, three different things, but three different aspects of the same thing. The critic who limits himself to the study of inner form, to the consideration of isolated passages and the analysis of "texture," may indeed serve the purposes of comparative study (Auerbach's interest is here), but he cannot very well be expected to come up with a satisfactory critical account of a whole work, any more than an anatomist could describe an elephant (or for that matter, a mouse) in terms taken from cellular physiology. Accordingly, I think it necessary to see what, if any, important or useful connection can be established between inner form and structure or genre.

Outer form, or genre, is wholly a matter of convention, though the convention may grow naturally out of the works of literature actually being produced. The important point is that outer form comes into existence with the first finished work in any new genre and is thus after the fact. When a genre already exists it exerts only a limiting effect upon new work, excluding many possibilities but prescribing none. I suspect, indeed, that whatever causal relation may be established is the other way round: the inner form of *Macbeth* is not what it is because Shakespeare set out to write a tragedy; *Macbeth* is a tragedy because that is the outer form consistent with the kind of vision it displays. Inner form is thus the cause of outer form, and a viable new genre comes into being only when a new outer form is needed to hold a new kind of vision. The novel itself, as Ian Watt has ably shown,[10] is to be thought of, not as owing its existence to the miscegenation of comedy and epic, but as the natural consequence of a new popular epistemology which looked upon the particulars of sensory experience as possessing a superior reality to the universals which could only be derived empirically from that experience. The distinctive outer form of the novel, in other words, came into being because of a new and distinctive view of what was real in experience.

A similar relation can be demonstrated between inner form and structure. Structure, according to my earlier account of it, is intermediate between inner and outer form; it is vision already objectified and made concrete in art, and at the same time it is the empirical basis of the conception of genre. A somewhat more vexing problem than understanding the theoretical relations of the various aspects of form is the establishment of a critical procedure in which the apprehension of inner form will assist us to the apprehension of structure or outer form, and vice versa. How can we estimate, that is, whether the inner form is perfectly commensurate with the structure that enfolds it? This, after all, is one of the main questions for criticism to answer.

One problem which has long occupied theorists of both literature and music—two arts which have in common a temporal dimension—is to explain the way in which one apprehends structure (or, for that matter, genre). It would seem to be impossible to make definitive judgments about either before hearing or reading the work in its totality. For nearly half its length *Measure for Measure* seems to hold in reserve the option of turning into a tragedy or a comedy, and it is difficult to know which it is to be until the play is over. A similar difficulty arises with musical works, for how are we to tell whether a given composition will be binary or ternary in structure until we have heard it through? And how, therefore, can we distinguish between the first movement of a sonata and a simple song? Northrop Frye's solution, that the *pattern* (i.e., the spatial organization) of music is to be approached through the printed score,[11] is I think less satisfactory than Sir Donald Tovey's. Tovey suggests that we can distinguish between binary and ternary forms by noting whether the first clause comes to rest on the tonic or not. If it does, then we do not need to hear the subsequent B and A clauses to reach the conclusion that we are listening to a ternary form, not a binary, and we are also aware, if we possess any musical sophistication, that we are hearing something structurally more elaborate than a song.[12] The principle opened up here seems to me to have almost limitless possibilities. What Tovey is in fact suggesting is that structural form is not only implicit but discernible in musical texture. A few bars of a Haydn quartet, he argues, do more than lay down a quite different musical idiom from a Bach fugue; they posit a whole new range of structural possibilities. In the terms of the present discussion, the inner form establishes and communicates the structure.

The applicability of this principle to literature may be briefly tested by comparing two short passages of widely different kinds to see whether the quickly apparent differences in narrative texture do not immediately reveal enormous potential differences in organization. I shall begin with the opening of one of the tales from *The Arabian Nights*. The first will do as well as any:

It has been related to me, O happy King, said Shahrazád, that there was a certain merchant who had great wealth, and traded extensively with surrounding countries; and one day he mounted his horse, and journeyed to a neighbouring country to collect what was due to him, and, the heat oppressing him, he sat under a tree, in a garden, and put his hand into his saddle-bag, and ate a morsel of bread and a date which were among his provisions. Having eaten the date, he threw aside the stone, and immediately there appeared before him an 'Efreet, of enormous height, who, holding a drawn sword in his hand, approached him, and said, Rise, that I may kill thee, as thou hast killed my son. The merchant asked him, How have I killed thy son? He answered, When thou atest the date, and threwest aside the stone, it struck my son upon the chest, and, as fate had decreed against him, he instantly died.[13]

By this time the reader knows, among other things, that this story is going to be simply constructed and relatively short. It is probably impossible to discount wholly the effect of the reader's prior knowledge and experience, for unless he is extraordinarily naïve and unsophisticated he can hardly fail to recognize the emergence of an all but universal folklore pattern. Still, I think that his expectations may be said to be formed by his response to and judgment about certain intrinsic qualities of the narrative. He recognizes, so to speak, that the valence of the narrative ingredients is too low to permit either a very large or a very complex structure. The unnamed hero, identified simply as a wealthy merchant, is thrust upon his destiny in fewer than two hundred words. The speed with which the predicament develops suggests the speed with which it is to be solved, and in fact the resolution turns out to be direct and abrupt. The tale achieves such magnitude as it possesses less by the extension or involution of its own substance than by the introduction of three new stories. Furthermore, the logic of the denouement is of a piece with that of the complication, for the 'Efreet "forgives" the merchant because three chance passers-by are able to tell wonderful stories. The texture of the opening paragraph obviously does not give away the ending, but it does announce something about the scale and complexity of the story and establishes the operative canons of probability.

Some further inferences are possible. The very sparseness and rapidity of the narrative exclude certain kinds of interest. For one thing, the narration is quite unconcerned with the psychological qualities of experience. The only phrases which hint at

the merchant's own thoughts or feelings—"to collect what was
due him" and "the heat oppressing him"—serve no purpose beyond the explanation of his actions; they simply give the
reason for his journey and the reason for his pausing to refresh
himself. And when the menacing figure of the 'Efreet confronts
him, not a single word indicates the merchant's surprise or terror; his question expresses only his curiosity to know the cause
of the threat. The narrative thus clearly lacks any adequate
basis for a fully empathic response to the merchant's experience,
and that experience is realized only in the most perfunctory
way. Another kind of interest which seems to be excluded is the
reader's potential moral involvement. The passage quoted asks
for no moral commitment from the reader at all, demands no
motion of praise or condemnation toward persons or actions.
Events proceed according to their own inscrutable logic, but
they do not "mean" anything in moral or human terms. It is
just this quality, the lack of moral point or tendency, that Coleridge chose to admire in the tale and led him to offer it as a
model of what he had attempted in "The Ancient Mariner." [14]
It is difficult, however, to like or approve a tale because of
what it excludes, so it seems likely that the exclusion produces,
or is attended by, certain positive qualities. In this case it is
clearly the reader's curiosity, his capacity for wonder and
surprise, rather than his humane or moral sentiments, that the
tale seeks to excite and sustain. The negative evidence is the
lack of a focus for moral or humane concern; the positive
evidence is the blunt, unapologetic introduction of supernat-
ural agencies obedient to necessities which remain occult. This
judgment rests on the evidence supplied by the quoted passage, but it may be relevant to point out that it is anticipated
by a frame story which makes the narrator's very life dependent on her playing successfully on her auditor's curiosity,
and it is confirmed by the subsequent development of the story,
for the merchant's own life is saved by the ability of the three

interlopers to outdo one another in telling improbable tales. Both inner form and structure combine in the statement of what may be thought of as the central theme of *The Arabian Nights*, the magical and persuasive powers of the narrative art.

It is not difficult to find narratives which differ radically from Shahrazád's simple but interlocking tales. Here, for example, is the well-known opening of *Pride and Prejudice*:

It is a truth universally acknowledged, that a single man in possession of a good fortune, must be in want of a wife.

However little known the feelings or views of such a man may be on his first entering a neighbourhood, this truth is so well fixed in the minds of the surrounding families, that he is considered as the rightful property of some one or other of their daughters.

"My dear Mr. Bennet," said his lady to him one day, "have you heard that Netherfield Park is let at last?"

Mr. Bennet replied that he had not.

"But it is," returned she; "for Mrs. Long has just been here, and she told me all about it."

Mr. Bennet made no answer.

"Do not you want to know who has taken it?" cried his wife impatiently.

"*You* want to tell me, and I have no objection to hearing it."

This was invitation enough.

"Why, my dear, you must know, Mrs. Long says that Netherfield is taken by a young man of large fortune from the north of England; that he came down on Monday in a chaise and four to see the place, and was so much delighted with it that he agreed with Mr. Morris immediately; that he is to take possession before Michaelmas, and some of his servants are to be in the house by the end of next week."

"What is his name?"

"Bingley."

"Is he married or single?"

"Oh! single, my dear, to be sure! A single man of large fortune; four or five thousand a year. What a fine thing for our girls!" [15]

This is clearly a whole new order of fiction, and it is scarcely possible to find any common ground at all, except what is provided by the general observation that both specimens belong to a story-telling art. In spite of the relative tameness of its subject, Jane Austen's story is obviously more dramatic than Shahrazád's; it is more detailed (the characters have names and personal idiosyncrasies), and the reader is brought closer to the action by the finer texture of the style, and by the devices of representation. The dialogue in both stories serves the purposes of exposition by telling the reader what he needs to know. But while the dialogue in the first story is nothing more than exposition, in the second story it becomes the actual stuff of the narrative. Here the dialogue succeeds in doing what it fails to do in the earlier example: realizing the confrontation of two people and rendering the thrust and parry of real conversation. Even Mr. Bennet's silences are made to contribute to this process of dramatization.

The specificity and dramatic qualities of Jane Austen's art are obvious enough, and have been commented upon many times before. What may be less obvious is the way in which the inner form revealed in this opening page serves to determine the structural possibilities of the story. Unlike the *Arabian Nights* tale with its flavor of improvisation, permitting us to infer only that the story will be simple, improbable, and short, the opening of *Pride and Prejudice* gives away overtly and at once the full range of the novel's concerns, and it supplies a powerful hint about the shape of the plot. Shahrazád's narrative seems to acknowledge no regulating law at all, but Jane Austen begins with an aphorism that supplies a conceptual framework for the narrative to follow: "It is a truth universally acknowledged, that a single man in possession of a good fortune, must be in want of a wife." The relevance of character and incident to an explicit shaping idea at once becomes clear. It does not matter that the aphorism is plainly ironic, for though the "universality" of its truth may be doubted, its relation to subsequent events is unaffected. The irony does, however, complicate the narrative texture, multiplying all the possible meanings by two.

But lest the reader assume too readily that the story to come will provide a straightforward demonstration of the truth of the aphorism, Jane Austen introduces another kind of complication in the dialogue between Mr. and Mrs. Bennet. The reader is here made aware of very subtle tensions that pull athwart the main uncertainty of the novel: will one of the Bennet girls get Mr. Bingley, or will she not? The reader must recognize that the opposition of different orders of sensibility in the brief conversation between Mr. Bennet and his lady is premonitory of a range and kind of complicating forces that will not permit a simple or easy resolution, and he knows that the story he is entering upon can easily sustain, out of its own momentum, the narration that will fill the 400-page volume he holds in his hand. In the terms of my earlier analogy, the opening bars of this composition contain the thematic richness to allow, and even to require, a full development, and they are stated in such a way as to lay down at least the general outlines of that development.

It would be absurd to suppose that so delicate a matter as criticism can be undertaken by rigorously applying generalizations about form, no matter how firmly they may be grounded, and I have no intention, in the essays which follow, of using a doctrinaire formula or a wholly a priori method of analysis. Criticism may begin anywhere—with a focus of irritation within the work or a prevailing critical judgment about it, with a bothersome word or phrase as well as with a generalized proposition—and its conclusions cannot be forced. Nevertheless, the critic who would not be wholly subjective must be guided by reasoned convictions about the art he proposes to discuss, and I have accordingly tried to make clear the assumptions which have, with varying degrees of closeness, directed the studies which follow. Before proceeding to specific cases, however, I should like to summarize briefly the theoretical position I have been developing.

Central to the critical discussion of literature is the concept of form, of which I distinguish three aspects: outer form, structure, and inner form. Outer form, or genre, is conventional and extrinsic and may be predicated without change of any number of literary works, as "picaresque novel" may describe *Gil Blas, Don Quixote, Roderick Random,* and many other particular works. As its name implies it is inevitably abstract and generalized and may be thought of as that portion of any work which is common to all works of the same kind. Its primary utility as a concept is thus for the literary historian or the synoptic theorist. Structure, which exists in literature as *mythos* or *dianoia* (plot or theme), is the particular which is universalized by outer form, but it too can be abstracted from the work it forms, as the frame of a building, for example, can be considered apart from the siding. Inner form, finally, is the formative principle itself, which can never be separated from the matter it forms. I have chosen to equate it with vision because I believe it to be a prerequisite of the imaginative process (like Kant's categories of perception), whether we regard that process as taking place in a moment of inspiration or through long tedious hours of composition. The order in which these three aspects of form come into being is clearly opposite to the order in which I have here taken them. Inner form precedes structure, as structure precedes outer form. One must of course grant the critic license to begin and end with any aspect of form which particularly interests him; nevertheless, the critical procedure which might be described as centrifugal because it works from the center outward promises to be both theoretically sound and practically rewarding.

CHAPTER II

The Two Heroines of

Moll Flanders

It is indeed an opinion strangely prevailing amongst men, that houses, mountains, rivers, and in a word all sensible objects, have an existence, natural or real, distinct from their being perceived by the understanding.
—BERKELEY, *Principles of Human Knowledge*

The title page of *Moll Flanders* makes a valiant, if rather long-winded, attempt to tell us what the book is about: "The Fortunes and Misfortunes of the Famous Moll Flanders, &c. Who was Born in Newgate, and during a Life of continu'd Variety for Three-score Years, besides her Childhood, was Twelve Year a Whore, five times a Wife (whereof once to her own Brother) Twelve Year a Thief, Eight Year a Transported Felon in Virginia, at last grew Rich, liv'd Honest, and died a Penitent" and so on.[1] Presumably this serves much the same function as the blurb on the jacket of the modern novel, to alert the prospective buyer to the kinds of experience he may expect to read about. Modern advertising techniques are somewhat more subtle, tending rather to suggest than to state, but the comparison serves chiefly to engender the dispiriting reflection that popular novels then and now deal with much the same thing. To the easily jaded reader, in fact, *Moll Flanders* seems to offer a wearisome and repetitious account of its heroine's vices and crimes.

Fortunately, perhaps, jacket blurbs and their eighteenth-century counterparts rarely tell the whole truth about a book, and they yield only a very crude idea of what the book they describe is about. If *Moll Flanders* were the factual account it pretends to be, then the catalogue given on the title page would indeed be an adequate description of its subject matter, but since the book is plainly fictitious and its characters and incidents imaginary, the real subject matter is not the incidents in themselves, but the incidents as seen from a particular point of view. The subject of the novel, that is, includes everything that Defoe's imagination seizes as relevant to, or part of, the event. Since the novel purports to be written by the title character, a certain amount of confusion naturally arises as to whether any given detail is to be referred to Defoe's own normal or habitual mode of perception or to the characterization of Moll. But the confusion can be cleared away by assuming what in fact seems obvious, that Defoe was capable of a more or less complete imaginative identification with his heroine. I do not mean that Defoe writes about himself under the guise of Moll, but that he has succeeded, apparently, in putting himself in her place and seeing with her eyes.[2] If this is true, as I believe it to be, it is possible to regard every detail as relevant to the characterization of Moll and at the same time conformable to Defoe's ordinary mental processes. Thus there is no inconsistency in speaking of *Defoe's* imagination as the instrument which consciously or unconsciously shapes *Moll's* perceptions and responses.

If one is to take *Moll Flanders* as an imaginative work rather than as an autobiography, the best way to get at its subject matter is not to perform an act of historical reconstruction, but to examine closely the verbal texture in which the novelist's imaginative vision is embedded, for it is here that one encounters the selection and arrangement of details, the modulations of tone, and the very rhythms of thought which make the narrated incidents significant. To stop with an identification of the incident is to miss nearly everything of importance to the novel as novel and to deprive oneself of the means of distinguishing between radically different modes of narration which happen to present incidents of the same kind. Though *Moll Flanders* and *Fanny Hill* both offer accounts of a long series of sexual encounters, they have virtually nothing else in common, and it would certainly be misleading to say that they are about the same thing.

Almost any page of *Moll Flanders* provides the means of forming a fairly accurate judgment of the novel's major concerns. Take, for example, this description of one of Moll's earliest thieving forays:

Going thro *Aldersgate-street*, there was a pretty little Child had been at a Dancing-School, and was a going home all alone, and my Prompter, like a true Devil, set me upon this innocent Creature; I talk'd to it, and it prattl'd to me again, and I took it by the Hand and led it a long till I came to a pav'd Alley that goes into *Bartholomew-Close*, and I led it in there; the Child said that was not its way home; I said, yes, my Dear, it is, I'll show you the way home; the Child had a little Necklace on of Gold Beads, and I had my Eye upon that, and in the dark of the Alley I stoop'd, pretending to mend the Child's Clog that was loose, and took off her Necklace, and the Child never felt it, and so led the Child on again: Here, I say, the Devil put me upon killing the Child in the dark Alley, that it might not Cry, but the very thought frighted me so that I was ready to drop down, but I turn'd the Child about and bad it go back again, for that was not its way home; the Child said so she would, and I went thro' into *Bartholomew-Close*, and then turn'd round to another Passage that goes into *Long-lane*, so away into *Charterhouse-Yard*, and out into *St. John's-street*; then crossing into *Smithfield*, went down *Chick-lane*, and into *Field-lane*, to *Holbourn-bridge*, when mixing with the Crowd of People usually passing there, it was not possible to have been found out; and thus I made my second Sally into the World. [II, 7]

In the absence of those qualities of vividness and movement that we have come to demand in fiction, this passage creates an illusion of extraordinary simplicity and artlessness. There is only the most perfunctory attempt to describe or vivify the child; it (even the sex remains in doubt for several sentences) is "pretty," it "prattles," and it wears a necklace of gold beads and a pair of clogs. Clearly the child is seen only as an object to be robbed (or perhaps murdered) and is given no existence of its own. The rhythm of the prose, too, seems not only artless but clumsy: "The Child had a little Necklace on of Gold Beads, and I had my Eye upon that, and in the dark of the Alley I stoop'd, pretending to mend the Child's Clog that was loose, and took off her Necklace, and the Child never felt it, and so led the Child on again." Among these jogging and monotonous clauses the action that we feel ought to be made climactic—the actual theft—is buried among actions of much less consequence, and the whole account is drained of its potential drama. Finally, the lengthy, unnecessarily specific description of Moll's retreat is quite out of proportion to the magnitude of the event or to its capacity to engage the reader's interest.

This apparent artlessness actually conceals Defoe's special kind of art. For one thing, the seemingly unformed quality of the narration disarms our suspicion that the whole business is simply invention and thereby helps to convince us that the story is true. Still more important, however, the same qualities which suggest the absence of artifice—the random selection of details, the anti-climactic order, the flabby prose—serve to define the qualities of the perceiving mind, and these qualities are as integral to what Defoe has to deliver in the passage as the events themselves. They are, in other words, an important part of the subject matter of *Moll Flanders*. If Moll is innocent of rhetoric, the details she supplies ought to be a reliable index of

what is uppermost in her mind. What she in fact notices are
the details which are of practical significance to her immediate
purpose: the necklace as an object of desire, the clog as a pretext for the necessary sleight of hand, the maze of streets as an
avenue of escape. It would be a mistake, however, to assume
that Moll is here reasoning logically, or even that her mind is
significantly engaged. What the narrative suggests is the automatic, reflexive action of one who sees something desirable,
seizes it, and runs away.

The simplicity of the narrative is not inherent in the event
but in Moll. What is excluded is therefore at least as significant
as what is included. The event raises all kinds of psychological
and moral issues which remain outside the focus of Moll's attention, but the reader's awareness of them sharpens his apprehension of the deficiencies in her. In a rapidly paced narrative,
of course, no one could expect commentary, but Moll's narrative is not rapid, and it does afford her leisure to introduce what
strike the reader as irrelevant details (some of the street names,
for example) as well as what passes for moral reflection. "My
Prompter," she says, "like a true Devil, set me upon this innocent Creature," or, a few lines later, "the Devil put me upon
killing the Child in the dark Alley . . . but the very thought
frighted me so that I was ready to drop down." Moll is simply
incapable of real insight into the mysterious chasm that sepa-
rates the impulse from the action; she thinks of herself as the
passive agent of some force outside herself, working its will on
her except when she is incapacitated by fear. Nor has she any
conception of the nature of guilt. She does recognize that the
deed is wrong by the conventional standards which she accepts,
and she is capable of being shocked, but not of realizing her
own moral responsibility. Again the convenient devil permits
her to view the action as though she were not involved in it.
She is incapable of sympathy or fellow feeling with the child
(who remains an "it"), and is apparently restrained from harm-

ing the little girl by fear of the consequences rather than by
pity or moral revulsion. The consciousness that is revealed to
us in this passage is a perfectly pragmatic one; if there is no
psychological awareness and no moral sensitivity, there is likewise no aesthetic response to experience. The single adjective,
"pretty," predicated of the child, is the only concession to the
quality of experience, and it marks a response so generalized,
so vague, and so unreflective as to be negligible. It is safe to
assume, I think, even on the relatively slender basis of the passage quoted, that *Moll Flanders* is to be more concerned with
the practical problems of Moll's uneasy mode of existence than
with the moral or aesthetic implications of her experience. If
the book teaches a lesson, as Defoe piously assures us, it has
nothing to do with the wages of sin; it is a lesson in how to
succeed at the confidence game.

The presumptions afforded by this passage are confirmed by
the novel as a whole. That Moll is incapable of savoring her
life, that the aesthetic impulse is deficient in her, is perhaps
most clearly shown in the rendering of her sexual experiences,
of which the first, with the elder brother of the Colchester
family, is typical. Several times she declares a passionate and
enduring attachment to him, and yet her encounters with him
are curiously cold. "His Words," she says at one point, "fir'd
my Blood; all my Spirits flew about my Heart, and put me
into Disorder enough" (I, 17). But at the crucial moments she
is always perfectly passive: "Perhaps he found me a little too
easy, for I made no Resistance to him while he only held me
in his Arms and kiss'd me; indeed I was too well pleas'd with
it, to resist him much" (I, 18). And the supreme moment when
Moll irrevocably sacrifices her innocence passes like this: "I
made no more Resistance to him, but let him do just what he
pleas'd, and as often as he pleas'd; and thus I finished my own
Destruction at once" (I, 25). Prudery can account for her (and
Defoe's) reticence in the description,[3] but it cannot altogether

account for the passivity of the role she assigns herself or for the striking absence of feeling. The flatness and coldness of this description, which is typical of many, are a sufficient guarantee against any indecency or pornographic intent, but what is more important, they demonstrate convincingly Moll's indifference to purely sensory enjoyments or at least her complete inability to render the sensuous quality of life.[4]

A secondary implication, but one of far-reaching consequence in the novel, is that Moll is both unfeeling and inarticulate in the realm of human relations. There is a noteworthy disparity between the love she professes to feel for the man who has ruined her and the coldness with which she describes her relations with him. "I lov'd him," she asserts, "to an Extravagance, not easy to imagine" (I, 54), but the statement carries no conviction at all. When she learns that the younger brother, Robin, intends to make her his wife, her first thought is that her entanglement with the elder brother will effectually prevent her from accepting even so advantageous an offer. Her declaration of love thus becomes simply a face-saving device which will enable her to assume the martyr's role when her erstwhile lover offers to stand aside. She can shield herself from the imputation both of promiscuity and of naked self-interest by affecting a broken heart at doing what her own interest demands—marrying Robin. "Interest," she declares with a kind of cynical resignation, but perhaps also with a hint of complacency, "banishes all manner of affection."[5]

In a hundred ways Moll reveals her essential want of feeling for others, or at any rate her want of a feeling strong enough to survive the first hint of conflict with her own interest. The result is that her protestations of feeling always ring false, both because we are already convinced that her capacity for feeling is slight and because her protestations have a way of becoming extravagant in themselves. When, toward the end of the book, she encounters the surviving child born of her incestuous marriage to her brother, her circumstances will not allow her to make herself known, but she watches the young man with mute adoration, and when he has passed she lies down, weeps, and kisses "the Ground that he had set his Foot on" (II, 152). It is scarcely conceivable that this feeling can be genuine, when we remember the number of children that Moll has cheerfully abandoned in her long career. Of her two first-born she remarks serenely, "My two Children were indeed taken happily off of my Hands by my Husband's Father and Mother, and that was all they got by Mrs. *Betty*" (I, 57). It is true that she shows great scrupulosity in disposing of the child of her bigamous marriage to Jemmy, her "Lancashire husband," but she has her own conscience to quiet, and even more important, she has the good opinion of her "governess" to preserve. Whatever maternal feeling Moll has never prevents her from disposing of her children when they become inconvenient to her, and whatever violence is offered to that maternal feeling by the separation always heals quickly.

Moll's relations with other people, whether based on sex, affection, gratitude, or common interest, and whether or not they are confirmed by legal or religious ties, generally prove casual. When these relations are disturbed or disrupted Moll never seems to suffer any lingering regrets. "When I was about fourteen Years and a quarter Old," she observes, "my good old Nurse, Mother I ought to call her, fell Sick and Dy'd" (I, 11). Nothing more than that; the death of the only mother Moll has ever known is drained of all feeling and significance, except that it serves to mark an era of Moll's life (the looseness of the "about" is curiously canceled by the precision of the "quarter"). And when the marriage bond begins to prove inconvenient, Moll has no hesitation about abrogating it by mutual consent. She "divorces" three husbands in this way (if we include the dissolution of the incestuous marriage to her brother), though she is later reunited with her Lancashire husband. Relations based on a temporary union of interest never engender any feelings of loyalty or affection. On one occasion, in fact, when one of Moll's accomplices in crime has been caught, she is on tenterhooks of fear and apprehension that he will implicate her until she receives "the joyful News that he was Hang'd," adding callously, "which was the Best News to me that I had heard a great while" (II, 36). The surprising thing is that there is not a hint of malice in her nature; she is uniformly good tempered in prosperity, and she is never vindictive in adversity. The simple truth of her character is that human feeling is always subordinate to practical interest.

Only two of Moll's attachments endure. Her liaison with Jemmy, her Lancashire husband, though temporarily suspended when it proves mutually embarrassing, is resumed toward the end, and Moll gives us a sentimental portrait of the two repentant sinners confronting the evening of their lives together. The two seem perfectly congenial; they are understanding and tolerant of each other's failures, but their union is not cemented by any deep feeling. Once again it is practical convenience that determines the durability of their relation. Jemmy, though we are led to believe that he has passed the interval of his separation from Moll in making a name for himself as a fearless and desperate highwayman, proves to be a cipher in adversity, and the task of cushioning the shock of their transportation to Virginia (she as a felon, he as a voluntary exile, since the evidence to convict him is lacking) falls altogether on Moll, whose resourcefulness and practical acumen are here put to their severest test. Throughout this last stage of the novel it is Moll's personality which is clearly dominant, and her husband, who is by now simply one of her dependents, has too little spirit and will to put any stress on their union, to make of it, that is, a dynamic interrelation between two people who are autonomous and fully alive. Like the child she had earlier robbed, he has been reduced to the status of a thing.

The other enduring attachment into which Moll enters is to the woman she calls her "governess." The growth of this connection is constant, and it survives every change in Moll's circumstances, but the fact does not after all disprove Moll's deficiency of human feeling. The governess is a curiously chameleonlike figure, whose nature seems continuously to be changing to suit Moll's physical and spiritual needs at any given moment. She first appears in the novel when Moll, having separated from her Lancashire husband, is in need of the services of a midwife who will not only raise no scruples of her own but will insulate her clients from the usual "parish impertinences" and attend to the disposition of the child afterwards (unless, of course, the child should conveniently die and save two pounds ten in christening expenses). Moll is not without money at this point, so her primary need is not so much for material care as it is for psychological nourishment; she needs to be assured that she is respectable, and the governess's worldliness and tact combine to provide the requisite comfort: "Every word this Creature said was a Cordial to me, and put new Life and new Spirit into my very Heart" (I, 173). What makes this relation difficult to understand is that we are provided no insight into the midwife's motives; her terms, by Moll's own admission, are dirt cheap, and she goes out of her way to cosset Moll by sending her own maid with "a Chicken roasted and hot, and a Bottle of Sherry" (I, 178). Moll accepts this attention without question and is certainly at no expense of spirit to sustain the friendship which is to last out her lifetime, but her very inertness forces the reader to draw his own conclusions.[6]

Some years after this lying-in Moll encounters her governess again, but the circumstances of both have changed for the worse. The governess is now a "pawnbroker," a euphemistic term for fence, and Moll herself has changed her life from whoring to thieving. The possibilities for fruitful collaboration are obvious, and the former intimacy between them is renewed. The most suggestive feature is that as Moll passes successively through all the possible levels of depravity, she always finds her governess there before her, ready to offer material aid or spiritual comfort as needed. When Moll slyly approaches her governess on the subject of her own thefts she is met, not by outraged morality, but by encouragement, which surprises even the incurious Moll, whose sensitivity to other people, as we have seen, is slight: "This," she records, "gave me a new Notion of my Governess" (II, 14). Even at the most dramatic change in Moll's fortunes—her arrest, conviction, and condemnation—the governess's moods anticipate Moll's, for though the governess is never arrested, she, too, suffers a change of heart and becomes a penitent. We last hear of her engaged in her usual untiring (and unremunerated) efforts in Moll's behalf. The constancy of this friendship through all the vicissitudes of fortune reveals no special quality of feeling in Moll. Moll is simply using her governess, and the suspicion must arise that the converse is also true, that the governess's early and otherwise inexplicable attentions to Moll are motivated by her expectation that Moll will prove a tractable and profitable pupil in the ways of crime. The governess's continued care of Moll, after Moll's conviction and her own change of heart, presumably arises from the uneasiness of her conscience toward a person she feels she has injured. The apparent changes in the governess's character are not really changes at all; Moll is simply learning more about her, and characteristically (for Moll never sees anything more in other people than the side that happens to be exposed to her at the moment—just as children are "pretty," her companions are always "agreeable") her original quite superficial impression is constantly being revised to accommodate new information. The chief significance I find in the development of this relation is that it reveals Moll's incapacity to know other people or to enter into their feelings because her vision is limited to the field of her own concerns and interests.

Moll's professions of moral sentiment are as specious as her protestations of affection. She is constantly making her moral sentiments explicit, and we very quickly learn that Moll's moral values are highly conventional, even a shade puritanical. When she yields to the elder brother in Colchester she speaks of chastity in terms that would do credit to Pamela: ". . . thus I finish'd my own Destruction at once, for from this Day, being forsaken of my Virtue, and my Modesty, I had nothing of Value left to recommend me, either to God's Blessing, or Man's Assistance" (I, 25). This is typical of Moll's moral valuation in that it is both extreme and unequivocal; she rarely minces words or stoops to euphemism. When her seducer's delicacy hesitates over the choice of a term to describe her relation to him she immediately suggests "Whore" (I, 36), and on another occasion, some years later, she seems to relish applying to herself "that unmusical harsh sounding Title of Whore" (I, 121). Moll might be described, in fact, as a kind of moral masochist, so clearly does she enjoy the stringency of her own judgments of herself.[7] One is reminded of Alice, scolding herself so severely that she bursts into tears.[8] Moll's horror at the thought of incest (I, 90) or abortion (I, 180) is predictable in the light of the orthodoxy of her other values, but her puritanical streak is incongruous. What kind of moral sense prompts a self-confessed whore and thief to plume herself on the fact that she has never stooped to "the baseness of Paint" (II, 54)? She is fond of homiletics and never fails to point the moral of an episode; her account of the robbing of the child is attended by a rebuke to the vanity of parents, but the supreme irony is that after she has given herself to a drunken "gentleman" in exchange for the opportunity of rifling his pockets, she launches into a superb denunciation of drunkenness and lechery (II, 43).

But that Moll's moral stance is all pretense, that her values are false, is clearly demonstrated, not so much by the disparity between her professed beliefs and her behavior, as by the fact that the disparity does not seem to damage her complacency. After she has robbed a family whose house was on fire, she has this to say about her taking such an advantage over the misfortunes of others: "I confess the inhumanity of this Action mov'd me very much, and made me relent exceedingly, and Tears stood in my Eyes upon that Subject; But with all my Sense of its being cruel and Inhuman, I cou'd never find in my Heart to make any Restitution: The Reflection wore off, and I quickly forgot the Circumstances that attended it" (II, 22). The insensitivity she acknowledges here is redoubled by the fact of her acknowledgment. Most suggestive of all, perhaps, is the indication we are given that moral distinctions are not real, since they exist only in our awareness of them. Of her incestuous union with her brother she remarks, "O! had the Story never been told me, all had been well; it had been no Crime to have lain with my Husband, if I had known nothing of it" (I, 90). So ends her catechism.

If Moll's morality, as I have sought to demonstrate, is indeed sham, then there is good reason to suspect the genuineness of her remorse when she is ordered for execution. One might even question whether she understands what penitence is. Her first groping toward repentance when she understands that she is in peril of her life is, as she is herself aware, "nothing but Fright, at what was to come" (II, 107). But she takes comfort in her protestation that now she has begun to think, which is "one real Advance from Hell to Heaven," though Moll's "thought" does not take her beyond an extremely vague and not at all convincing eschatology: "The Word Eternity represented itself with all its incomprehensible Additions, and I had such extended Notions of it, that I know not how to express them: Among the rest, how absurd did every pleasant Thing look?

I mean, that we had counted pleasant before; when I reflected that these sordid Trifles were the things for which we forfeited eternal Felicity" (II, 114). Moll's contempt for "sordid Trifles" turns out in the sequel to have been a very temporary state of mind. The further progress of her remorse, under the tutelage of a minister, is rapid, particularly when she understands that divine mercy demands nothing more from her than "being sincerely desirous of it, and willing to accept it; only a sincere Regret for, and hatred of those things which render'd me so just an Object of divine Vengeance" (II, 115). Penitence, in this view, exacts only a gesture of surrender, and Moll embraces it with "a secret surprizing Joy." When the danger is over, of course, Moll reverts to her worldly concerns but maintains the role of penitent, by which she succeeds in hanging onto the cake she has already eaten. She is aware of no inconsistency, however, and the reader is confirmed in his suspicion that Moll's nature has never been really touched by moral concerns.

I have dwelt at such length on those aspects of life which *Moll Flanders* is not centrally concerned with, because the book misleads us as to what it is really about. In his character as editor Defoe insists in the Preface that the main interest of the novel is in its moral teaching, while simultaneously, in his character as impresario for Moll, he appeals in the long descriptive title to the reader's prurience. Even more important, the novel itself, by making Moll's moral posturing such an obtrusive ingredient of her characterization, can be misleading if the reader takes Moll's moral professions at face value. What I am, in fact, suggesting is that the novel is ironic in that it seems to say one thing and actually says another. The point is not a new one; that *Moll Flanders* is organized by ironies of one kind or another has been argued by, among others, Dorothy Van Ghent and H. L. Koonce (in works already cited), but the issue of Defoe's intention ought perhaps to be confronted. This is the

question which troubles Ian Watt, who, though not disposed
to deny the existence of irony in the novel, disputes that it is
under Defoe's conscious control.⁹ I see no way to prove or
disprove the consciousness of the control, but the existence of
the control is, I believe, demonstrable in the organization of the
novel. At any rate my own object in what follows is to draw
attention to what seems to me a consistent principle of organization. In the meantime, perhaps, the issue of intention need
not become too intrusive if we can manage to think of the
second, or ironic voice as emanating from Moll herself.

Moll's pretense of a moral preoccupation, equally with her
manifest indifference to the psychological and aesthetic aspects
of experience, ought to direct our attention to the fact that the
subject of the novel is not conceived in any of these ways, and
in fact it has been generally recognized that the consciousness
which is ordering the experience recorded in the novel is fundamentally concerned with practical matters. Throughout her
life Moll remains true to her childhood ambition to be a gentlewoman, which means, apparently, not going into service or
doing housework (I, 8). Her motives are primarily economic,
having less to do with social status than with physical and
material well-being, and they constitute the mainspring of her
character, though as she grows older she conceals this naked
acquisitive drive under various disguises, including her puritanical morality. One or two suggestive evidences of what Mark
Schorer, echoing a good deal of earlier commentary, calls "the
mercantile mind" ought to be enough.¹⁰ Of the tragedy of
Moll's own coming into the world, of her mother's disgrace
and transportation, only a single specific detail clings in her
memory: her mother's crime was "borrowing three Pieces of
fine *Holland*, of a certain Draper in *Cheap-side*" (I, 2). Among
the agitations of her conscience after her own first exercise in
theft she does not fail to cast up a rigorously exact account of
the booty: "There was a Suit of Child-bed Linnen in it, very

good and almost new, the Lace very fine; there was a Silver Porringer of a Pint, a small Silver Mug and Six Spoons, with some other Linnen, a good Smock, and Three Silk Handkerchiefs, and in the Mug in a Paper, Eighteen Shillings and Sixpence" (II, 5). And why does she bother to reproduce in toto all three of the midwife's bills when only a single one is applicable? Her inevitable response to experience, of whatever kind, is that of the bookkeeper; the first task is to calculate profit and loss. In this respect at least Moll is very much like Robinson Crusoe; both are centrally concerned with the elementary problem of survival, and beyond that with whatever material amenities a hostile environment can be made to provide. But there is this significant difference between Moll and Crusoe; his principal victory must be won against non-human enemies, but her struggle is with society itself. Crusoe's situation intensifies the practical problems of his life, but it relieves him altogether of the moral and social problems which confront Moll and which she must solve or evade if she is to deal successfully with the larger, more fundamental, and more engrossing problem of economic survival. In *Robinson Crusoe* the fundamental narrative interest and the basic lineaments of the narrator's consciousness are not overlaid by the distracting complications always present in *Moll Flanders*, which for this reason is a less straightforward, but more interesting, novel.

If the novel's substance, as I have been arguing, is revealed to us through the consciousness of the narrator rather than through the crude cataloguing of incident attempted in the descriptive title of the work, it may be fruitful to turn to the same source for an understanding of the way in which that substance is ordered. One structural principle, of course, is already implicit in the autobiographical format, but the structure so imparted to the novel is very loose and is consistent with a wide variety of artistic or rhetorical purposes. What needs to be established, if possible, is an artistic principle of structure, one that will not only impose unity but make it meaningful. It is clear that the events themselves, considered apart from the way in which they are seen and described, belong to no coherent system. Their order, it is true, is determined in part by the autobiographical plan and by the facts of biology, but there is no inner compulsion that moves us irresistibly from the beginning of Moll's story to the end. Often, indeed, the narrative comes to a halt, as when Moll marries and finds an acceptable mode of life, and it can be made to move forward again only by gratuitously killing off her husband and confronting her all over again with the problem of making her way in the world. In Aristotelian terms, the whole novel consists of "middle," and so no useful purpose can be served by attempting to discover and define a "plot," but it is almost equally unsatisfactory to locate the novel's unifying principle in "character," meaning the Moll who acts and suffers as distinct from the Moll who perceives and narrates. Moll's character, in this sense, undergoes too little change to make its development the sustaining interest of the novel. Furthermore, her character is too simple to permit building the novel around its exposition; we understand Moll as fully as we are going to by the time we are halfway through the book. What remains as a potentially fruitful organizing principle is the relation between Moll as character and Moll as narrator, the curiously devious process by which Moll apprehends and organizes the details of her own experience.

It is not possible, of course, to separate entirely a novel's form from its substance; to say what the novel is about is necessarily also to say a good deal about the way it is put together, for the matter is never conceived without form, and the imaginative act which produces the narrative persona also determines the ways in which it will operate to impose order on the narrative. "Order" is here taken to mean not only sequence but proportion and emphasis, since even a narrative art can be arranged in other than chronological ways. Nevertheless, though substance implies form, it is still possible, and even fruitful, to talk about form as something different from substance.

I have been examining the details of Moll's story in an effort to determine as precisely as possible the motions of her mind; it is time now to look at the aggregate of these details to see what kind of artistic coherence and unity the novel possesses. For reasons already given I do not think that Moll's purpose (as explained and endorsed by Defoe in the Preface) satisfactorily explains either the selection of detail or its ordering in the novel as a whole. The pattern of temptation, sin, and redemption through suffering, which Defoe as editor tries to force on the narrative, does not really serve to organize it. What does lend coherence to the story is to be sought, I believe, within the fabric of the narration, and specifically within Moll's consciousness as she observes her objective "self" in the role of heroine. Since the novel as a whole is obviously episodic, and the story is continually reaching a full stop, it will be convenient to consider the structure of various episodes, taken singly, before attempting to say anything about the forces of coherence which forge them into a whole.

The first major unit in the novel, bound together by characters, events, and locale, is the Colchester episode, beginning with the death of Moll's foster mother and Moll's subsequent entry into the Colchester household where she occupies a vaguely defined position as protégée and companion and ending with her marriage to Robin, the younger of the two brothers. Now Moll, though professing to care nothing for him, is impelled by the strongest force of her character, her longing for material security and well-being, to desire this marriage, but there are two important obstacles. The first is that she has no fortune, and this lack unites the family against her in spite of the fact that they all admire her. But, as one of the daughters cynically remarks: "If a young Woman has Beauty, Birth,

Breeding, Wit, Sense, Manners, Modesty, and all to an Extream; yet if she has not Money, she's no Body, she had as good want them all; nothing but Money now recommends a Woman" (I, 15–16). She can, of course, marry the young man without his parents' blessing, but since he is the younger son, their prospects necessarily depend on the good will of his parents. The second obstacle is that she has naïvely allowed herself to be drawn into a liaison with the elder brother, without the precaution of agreeing on a fixed settlement. In spite of her professed passion for this brother, Moll would gladly marry his brother and exchange her present precarious situation for a secure and respectable one, and the elder brother, too, would not be averse to such a convenient method of relieving himself without embarrassment from a position that threatens to become both tiresome and awkward. But Moll realizes that she must proceed with caution, for if she accepts this solution with alacrity, then she risks alienating the elder brother by wounding his vanity. She knows, though she is curiously late in acknowledging it to the reader, that she runs the risk "of being drop'd by both of them, and left alone in the World" (I, 55). Moll's master stroke of policy is to declare her undying love for the elder brother and her perfect confidence in his intention to make an honest woman of her. "It took from him," she remarks smugly, "all Possibility of quitting me, but by a down right breach of Honour, and giving up all the Faith of a Gentleman which he had so often engaged by, never to abandon me, but to make me his Wife as soon as he came to his Estate" (I, 47–48). The result is that Moll has converted one of her most serious disadvantages into an advantage, and henceforward the elder brother will be assiduous, not only to persuade her to consult her own advantage by marrying Robin, but to take her part with the rest of the family in overcoming their objection to the match.

That objection is finally overcome, in part by the elder

brother's solicitation, but more importantly by another of Moll's finesses. She simply refuses Robin's offer, and in doing so she attempts (with considerable success) to deceive everyone. To Robin and his parents and sisters it appears that Moll's refusal stems from loyalty to the family and an unwillingness to be the instrument of a schism; to the elder brother it appears that Moll loves him so single-mindedly that she cannot think of making Robin her husband; to the uncritical reader it appears that Moll, being entangled with the elder brother, is unable to break that entanglement so as to permit her to consult her own material and worldly advantage by marrying Robin. To everyone Moll appears in a favorable light because of her unselfishness and her constancy, but the superb irony of all this is that Moll's enjoyment of the good opinion won by her renunciation is not going to cost her the usual price; she is going to have Robin too.

This episode is a remarkably skillful and self-contained little comedy, though its neatness tends to be obscured by the diffuseness and apparent artlessness of Moll's narrative style. But its chief interest and importance in the present discussion is the insight it can be made to yield into the structure Moll imposes on her experience. What is central to her account is not the end achieved but the process of achieving it. Her own little epilogue is suggestive:

It concerns the Story in Hand very little to enter into the farther Particulars of the Family, or of my self, for the five Years that I liv'd with this Husband, only to observe that I had two Children by him, and that at the end of the five Years he died . . . and . . . left me a Widow with about 1200*l*. in my Pocket. [I, 57]

Obviously the prize, once gained, is of no further interest, and Moll proposes to give us no account at all of the five years of her married life, a period of time which is measured for her characteristically by the bearing of two children and the acquisition of £1,200. What is of paramount interest to her in this whole episode is clearly the means by which the prize is gained, but we must beware of taking her own valuations or interpretive comments too literally. For one thing she is inclined to insist too strongly, as we have seen, on the importance of her own feelings in constituting her dilemma.

Moll's relation to the reader is not an entirely honest one; she is creating a character for us which differs in many respects from the character she presents to other personages in the story, but which is equally far removed from what we may presume to be her real character. In fact, the secret of Moll's worldly success, here and later, is in her ability to assume whatever role is appropriate to her immediate purpose. Here, of course, she differs most radically from Crusoe, who is always himself, since his problem is simply to wrest his subsistence from stubborn Nature. Moll has to get what she wants from other people, a process which involves a duplicity foreign to Crusoe's nature. But Moll's role-playing is more than a technique of her lifelong confidence game; it is, in an important sense, the very center of her being. In the assumption of a specious identity Moll comes as close as she ever can to the disinterested enjoyment of life; her account of the praise lavished on her by the family for her loyalty and abnegation, and of her own "sincerity" in confessing the whole matter to them, breathes her delight in the deception, the special piquancy of which resides in its perfectly ironic quality. Moll knows that she is exactly the opposite of what the family thinks her.

It is not enough, however, to say that Moll enjoys playing a part; she only becomes truly alive when she does. With all her strength and resourcefulness Moll is essentially weak. There is no drive in her character except the vegetable tropism that draws her to comfort and security, and she possesses no inner life at all. A most suggestive passage occurs during her visit to Lancashire, where she falls in with a Roman Catholic family:

The Truth is, I had not so much Principle of any kind, as to be Nice in Point of Religion; and I presently learn'd to speak favourably of the *Romish Church;* particularly I told them I saw little, but the Prejudice of Education in all the Differences that were among Christians about Religion, and if it had so happen'd that my Father had been a *Roman Catholick*, I doubted not but I should have been as well pleas'd with their Religion as my own. [I, 150]

Moll is clearly what David Riesman would call an "other-directed" person; she has no character or personality of her own, only what she reflects of the society she happens to be in. On Crusoe's desert island she would cease to exist. Her play-acting, therefore, is more than a practical stratagem, more than an amusement, it is the very breath of life, for with no identity of her own Moll must be continually borrowing one.

The attitude at the focus of the first major episode of the novel serves as the center around which all the details are grouped, and this attitude is also, I believe, the center of the novel as a whole. From her childish attempt to assume the role of gentlewoman to her final exit in the character of a penitent, the keen edge of Moll's confrontation of life is pretending to be somebody she is not. Her very name is an assumed identity, for she assures us that Moll Flanders is only a stage name, signifying nothing of her true identity, but only what would now be called her "public image," for Moll's celebrity is considerable (II, 30). Throughout the later part of her career, in fact, Moll relies heavily on stagecraft. "I had several Shapes to appear in" (II, 57), she acknowledges on one occasion, and she owes her survival after one exploit to the fact that she has disguised herself as a man, and her true sex is unknown to her accomplice.[11] Sometimes, on the other hand, her disguises prove less happy, though the difficulties they involve her in are not practical but psychological. When, for example, she puts on the dress of a beggar woman, she complains that the disguise is "uneasy" and attributes the feeling to her natural abhorrence of "Dirt and

Rags" (II, 75), but the reader is inclined rather to suspect
that Moll is uneasy as a beggar because she does not have a firm
enough sense of her own identity to remain unaffected by the
imposture, and of course beggary is Moll's veritable hell.[12]

Most conspicuous of all, however, in the second half of the
novel is the affair of the mercer, which occupies such a seemingly disproportionate space in Moll's account of her thieving
exploits. Briefly, Moll has dressed as a widow (she thinks of it
as a disguise, though she is indeed a widow) and ventured forth
"without any real design in view, but only waiting for any thing
that might offer" (II, 61). She hears the cry of "Stop Thief!"
and presently finds herself dragged into a mercer's shop and
accused of theft, for the shop, it appears, has been robbed by a
woman in widow's weeds. After receiving a good deal of abuse
with only a formal protest, Moll, who is enjoying the role of
injured innocence (her innocence, of course, is only technical,
since she has had robbery in her heart) and at the same time is
aware of the practical possibilities of her situation, secures her
witnesses for an action against the mercer and his assistant.
When the real thief is brought in, Moll's case is unshakable, and
the mercer eventually has to settle for £150, her attorney's
fees, "a Suit of black Silk cloaths," and "a good Supper into the
Bargain" (II, 73). When Moll arrives to collect this blackmail
she carries it off in grand style:

When I came to receive the Money, I brought my Governess
with me, dress'd like an old Dutchess, and a Gentleman very well
dress'd, who we pretended Courted me, but I call'd him Cousin,
and the Lawyer was only to hint privately to them, that this
Gentleman Courted the Widow. [II, 73]

Since her case is already won, it would appear that this little
scene is to be staged for its own sake. Moll would like to play
the piece out in her character of a respected but maligned
widow. Here, as so prominently elsewhere in the novel, Moll

contemplates herself, not as the innocently covetous thing she is underneath her various disguises, but as the person she appears to be, gaining a few moments of wider and intenser life by accepting the image of herself that a temporary circumstance has offered her.

The organizing principle of the novel, the principle that ultimately controls order, proportion, and emphasis, is implicit in this double function of Moll to serve, so to speak, as both subject and object. Her consciousness not only reveals the subject to us, it *is* the subject. The effect is a kind of irony, or double vision, but since the novel offers us a number of different, perhaps equally pervasive ironies, it will be necessary to make a careful distinction. There is, for example, the irony implicit in Moll's assumption that the guilt of her life is her own rather than that of the heartless and venal society that has produced her. There is also irony of a particularly devastating kind in Moll's innocent acknowledgment (made overtly only once, but it underlies her whole moral attitude) that an immoral act is· nullified if the perpetrator is ignorant of its moral bearings. The agent's ignorance, in other words, not only excuses him, it changes the nature of his act. This amounts to confusing the morality which is an inward condition of mind and spirit with that which is only reputation. But the fundamental, shaping irony of *Moll Flanders* is the double vision of the heroine.

Since she herself is unconscious of the irony, it might in fact be better to revert to a distinction analogous to, but not identical with, the one already made, between the Moll who acts and suffers and the Moll who perceives and narrates, so that the duality in her vision is really a duality in herself. One of her selves, the one whose impoverished sensibility is displayed to us in the very texture of the prose, is brutal in its simplicity. She is a kind of vegetable, reaching toward the means of subsistence as a plant reaches toward the light, not by conscious effort, but by some mysterious inherent energy. The other Moll, the unconscious creation of the first, is less the image of what she herself would like to be than of what society would constrain her to be, and her intermittent existence in the various roles she assumes is to be explained not by her conscious or unconscious aspirations, but by her desperate need to escape from the confinement of her nakedly acquisitive self. Her puritanical system of moral valuations, for example, serves in much the same way as her widow's weeds or duchess's costume to confer upon her a moral nature, but one that is quite superficial. Without framing the distinction to herself, Moll realizes that it is better to be a sinner than to be nothing at all. Among the many deceptions that Moll practices, the last and cruelest is of herself, because she has apparently come to take her assumed self for her "real" one. At any rate, she confronts us, finally, in the altogether unearned and unconvincing character of a penitent. What prevents the deception from taking us in, too, is that Moll's undramatic self is there as well, imparting its own unmistakable quality to the narration.

This fundamental irony, produced by the reader's continuous and simultaneous awareness of the two sides of Moll's nature, transforms what would otherwise be a dreary and tedious chronicle of petty deceptions and crimes, unadorned by sensuousness or vividness of description, into a clearly focused and coherent story. Obviously *Moll Flanders* can lay no claim to being tightly constructed, and certainly a great part of its characteristic quality would be destroyed by any effort to contain its substance within the rigidities of a dramatic plot. Nevertheless, the novel does have a more or less clearly defined center in the competing concerns of the two Molls, producing a continuous abrasion that gives to the novel both edge and form. The novel's coherence is a product of its inner form, which has succeeded in energizing and bracing up an otherwise limp and flaccid structure. The difference between the loose and episodic account which *Moll Flanders* has been taken to be and the ironically focused narrative I have attempted to describe may not be very great, but it is enough to transmute a book full of Defoe's skillful and circumstantial lies into what may truly be called a novel with an imaginative center of its own.

CHAPTER III

The Problem of Pamela

For that peerless princess pressed him so closely,
Lured him so near the line, that her love
He must gladly accept or ungraciously spurn.
He cared for his courtesy, lest uncouth he prove,
Still more for the mischief should he commit sin
And basely dishonor the house and his host.
            —*Gawain and the Green Knight*

Richardson's critics have always tended to divide themselves into the pamelists and the antipamelists. Since the publication of *Pamela* in 1740 few readers have been able to maintain
a proper critical reserve, either toward Richardson himself or
toward his heroine. Thus Aaron Hill's unctuous praise quickly
overflows the bounds of his turgid prose into his turgid heroic
couplets:

O PAMELA!—what native charms were thine!
Nervously soft, and modestly divine!
High, without straining, was thy matchless flight,
And all unmix'd with pain, thou gav'st delight! [1]

On the other side, Fielding's derisive laughter in both *Shamela*
and *Joseph Andrews* is too well-known to require comment.[2]
Richardson's modern readers, though appreciably fewer than
those of his own day, are often no less strongly partisan in their

judgments. Joseph Wood Krutch assails Pamela in a tone that can only be described as savage:

The character of Pamela is one so devoid of any delicacy of feeling as to be inevitably indecent. She seems to have no sense of either her own or any possible human dignity and she can be admired only if a dogged determination to resist violation is considered to be, by itself, enough to make her admirable. Despite the language of pious cant which she speaks with such fluency there is no evidence that she has the faintest conception of that disinterestedness which alone can give piety a meaning.[3]

A modern pamelist, B. L. Reid, responds to Krutch's onslaught (of which he quotes a different, but not dissimilar, specimen) with "amazement and a kind of detached rage." He declares that "there is no real evidence for such a view," that Krutch is "guilty of a serious misreading, at the very least of an exaggeration equal to falsehood," and that Krutch's strictures against the book are "finely emphatic, but . . . simply untrue." [4] That feelings still run high over a book now generally dismissed as a historical curiosity is a convincing and effective refutation of the claim that *Pamela* is dead. Only the book's vitality can explain Krutch's animosity or Reid's chivalrous rebuttal.

The argument has consistently sought moral grounds. The antipamelists charge that Pamela is either a shameless and hypocritical schemer (Fielding), or a sententious prig (the orthodox view), or both (Krutch). Pamela's sudden capitulation to Mr. B. is taken, at best, as the expression of a simple-minded, hopelessly commercial ethic, naïvely translated into sentimental platitudes. At its worst it is seen as the triumph of acquisitiveness, consciously cloaked by a specious "virtue." As Shamela puts it, with admirable succinctness, "I thought once of making a little Fortune by my Person. I now intend to make a great one by my Vartue." [5] Fielding's parody, here and in *Joseph Andrews*, is brilliant, but Fielding and his successors in the antipamelist tradition are beating a dead horse (if, indeed, that horse ever lived). The trouble is partly that Pamela is too easy a target for that kind of sport, but an even greater objection is that such a line of attack leaves untouched whatever it is that accounts for the book's artistic vitality. Yet Reid takes up the defense of *Pamela* on precisely the grounds selected by its assailants. He maintains, first of all, that the novel succeeds in achieving what James called "solidity of specification," that primary virtue of all fiction, and is thus libeled by critical efforts to classify it as "sentimental" in neat opposition to another class of novels to be denominated "realistic." This argument has some relevance to the moral issue as I have defined it, because it attempts to remove, or at least to soften, the imputation of sentimentality as undermining the book's ethical validity. But Reid's second argument meets the moral objections head on. In effect, he accuses the antipamelists of excessive scrupulosity and asserts the value of Richardson's "sturdy pragmatism" as the basis of a practicable moral system which is far from despicable. Reid's purely defensive tactics meet, I suppose, the moral objections to *Pamela*, at any rate in their baldest and crudest form, but they do not and cannot give us any insight into what constitutes that novel's positive artistic value. Of course Reid is aware of the limitations of his argument. He concludes, in fact, by declaring that the "very considerable artistic achievement" of the novel depends on Richardson's knowing "how to keep the anesthetic of Puritan morality from immobilizing life." This amounts to a concession that the artistic value of Richardson's novel is independent of, if not in spite of, the ethical substructure.

My point is that in all this coil of statement and counter-statement, the essential fact about Richardson's novel has somehow been missed. The combatants have divided over issues which are unimportant or even irrelevant to the determination of *Pamela's* artistic worth. *Pamela* is about morality only in the way that *Robinson Crusoe* is about an island; the "subject" in both cases is really only a means of limiting the sphere of action (not of "immobilizing life," therefore, but of determining the range of its operation). The moral system of the novel, precisely because it is not disinterested, provides no motives for action; it can do no more than define the permissible limits of action, the springs of which (the antipamelists will be quick to point out) lie in the sexual and acquisitive instincts, but also, and much more richly and subtly, in the complex social attitudes that the novel describes and that are much closer to its artistic center than its relatively crude ethic. William M. Sale, Jr., has defined Richardson's subject matter as the impact of the "new" men and women of the middle classes upon the older world of the aristocracy. Richardson's primary concern, in this view, is with the social consequences of such an interpenetration of classes, rather than with the incidental moral dilemmas it may give rise to.[6] This seems to me a vastly more fruitful way to represent the *donnée* of Richardson's fiction than the conventional one, and though Sale is inclined to dismiss *Pamela* as a relatively crude formulation, I propose, in the rest of this chapter, to examine that novel very much on Sale's terms, to shift my emphasis away from those moral questions which have too long monopolized discussion, and to concentrate on the purely social dilemma which confronts Pamela. It is this social dilemma, and Pamela's response to it, which I believe gives integrity to the novel as an artistic structure, an integrity invariably overlooked by the moralists who persist in talking about the book as though it ended with the first volume.

Let me begin by clearing the ground a little. That Pamela is caught up in a purely moral dilemma, and that her attempts to solve that dilemma constitute the main, if not the only line of development in the novel are stubborn myths which die hard. A recent historian of the novel, Walter Allen, gives the conventional view: "There is Pamela, there is Mr. B. hot in pursuit of her virginity. Will she lose it? Will she? Won't she? The suspense is everything; and the screw is turned to the uttermost." [7] I am inclined to agree that "the suspense is everything." Surely one of the principal reasons for the avidity with which *Pamela* was read in the middle of the eighteenth century was its ability, at that time a novelty, to draw the reader into it, to make him aware of the necessity for choice, and to force him to share the agony of decision-making. Sale rightly points out that when Pamela is swept away into Lincolnshire, where her ability to mold events by her own will is closely restricted, the novel assumes the character of an "adventure story." I don't propose to enter into the reasons why the novel produces this effect of drawing the reader into it because they have been adequately explored. It is enough to say that the epistolary point of view and the minuteness of Richardson's representation have their share in producing the effect and set *Pamela* apart from *Moll Flanders*.[8] But surely Allen's formulation misrepresents the reasons for suspense. I cannot find that the novel introduces any credible evidence at all that would inspire me to doubt the ultimate triumph of Pamela's virginity. I cannot believe that her virginity is ever subjected to any real threat. Does the threat come from within? Here is Pamela's resolution, announced in Letter III:

But that which gives me most Trouble is, that you seem to mistrust the Honesty of your Child. No, my dear Father and Mother, be assur'd, that, by God's Grace, I never will do any thing that shall bring your grey Hairs with Sorrow to the Grave. I will die a thousand Deaths, rather than be dishonest any way. Of that be assur'd, and set your Hearts at Rest; for altho' I have liv'd above myself for some Time past, yet I can be content with Rags and Poverty, and Bread and Water, and will embrace them, rather than forfeit my good Name, let who will be the Tempter.[9]

This is the posturing of a fifteen-year-old girl, to be sure, but it is none the less convincing for that. Pamela may not be

wholly devoid of concupiscence, but her concupiscence is no
match for her dramatic sense. Sex holds out no such promise of
pleasure for her as the heroic posture of virtue affords easily
and safely. I can find no convincing evidence that the attractions
of Mr. B.'s person ever outweigh for her those of virtue. I am
not at all concerned to prove that Pamela's virtue is either
real or sham, but I cannot resist pointing out that one of the
strongest, though strangely neglected, indications that it is
after all fraudulent is just the point that I am here concerned to
make, that her virtue is never really tested in the sense that she
has to fight against her own inclination in order to preserve it.

A threat which must be taken more seriously is the one from
without. What if Mr. B. should rape her? We may quickly dispose of the relatively subtle moral justification that a girl does
not lose her virtue with her virginity if she does not give
consent. Obviously this would be little comfort to Pamela, for
whom virtue is simply equivalent to virginity, and who regards
chastity in purely technical terms. Violence, then, is a real
danger to Pamela's virtue as she conceives it, but how serious is
Mr. B.'s threat of violence? The first encounter in which he
offers force is suggestive. Pamela records that "he by Force
kissed my Neck and Lips," and proceeds to describe the sequel:

He then put his Hand in my Bosom, and Indignation gave me
double Strength, and I got loose from him by a sudden Spring,
and ran out of the Room; and the next Chamber being open, I
made shift to get into it, and threw-to the Door, and it locked
after me; but he followed me so close, he got hold of my Gown,
and tore a Piece off, which hung without the Door; for the Key
was on the Inside.

I just remembered I got into the Room; for I knew nothing
further of the Matter til afterwards, because I fell into a Fit with
my Terror; and there I lay, till he, as I suppose, looking through
the Key-hole, 'spy'd me upon the Floor, stretch'd out at Length,
on my Face; and then he call'd Mrs. *Jervis* to me, who, by his

Assistance, bursting open the Door, he went away, seeing me coming to myself; and bid her say nothing of the Matter, if she was wise. [I, 31–32]

As a rapist Mr. B. is singularly inept. So much so, in fact, that I am impelled to believe him when, a few pages after the scene reported above, he declares to Mrs. Jervis, in Pamela's presence:

I think her very pretty, and I thought her humble, and one that would not grow upon my Favours, or the Notice I took of her; but I abhor the Thought of forcing her to any thing. I know myself better, said he, and what belongs to me: And, to be sure, I have enough demean'd myself, to take Notice of such an one as she; but I was bewitch'd by her, I think, to be freer than became me; tho' I had no Intention to carry the Jest farther. [I, 35–36]

Pamela's chastity is safe, it would appear, because of a kind of dual safety-device. On the one hand is Pamela's own propensity to throw a fit or to faint when hard-pressed, a mechanism which Ian Watt happily christens her "sociosomatic snobbery," because it is the unconscious expression by her body of her social aspirations. On the other hand, Pamela's chastity is guarded by Mr. B.'s more conscious form of snobbery; he regards rape as beneath him because it is a concession that he must resort to force to have what is his by a kind of *droit de seigneur*. Furthermore, it becomes clear in this encounter, as well as in the others scattered over the first half of the novel, that the courtship of Mr. B. and Pamela is a kind of game, subject to a set of rules which he, at least, understands perfectly. It is permissible, for example, to attempt to frighten Pamela into acquiescence by threats of violence, but it is clearly against the rules to apply *force majeure* or to carry on the game when her power of choice is suspended. A more difficult problem is to ascertain whether Pamela herself understands that the threat of force is illusory. Yet even here, I think, the evidence points to her

awareness. She is present (and conscious) when Mr. B. dis-
claims to Mrs. Jervis the use of violence, and the agitation she
subsequently displays whenever Mr. B. resorts to force is
perfectly consistent with her awareness that he will always stop
short of rape. Her agitation is, in fact, more convincingly
explicable as the expression of her outraged sense of decency
than as an index of her fear. In any case, it seems to me absurd
to suppose that the reader's suspense derives from his uncertainty as to whether Mr. B.'s designs will succeed, and still
more absurd to claim that Pamela herself confronts a real moral
choice. The problem, then, remains. How are we to account
for the suspense which the reader actually does experience?
How can we define the dilemma that Pamela faces?

One of the most striking characteristics of the world represented in *Pamela*, particularly when we compare it with those
in *Moll Flanders* or in Fielding's parody, *Joseph Andrews*, is
the tightness and clarity of its social structure. Whether or not
these qualities may be predicated of the historical reality, they
nevertheless accurately describe the world of the novel in which
Pamela has her existence. At the apex, of course, is the squire,
Mr. B., with his estates in Bedfordshire and Lincolnshire, and
his connections in the peerage. He is the sole and exclusive
representative in the novel of temporal power, suggested by the
fact that he is in the commission of the peace and amply and
clearly demonstrated by his entire freedom from restraint by
any superior authority. He is a law unto himself. Moreover, he
is even free of the moral suasions which would normally be
applied by the representatives of the Church. Mr. Williams, the
only clergyman very much in evidence, is not beneficed, and
he is entirely dependent upon Mr. B. for preferment. And if
this does not give Mr. B. sufficient control over him, that control is reinforced by the terrible potency of money. Mr.
Williams is in the squire's debt, and Mr. B. can accordingly
have him jailed at his pleasure. Downward from Mr. B., the

hierarchy is clearly defined. After the parson we have the tenants, to whom Pamela appeals in vain for help, and then the "upper" servants, Mrs. Jervis, for example, or Mrs. Jewkes, and finally the "lower" servants, like John, the footman who carries Pamela's letters. Outside this hierarchy, but clearly related to it, are Mr. B.'s neighbors, who are bound to him by strong ties of class loyalty. The only person in the novel whose position in the orderly social structure is ambiguous is Pamela herself, and perhaps also her parents. Pamela is a kind of articled servant, who receives no wages and is thus low in the social scale, but her close personal relationship with Lady B. gives her some claim to social equality with Mrs. Jervis. It is certainly suggestive that she has been educated above her station by the kindness of her mistress. Her parents, too, occupy a somewhat ambiguous place in the world. Her father is an educated man who has had a school, but he has suffered reverses and now lives precariously in the humblest station of all, that of an agricultural laborer.

The novel begins with the death of Lady B., an event which precipitates a crisis for Pamela, both because it permits the un-welcome attentions of Lady B.'s son and because it leaves her without a clearly defined position in the household. Her prob-lem, then, is twofold, how to defend her chastity and how to consolidate her social position in the world presided over by Mr. B. I have already given my reasons for thinking that the first is a problem which presents no real difficulty for Pamela, but it is itself the key difficulty in the solution of her second problem. The delicacy of her situation consists in this: that her virtue requires her to say No to Mr. B., while her role as a servant requires her to be obedient to his wishes. To refuse him is easy enough; what is difficult is to refuse him without doing violence to the master-servant relationship. Watt has traced the descent of Richardson's handling of love to the medieval con-ventions of courtly love, and the connection is by no means farfetched. Pamela's problem, in my view of the novel, is after all not essentially different from the one faced by Gawain when, tempted by the solicitations of his host's lady, he must not only fulfill the demands of honor by refusing her but must also fulfill the demands of chivalry by refusing her in such a manner that he will not give offense. Pamela's problem is actually more difficult than Gawain's, for where he can rely on a fully worked-out, explicitly formulated set of rules, the doctrines of courtly love, Pamela is entering upon a game (to revert to a metaphor I have earlier made use of) whose rules she is ignorant of. She is constantly under the necessity of improvising ways of acting to meet the emergencies of the moment. Here, I believe, is the center of interest, the "suspense," if I must use that term, of the novel considered as novel. Let us look at a few of the situations in which Pamela's extraordinary social address is called into play and tested.

The first occasion where she is put on her mettle is the original scene in the summer-house:

One Day he came to me, as I was in the Summer-house in the little Garden, at work with my Needle, and Mrs. *Jervis* was just gone from me; and I would have gone out; but he said, No, don't go, *Pamela;* I have something to say to you; and you always fly me, when I come near you, as if you were afraid of me.

I was much out of Countenance, you may well think; but said, at last, It does not become your poor Servant to stay in your Presence, Sir, without your Business required it; and I hope I shall always know my Place.

Well, says he, my Business does require it sometimes, and I have a Mind you should stay to hear what I have to say to you.

What he has to say turns out to be no particular surprise to anyone, least of all to Pamela, and she tries to break away:

I would have given my Life for a Farthing. And he said, I'll do you no harm, *Pamela;* don't be afraid of me. I said, I won't stay.

You won't, Hussy! said he: Do you know whom you speak to?
I lost all Fear, and all Respect, and said, Yes, I do, Sir, too well!—
Well may I forget, that I am your Servant, when you forget what
belongs to a Master.

I sobb'd and cry'd most sadly. What a foolish Hussy you are!
said he; Have I done you any Harm?—Yes, Sir, said I, the greatest
Harm in the World: You have taught me to forget myself, and
what belongs to me; and have lessen'd the Distance that Fortune
has made between us. [I, 18-19]

Pamela's sense of her own position, its privileges as well as its
responsibilities, is already fully developed, and she is quick to
take advantage of Mr. B.'s tactical blunder in reminding her of
her inferior status, by taking refuge in her inferiority. She has
neatly turned her principal disability into an impregnable
fortress. Mr. B. is badly beaten in this encounter.

Once Pamela's fears about Mr. B.'s sinister motives have
been confirmed, the question which has always proved trouble-
some to Richardson's admirers arises: why doesn't she just go
home? That she does not has generally confirmed the antipamelists in their suspicions of her ulterior motives, and it has
led her admirers to the reluctant admission that in this matter
Richardson has simply proved himself inept and has allowed
the strings to be seen. I do not know that any amount of special
pleading can do away with the patent clumsiness of some of
Richardson's stratagems; the forcible abduction and the cow in
the pasture are awkward and transparent devices at best. Yet
according to the view of the novel that I am here advancing, it
seems to me that her real problem cannot be solved by just
going home. If her sole objective is to preserve her chastity,
then the obvious solution is to go. If her objective is to snare
Mr. B., then the wisest course might be to do the same; after
all, that turns out to be the trick by which, in the cynical view
of her conduct, she finally catches him. But if her objective is
to maintain and consolidate her social status, then to withdraw

would be a confession of defeat; it would not only annihilate everything she has gained (Mr. B. threatens to withhold her "character"), it would deprive her of her very class identity. I believe that in this case what has been taken as the merest rationalization of her delay in returning to her parents—her concern over the state of her wardrobe—is in fact a soundly conceived revelation of Pamela's character and values. She is perfectly willing to move either up or down in the social scale, but she insists always on having her status known and recognized. With typically Richardsonian prudence she will not leave one position until the next is prepared, and though she is willing to resume her life as the daughter of a farm laborer she is unwilling to do so until she can dress the part, until, that is, she can display to the world that she seems what she is.

In arguing that Pamela's central concern is with the clear and unambiguous definition of her social identity, I do not want to imply that she is unambitious or that she would just as soon be a lady's maid as a lady. On the contrary, her whole set of values, her whole range of conduct (even her fainting, as Watt suggests), is expressive of her social aspirations. The very fact that she is jealous of her chastity is an assertion of her (perhaps unconscious) desire to make common cause with the aristocracy, for who ever valued chastity in a servant? Mr. B. sees her, ironically, as a kind of Lucretia, that most aristocratic of virgins, because of the utter intransigence of her ideas about the sacredness of her body. The only qualification I would insist upon in acknowledging that Pamela is a climber is that she always demands full recognition of her right to whatever social niche she is called upon to occupy. She will not have the appearance of the thing unless she can also have the thing, and vice versa. The ultimate defeat, in her view, is to lose one's social orientation, to forfeit one's standing in a world which is both rigidly hierarchical and completely hermetic. It is significant that Miss Sally Godfrey, a victim of Mr. B.'s libertine

ways, is to be commiserated less because of the agitations of
her conscience than because she has become, literally, *déclassée*.

As the novel progresses Pamela proceeds from one dilemma
to another, for Mr. B. is nothing if not pertinacious, and the
social difficulty of her situation becomes increasingly demanding, while the moral problem remains the same or even
disappears altogether. To the arguments of Moloch, Pamela
responds as we have seen; the arguments of Mammon require a
subtler technique of repulsion. Yet even here Pamela is equal to
the difficulty, and her written reply to Mr. B.'s infamous
"articles" is a masterpiece of diplomacy no less than of logic.
"Forgive, good Sir," she writes, "the Spirit your poor Servant
is about to shew in her Answer to your ARTICLES. Not to be
warm, and in earnest, on such an Occasion, as the present,
would shew a Degree of Guilt, that, I hope, my Soul abhors. I
will not trifle with you, nor act like a Person doubtful of her
own Mind; for it wants not one Moment's Consideration with
me; and I therefore return the ANSWER following, let what will
be the Consequence" (I, 256). Pamela is extraordinarily adroit in
parrying the squire's frequent attempts to put her morally in
the wrong or to force her to assume a false position in replying
to his importunities. She can swear with a clear conscience that
her relations with Williams have been innocent, but she is
aware of the implications of her so swearing, and she makes
clear that she does so only to avoid the imputation of being
"forward and artful."

The screw is given another turn when Mr. B., finding both
force and money unavailing, changes from a lion to a lamb and
lays siege to Pamela's virginity with all the arts of politeness.
Now neither injured innocence nor moral indignation will
work for Pamela, and she must conceal her mistrust and her
countermoves under an aspect of humility and complaisance.
Mr. B., with the grossest kind of unfairness, attempts to make
Pamela his confidante, and without offering her marriage he

hints at its possibility and then requires her to give him advice. She has been led to a stream and invited to leap it. If she jumps she is likely to miss her footing and fall, but if she declines to jump then she has made a choice which may prove irrevocable. Pamela's power of equivocation is equal to the demands put upon it; she gives him the advice that her status with respect to him requires, but she succeeds in conveying the hint that if her status were different her advice might be too (I, 294). Mr. B.'s question gets the kind of answer it deserves. By this point in the novel it has become abundantly clear that Mr. B. is no match for Pamela, and that if Pamela is to go on to more brilliant triumphs, she must be provided with still more taxing social situations than Mr. B.'s poor brain can devise. He is himself aware of her abilities, and is inclined to arrogate to himself the credit for having sharpened her wits and enlarged her resourcefulness:

What the duce do we Men go to School for? if our Wits were equal to Womens, we might spare much Time and Pains in our Education. For Nature teaches your Sex, what in a long Course of Labour and Study, ours can hardly attain to. . . . I believe, I must assume to myself half the Merit of your Wit, too: for the innocent Exercises you have had for it from me, have certainly sharpen'd your Invention. [I, 317]

At any rate, Richardson does provide her with a wider, more challenging field for the display of her social prowess by the simple expedient of marrying her to Mr. B.

Nearly all the critics of *Pamela* have regarded with varying degrees of disfavor the fact that Richardson brings about the marriage too soon (at about the halfway point), and that the second half of the novel is therefore largely anticlimactic.[10] Now if we take the central dilemma of the book to be simply a moral one, such an objection is clearly compelling, for the moral dilemma is removed with Pamela's marriage. But if, as I have been arguing, we read Pamela's dilemma as social in nature, then there is no need to regard the second half of the novel as anticlimactic at all. If Pamela's efforts all along have been directed toward living up to the formal demands of her social position, then her marriage settles nothing, but rather precipitates her into a more difficult and trying situation than she has hitherto occupied. She has conquered Mr. B., but the rather more formidable obstacles of public opinion and the objections of the family have still to be dealt with. For this reason, the interest of the episodes which take place after Pamela's betrothal ought to be at least as great as that of the earlier ones, though Richardson's inveterate sentimental moralizing often gets in the way of the development of that interest. Even so, however, the scenes with the neighboring gentry, and especially with Mr. B.'s sister, Lady Davers, are among the most clearly focused and skillfully handled in the novel, and the dramatic conflict they depend on is essentially the same as in the earlier scenes.

During the period of her betrothal, Pamela occupies a position of some delicacy, for though she is still a servant she is nevertheless expected to live up to what will be expected of her as the squire's lady. Mr. B., intent upon displaying his prize to the quality of the neighborhood, invites a group who seem only too ready to be charmed by Pamela, but who in their condescension prove terribly embarrassing to her and subject her to one of her most trying ordeals. She is visited by Sir Simon and Lady Darnford and their daughters, accompanied by Lady Jones and her sister-in-law, and by the rector, Mr. Peters, with his family. Sir Simon is vulgarly facetious; his lady very elegant and condescending; the rector pious; and the younger ladies "affable, kind, and obliging" (as Pamela says), but also patronizing (they praise Pamela's figure in her servant dress) and not a little envious. Pamela comes through her ordeal brilliantly. She achieves just the right and precarious

mixture of humility and pride, displaying an awareness of the
requirements of the situation she is entering upon, but at the
same time conducting herself with just enough deference before these aristocratic ladies and gentlemen. When Lady Jones
passes her a compliment she returns it deftly:

I see very well [Lady Jones remarks], that it will be the Interest
of all the Gentlemen, to bring their Ladies into an Intimacy with
one that can give them such a good Example. I am sure, then,
Madam, said I, it must be after I have been polish'd and improv'd
by the Honour of such an Example as yours. [II, 61]

Pamela knows exactly the degree of familiarity which it is
proper, indeed necessary, for her to assume. She will drink a
cordial with her "Master's" guests because it will enable her to
propose their health, but she begs to be excused from sitting
down to dinner with them because she feels this would be
pushing matters too far too fast. Mr. B. is himself so charmed
by Pamela's social awareness that he threatens to hasten the
day of their marriage, which Pamela has coyly held off for at
least the following week.

But the most dramatic scene in the novel, and the one which
best illustrates all of the tensions to which Pamela is subject,
occurs after her marriage, when Lady Davers, Mr. B.'s sister,
attended by her maid and her nephew Jackey (Richardson's
unfortunate attempt to give us a beau), calls upon Pamela
during her Master's absence. The means by which this encounter is engineered are clumsy enough. Mr. B. is conveniently got rid of three days after his wedding by the stalest
and most transparent of contrivances, a sick friend, and Lady
Davers is received by Mrs. Jewkes, who sets up the misunderstanding on which the scene turns by telling her ladyship that
Pamela is not married, since the marriage has not yet been
publicly announced. Pamela, fluttered by the prospect of facing
Lady Davers, lingers in her closet until the last possible moment

and of course records her palpitations in her journal. Mrs. Jewkes, with thoroughly plebeian coarseness of sensibility, cannot understand why Pamela is fearful. "If it was me," she says, "I would put on an Air as Mistress of the House, as you are, and go and salute her Ladyship, and bid her welcome." Obviously, if she felt herself on the "right side of the hedge," Mrs. Jewkes would revel in the situation, but Pamela, though she may take her own secret joy of the encounter, is made of finer stuff than Jewkes, and she sees, as the servant mentality does not, that she must have Lady Davers on her side or forever suffer the stigma of usurpation. The encounter will indeed be a difficult one for her, since she will have to adjust somehow the conflicting demands of her condition, as the wife of Mr. B., and her quality, as the daughter of Goodman Andrews. Trembling, she descends to the ordeal, but in all her fearfulness she remains conscious of the figure she is cutting. She wears her gloves and carries her fan and resolves to "put on as good an Air" as possible. Lady Davers receives her with open scorn:

Where's your well-manner'd Deceiver gone, Child? says she.—Said I, When your Ladyship is pleased to speak intelligibly, I shall know how to answer.

Well, but my dear Child, said she in Drollery, don't be too *pert* neither, I beseech thee. Thou wilt not find thy Master's Sister half so ready to take thy Freedoms, as thy mannerly Master is!—So, a little more of that Modesty and Humility, that my Mother's Waiting-maid used to shew, will become thee better than the Airs thou givest thyself, since my Mother's Son has taught thee to forget thyself.

I would beg, said I, one Favour of your Ladyship, that if you would have me keep my Distance, you will not forget your own Degree.—Why, suppose, *Miss Pert*, I should forget my Degree, would'st thou not keep thy Distance then?

If you, Madam, said I, lessen the Distance yourself, you will de-

scend to my Level, and make an Equality, which I don't presume
to think of; for I can't descend lower than I am.—at least in your
Ladyship's Esteem! [II, 197]

Even though Lady Davers here suffers the disadvantages of her
ignorance, she is a more formidable, because a more spirited,
adversary than her brother. Pamela's point in this argument is
well-taken; her formal style of address is nicely matched to the
familiar thee–thou which Lady Davers slips into, but the
deliberate assumption of inferiority which paralyzed Mr. B.
does not work so well with Lady Davers, who simply beats the
argument down with a fine feminine disregard of logic. Pamela
quickly finds that she cannot soften Lady Davers's wrath by
words, but even the silence she resolves on has its perils, since
her tormentor provokes her by an impossible request; she
orders Pamela to pour wine for her. This apparently innocuous
request poses a nice dilemma for Pamela, because however
complaisant she tries to be, she cannot, as the wife of Mr. B.,
perform a menial service for her sister-in-law, at any rate not
when it is exacted of her as a duty. She therefore remains silent,
until Jackey forces the issue:

He arose, and brought the Bottle and Glass: Come, said he, Mrs.
Bride, be pleased to help my Lady, and I will be your Deputy. Sir,
reply'd I, 'tis in a good Hand; help my Lady yourself.—Why,
Creature, said she, dost thou think thyself above it?—And then
flew into a Passion; Insolence! continued she, this Moment, when
I bid you, know your Duty, and give me a Glass of Wine; or—
  So I took a little Spirit then—thought I, I can but be beaten.—
If, said I, to attend your Ladyship at Table, or even kneel at your
Feet, was requir'd of me, I would most gladly do it, were I only
the Person you think me; but if it be to triumph over one who
has received Honours, that she thinks require her to act another
Part, not to be utterly unworthy of them, I must say, I *cannot* do
it. [II, 205–206]

Lady Davers is finally forced to look at the truth, even though she has willfully closed her mind to the possibility, and she puts the question directly to Pamela, "Dost thou think thou art really married?" But Pamela has already discovered that to Lady Davers's questions there are no right answers, and furthermore, she is unable to face her adversary on equal terms. When Lady Davers gives her the lie direct, she can only reply, "I am not of Quality to answer such Language," for her social inferiority does not license a categorical denial. So to Lady Davers's direct question she offers a brilliant reply:

I see, Madam, said I, you are resolv'd not to be pleas'd with *any* Answer I shall return: If I should say, I am *not*, then your Lady-ship will call me hard Names, and perhaps I should tell a Fib. If I should say, I *am*, your Ladyship will ask me how I have the Impudence to be so,—and will call it a Sham-marriage. I will, said she, be answer'd more directly. Why, what, and please your Ladyship, does it signify what I think! Your Ladyship will believe as you please. [II, 209]

Pamela is in her native element here, and Richardson under-standably draws this scene out until it is one of the longest pieces of continuous action in the book. The scene is, in fact, a sort of epitome of the novel, at least insofar as it contains all the essential ingredients: the same arbitrary limitation of Pamela's freedom of choice, the same (ludicrous) threats of violence, the same fundamental opposition of wills, and the same kinds of skills displayed in Pamela's successful defense. But this scene does not distract us with a specious moral issue, and it there-fore permits the essential nature of Richardson's fictional technique to be seen.

Pamela's problem of achieving a viable social orientation is both intensified and complicated by her marriage, for that event casts her adrift from the class in which she has hitherto belonged. Accordingly, she must not only conciliate Lady

Davers, she must adjust her relationship to the servants, her erstwhile peers. In most cases Pamela's new social duty runs with her inclination; she enjoys effecting the reinstatement of the Bedfordshire servants who had invoked Mr. B.'s displeasure by siding with her, and she takes a perhaps not altogether innocent pleasure in serving as her husband's almoner. The scene in which she holds up her fingers to intimate to Mr. B. the precise degree his largesse should assume toward each of his servants is a cheerfully absurd indication of how quickly Pamela has learned the lesson of *noblesse oblige*. But in one case at least Pamela is torn by the threatened division of her class loyalties; it is hard for her to forgive Mrs. Jewkes for her allegiance to the very class Pamela now belongs to. That she can forgive her former jailer is less an indication of her charity or the sweetness of her nature than it is an index of her resolution to play the *grande dame*. Certainly with this gesture Pamela severs her ties with the past.

I do not want to rest my argument on the assumption of Richardson's conscious awareness that the central dilemma of the novel is not so much moral as social, because I am not certain how fully he understood the basis of his own art. But once we get beyond the elementary and obvious fact that Richardson thought of himself as a moralist, perhaps we can free ourselves for the recognition that his purposes embraced other ends besides the inculcation of virtue. It has often enough been pointed out that *Pamela* takes its origin in a volume of familiar letters and that Richardson's avowed purpose in that book was to provide moral instruction, but what is generally overlooked or ignored is that the usual and chief purpose of such a volume is to provide models of the correct and appropriate forms of language by which the unlettered can meet the demands of any conceivable social situation, that is, of any situation which can be met by a form of words sanctioned by tradition.[11] That Richardson should seek, not only to fulfill this perfectly obvious intention, but to furnish moral instruction as well is characteristic of him, but it tends to obscure the principal application of the work. Social rituals themselves are important, and their mastery—with or without the moral truth they embody—is an essential ingredient of the good life.

Similarly with *Pamela*. We have become so used to reading this novel exclusively as a moral fable that it is easy to miss the fact that its appeal is grounded not so much in the triumph of modest virtue as in the successful application of social formulas to a practical problem. As a moral treatise *Pamela* seems to me to take us very little further than the proposition implied by its subtitle, "Virtue Rewarded"; as a rendering forth of experience which is made interesting by the play of human motives and purposes, it offers a vastly richer field of speculation and inquiry than so narrowly didactic a purpose will suggest. I make no extravagant claims for the novel's artistic excellence. It seems to me, in fact, very badly flawed. For one thing, the central conflict has been arbitrarily simplified by such clumsy and transparent devices as the abduction and the cow in the pasture. For another, Pamela's social proficiency—best exemplified, perhaps, by her ability to produce a courtly compliment —is scarcely plausible, even if we recall her instruction at the hands of Lady B. And Richardson's crudeness in the portrayal of aristocratic manners and characters is hardly to be forgiven. Nevertheless, with all its defects, the novel reveals a fundamental coherence in its inner form that compensates in part for its structural flaws and suggests that Richardson has hit on a more viable mode of fiction than either Bunyan or Defoe. *Pamela* as a comedy of manners, as a tale of the social success of a flesh and blood heroine armed, not with abstract "Good Deeds," but with the world's own weapons, has a vitality that cannot be destroyed by its artistic crudity—or even by its moral pretensions.

CHAPTER IV

Joseph Andrews as Parody

So the whole thing has a happy ending! How
calm and peaceful would our life be always if a
messenger came from the king whenever we
wanted!
—BRECHT, *The Threepenny Opera*, trans.
Eric Bentley and Desmond Vesey

Shamela is such a devastating parody of *Pamela* that one
wonders why Fielding was impelled to attempt in *Joseph
Andrews* yet another attack on the same work. For all its
brevity *Shamela* is comprehensive; it parodies virtually every
aspect of its original—except perhaps its tediousness. There is
the apparatus of laudatory epistles (two such letters had
appeared in the first edition of *Pamela*, and others in the second
edition of February 14, 1741), the sententious garrulity of the
heroine, the admonitions of her mother, and the impotent
railing of the squire when his desires are frustrated. The events
of the story correspond to those in *Pamela* in remarkable detail,
though of course the compass is much smaller. Shamela's ordeal,
like Pamela's, is punctuated by an abduction into Lincolnshire,
an attempt at suicide, the proffer of a written contract of con-
cubinage, and an abrupt dismissal by the squire, and (again like
Pamela's) it terminates in the squire's abject surrender. Even
Pamela's charitable offices toward her former fellow servants

find their counterpart in Shamela's calculated generosity. All this is brilliantly effective, and it would seem that any attempt to improve on *Shamela's* pungent hilarity would be in vain.

Yet Fielding returned to the assault on *Pamela* in the following year with *Joseph Andrews*, in which the first ten and the last thirteen chapters constitute an explicit parody of Richardson's novel. Commentary has generally focused, however, on the central chapters of the novel, which contain no overt reference to *Pamela* at all. The opening and closing chapters have proved something of an embarrassment to those who, like Irvin Ehrenpreis, would prefer to regard *Joseph Andrews* as "autonomous." [1] The usual way of accounting for these embarrassing chapters is to assume that Fielding "forgot," during the central portion of the novel, that he was writing a parody and allowed the characters to take matters temporarily into their own hands.[2] In spite of an impressive weight of opinion on this point, I think it might be fruitful to explore the contrary assumption that Fielding, far from forgetting the design of making fun of *Pamela*, pursues that objective continuously throughout the novel, though my concern is less with Fielding's intention than with the coherence, or lack of it, in the imaginative vision which shapes the novel. It is the novel itself that I propose to examine.

Fielding's detestation of Richardson, as Digeon long ago pointed out, is centered upon Richardson's "devout admiration" (*admiration béate*) of his own heroine and the moral vision she displays.[3] Fielding's technique in *Shamela* was to assume the events of *Pamela* while he rejected the moral vision which ordered them. Pamela, in other words, emerges as Shamela, with her "true" motives revealed, not only to us, but to herself. Every line of her story embodies the recognition that her whole bearing toward the squire is hypocritical:

The poor Booby frightned out of his Wits, jumped out of Bed, and, in his Shirt, sat down by my Bed-Side, pale and trembling, for the Moon shone, and I kept my Eyes wide open, and pretended to fix them in my Head. Mrs. *Jervis* apply'd Lavender Water, and Hartshorn, and this, for a full half Hour; when thinking I had carried it on long enough, and being likewise unable to continue the Sport any longer, I began by Degrees to come to my self.[4]

Our delight in all this arises out of the awareness that the events described in Richardson's novel can be accounted for by radically different assumptions about character and motive from those which Richardson asks us to make. All we need to do is to assume that instead of being a pure and virtuous maiden Pamela is really an ambitious trollop, and the same pattern of events can be expected to follow.

Joseph Andrews employs exactly the contrary technique. Instead of adopting the events and rejecting the moral vision, Fielding ironically adopts the moral vision and refashions the events as a consequence of that adoption. For this reason the satiric technique of *Joseph Andrews* is less confining than the one employed in *Shamela*, and it opens up a much greater variety of comic possibilities. *Joseph Andrews* emerges as a novel which is perfectly capable of standing alone as a comic masterpiece in its own right, but at the same time it is continuously enriched by its relation to *Pamela*—a relation which begins in the simplest and most obvious devices of parody, but which unfolds into an extraordinarily subtle and far-reaching commentary on Richardson's ethical assumptions. The result is a more durably funny parody of *Pamela*, as well as a more searching critique of its morality, than we can get from *Shamela*.

Parody, in its most literal sense, is the imitation of a literary work for the purpose of ridicule. It reveals itself most obviously in the structure of a work, for in a parody the structure derives from the work imitated. But what is more significant for my own analysis, parody reveals itself continuously in the texture of the style, which exposes at every point the absurd disparity between the informing idea of the original and that of the parody. The parody which announces its presence in both structure and inner form may be taken to constitute a distinctive literary genre, one to which *Shamela* obviously belongs. The parody which is a matter only of inner form, in which the overt pattern of imitation disappears, is rather more difficult to recognize and define. Nevertheless, I believe that the expectations which Fielding establishes by the explicit parody in the first ten chapters of *Joseph Andrews* are not simply held in abeyance during the central forty-one chapters, to be met, finally, in the last thirteen. It seems to me both more natural and more useful to assume that the explicit and unmistakable comparison between *Joseph Andrews* and *Pamela* which is invited in the opening chapters of the former novel draws the reader's attention to that disparity between Fielding's moral vision and Richardson's which, in my view, most sharply defines the inner form of the entire novel. The double shift is thus not a betrayal of Fielding's satirical purpose; it is only a structural modification which permits the inner form to be more fully and effectively displayed. To test this assumption, I must begin with the explicit parody.

Pamela's simple-minded ethic is preserved intact in her brother, the titular hero of *Joseph Andrews*,[5] but it is made ridiculous by several devices. Most important, of course, is the fact that male chastity, though not inherently ridiculous, becomes absurd when it is insisted upon in apparent forgetfulness that it is not subject to the same threat of forcible privation as female chastity. A man who lives in fear of rape is inherently ridiculous. In the second place, Joseph's posture toward Lady Booby (and later Mrs. Slipslop) is both ridiculous and faintly, pathetically chivalrous because neither lady is equipped by nature for the role of seductress. Finally, there is the absurd sententiousness of Joseph's language when he declares that he will never allow his inclinations to get the better of his virtue. The climax of the encounter in which Lady Booby forces him from an eminently sane and reasonable stance into a ridiculous one is worth quoting in full:

"Your virtue! (said the lady recovering after a silence of two minutes) I shall never survive it. Your virtue! Intolerable confidence! Have you the assurance to pretend, that when a lady demeans herself to throw aside the rules of decency, in order to honour you with the highest favour in her power, your virtue should resist her inclination? That when she had conquered her own virtue, she should find an obstruction in yours?" "Madam," said Joseph, "I can't see why her having no virtue should be a reason against my having any: or why, because I am a man, or because I am poor, my virtue must be subservient to her pleasures." "I am out of patience," cries the lady: "did ever mortal hear of a man's virtue! Did ever the greatest, or the gravest men pretend to any of this kind! Will magistrates who punish lewdness, or parsons, who preach against it, make any scruple of committing it? And can a boy, a stripling, have the confidence to talk of his virtue?" "Madam," says Joseph, "that boy is the brother of Pamela, and would be ashamed, that the chastity of his family, which is preserved in her, should be stained in him." [6]

Fielding squeezes all the juice out of this ironic inversion, but it is clear that so simple a device of parody cannot very well sustain a two-volume novel, and he quickly enlarges the scope of the novel by abandoning the confining pattern of imitation. But though the open references to Richardson's novel disappear, at least for the time being, its moral assumptions remain at the focus of Fielding's satiric humor.

The most significant indication that Fielding is ready to drop the brilliant but not very subtle technique of having Joseph defend his virtue against the threats posed by his lascivious mistress is that he now (Bk. I, ch. 11) provides Joseph with a genuine human motive for his moral stance; we discover that Joseph's resistance to Lady Booby is not a prudish affectation of virtue after all, but the natural and laudable consequence of his being in love with Fanny.[7] But the same stroke which humanizes Joseph dulls his edge as an instrument of satire by depriving him of the rigidities of attitude and behavior which made the ridiculous inversion of the opening chapters effective. From this point in the novel Joseph's role is altered; now he is to become the romantic lead (though his simplicity remains functional both as comedy and as satire), and the main comic part is to be filled by Parson Adams. The reshuffling of roles here is doubtless a principal reason for the common supposition that Fielding has abandoned his original intention of ridiculing *Pamela*, but that intention is now to be achieved in a subtler, less direct way. The quixotic Adams, who comes to the fore in Chapter 14 of Book I, is the key to the transition.

Adams's derivation from Don Quixote is obvious and has often been analyzed.[8] Both Adams and Quixote are naïve idealists in a hostile world, a world that systematically frustrates their expectations and generally subjects them to indignities, or physical violence, or both. Both subscribe to ideals which are at once lofty and impracticable, and both have taken their ideals and their notions of the world from books. It should be noted, however, that Adams and Quixote are distinguished in at least one important way: Quixote's ideal is that of knight errantry, a manifest anachronism in the realistic seventeenth-century world that Cervantes provides him, but Adams's ideal is simply Christianity, as it was not only understood but professed by everyone in the novel. What makes Adams a quixotic figure is his unconsciousness of the disparity between professing Christianity and practicing it, a difference almost as wide, Fielding ironically suggests, as that between the romantic ideal of chivalry and the grubby materialism of the world Don Quixote really lives in. Like his literary prototype, Adams combines sublime dignity with ridiculous simplicity; he is simultaneously the patriarch whose role as pastor and paterfamilias charges him with the responsibility of giving spiritual guidance and counsel to others, and the naïve innocent whose ignorance of real evil makes him as virginal as Pamela.[9] In fact, Adams's character is in several important respects comparable to Pamela's. The essence of their likeness is that they both confront the world with an unbelievably simple set of moral axioms or formulas which they naïvely expect will open all doors and solve all difficulties for them. Adams is as literal-minded and unsophisticated in his acceptance of Christianity as Pamela can possibly be in her espousal of technical chastity. The difference, of course, is just that Pamela's formulas work and Adams's do not, and therein lie the main possibilities for parody which Fielding exploits in the central section of *Joseph Andrews*, for Adams is to become the principal instrument of Fielding's *reductio ad absurdum* of the moral view exemplified by Pamela. I do not want to suggest that Adams is a comic or satiric pastiche of Pamela; he is obviously a great deal more. My point is that having referred directly in the opening chapters to Pamela's moral posture, Fielding now seeks to discredit that posture by displaying to us in the character of Adams a moral literalism and simplicity that transcend Pamela's own, and at the same time a warm humanity that is at constant odds with the literalism and simplicity of his doctrinaire Christianity.

The similarity between the moral axioms of Parson Adams and those of Pamela is more than a matter of their simplicity. Both Adams and Pamela are committed to a doctrine of salvation by works. In this respect, of course, Pamela differs sharply from Shamela, who, it will be remembered, favored a sermon of Mr. Williams called "Be Not Righteous Overmuch," and who had studied the works of Mr. Whitefield. Adams and Pamela also share a naïve faith in Providence. Pamela recoils from the idea of suicide by reflecting on its impiety:

This Act of Despondency, thought I, is a Sin, that, if I pursue it, admits of no Repentance, and can therefore hope no Forgiveness.—

And wilt thou, to shorten thy transitory Griefs, *heavy* as they are, and *weak* as thou fanciest thyself, plunge both Body and Soul into everlasting Misery! Hitherto, *Pamela*, thought I, thou art the innocent, the suffering *Pamela;* and wilt thou, to avoid thy Sufferings, be the guilty Aggressor? And, because wicked Men persecute thee, wilt thou fly in the Face of the Almighty, and distrust his Grace and Goodness, who can *still* turn all these Sufferings to Benefits? [10]

Similarly, Adams repeatedly admonishes Joseph when Joseph seems inclined to despair. At one point, when the two men are bound back to back to the bedpost of an inn, and Fanny has been carried off by a lecherous squire, Joseph threatens to do violence to himself, and Adams remonstrates:

You are to consider you are a Christian; that no accident happens to us without the Divine permission, and that it is the duty of a man, much more of a Christian, to submit. We did not make ourselves; but the same Power which made us, rules over us, and we are absolutely at his disposal; he may do with us what he pleases, nor have we any right to complain. A second reason against our complaint is our ignorance; for as we know not future events, so neither can we tell to what purpose any accident tends; and that which at first threatens us with evil, may in the end produce our good. [Bk. III, ch. 11]

It is difficult to avoid the conclusion that Adams's recommendation of the comfortable doctrine of divine providence is an ironic commentary on Pamela's dramatization of her own pathetic innocence. The thrust becomes unmistakable when Adams, toward the end of the novel, once again reproves Joseph for his lack of patience under adversity but reveals his inability to accept his own teaching a moment later when he is told (erroneously, as it turns out) of his son's drowning. Only sorrow which is half affectation, Fielding implies, can find comfort in such facile reflections; real human sorrow is expressed less self-consciously. Both Adams and Pamela are extraordinarily literal-minded in their acceptance of moral precepts. To Pamela the injunction to live chastely conveys a perfectly precise meaning, one that can never be clouded by sophistries about the letter and the spirit. That Adams, too, accepts moral injunctions literally is attested by his disputes with Barnabas (Bk. I, ch. 17) and Peter Pounce (Bk. III, ch. 13), by the simple and irrefutable logic which leads him to ask Trulliber for money (Bk. II, ch. 14), and above all by the whole quixotic cast of his mind which blurs for him the distinction between appearance and reality. It is one of Adams's most conspicuous and characteristic traits that he is never able to distinguish between pretense and sincerity. Thus he is repeatedly deceived, by the "courageous" hunter who would have all cowards hanged but who takes to his heels at the first hint of danger (Bk. II, ch. 9), by the "generous" squire whose extravagant promises even the simple Joseph sees through (Bk. II, ch. 16), and by the humor-loving squire who takes advantage of Adams's simplicity to amuse his company with practical jokes (Bk. III, ch. 7). The fact is that Adams, being utterly devoid of guile, always believes literally everything he is told, and he is quite incapable of detecting even the most conventional literary artifice, as is suggested by his childlike response to the narratives of the lady in the coach or of Mr. Wilson. The former story, the fictitious "Leonora, or the Unfortunate Jilt," Adams accepts at face value, making no distinction between fact and fancy, for he has no disbelief to suspend. His interruptions reveal his own absorption in the story and his entirely uncritical acceptance of it, as well as a pamelesque concern with appearances. "Madam," he cries at one point, "if it be not impertinent, I should be glad to know how this gentleman was drest" (Bk. II, ch. 4), and it is Adams who most vehemently desires to hear the full text of the letters exchanged by Horatio and Leonora (Bk. II, ch. 4). Mr. Wilson's story is "true," but the events are relatively remote in time and place. Still, Adams's lively sympathies are actively evoked, and he cannot forbear his groans at the catalogue of Wilson's youthful follies (Bk. III, ch. 3).

That Pamela's moral tenets, simply held and rigorously followed, prove triumphantly superior to the accidents of existence, while Adams's conspicuously fail to do so, stems from the radically different assumptions made by Richardson and Fielding about the nature of the world in which moral precepts must be rendered operative. Pamela's simple-minded morality will work only—or so Fielding's satire proclaims—in the artificial and unreal world of Richardson's novel. Surely one of the most striking features of Pamela's ordeal is that it takes place in actual isolation—physical as well as moral—from the rest of the world. After the preliminary skirmishing and drawing of lines in Bedfordshire, the action is transferred to Mr. B.'s Lincolnshire estate where Pamela is effectively isolated from other human contact. She does, of course, encounter other people, but these people all belong to the social hierarchy of which Mr. B. is the pinnacle, and they are therefore solidly aligned on his side, except for the unhappy and unfortunate Williams. Under such artificial conditions, in such an arbitrarily restricted universe, Pamela's trial and triumph occur. The moral dilemma is further simplified in Richardson's novel by the conspicuous lack of guile in all the characters, except perhaps Pamela herself. This is, then, a closed world in which unexpected encounters seldom occur and in which vice rarely masquerades as virtue. Pamela, unlike Adams, is rarely deceived about anyone, and her moral choices are made easy by the fact that good and evil almost always wear their own semblance, uncomplicated by vanity or hypocrisy.

It is Fielding's principal device of parody to send a character armed with moral precepts as simple as Pamela's own into a world like the real one, at least insofar as it offers the possibility

of random and unexpected encounters with other human
beings, and insofar as it makes moral choices difficult because
vice is most often concealed under affectation. This degree of
realism seems to me perfectly consistent with Fielding's use of
the picaresque tradition; indeed the picaresque setting provides
just the right milieu for the testing of pamelesque virtue.
Fielding is careful to delineate this world before he introduces
Adams into it. After his dismissal by Lady Booby, Joseph sets
out on foot to rejoin Fanny in London, but he is at once set
upon by robbers, beaten, and left naked in a ditch. Just at this
moment a stagecoach arrives on the scene, and the postilion,
hearing Joseph's groans, pulls up his horses, but the coachman
orders him to drive on, because the coach is "confounded late."
A lady passenger, hearing the groans, inquires into the matter,
but upon being informed that they come from a naked man she
recoils in horror and asks the coachman to drive on. Two other
passengers interest themselves in the matter; an old gentleman
calls for the coachman to go on because he is fearful of the
robbers, but a young lawyer points out that the law may hold
them responsible for the young man's death, which observation
puts a slightly different complexion on the affair. Still, the
coachman refuses to admit Joseph to the coach unless someone
will pay his fare, which of course no one offers to do, and the
lady renews her objections to riding with a naked man. The
lawyer's view finally prevails, however, and Joseph is permitted
to enter the coach, though now his own modesty prevents
him, and he refuses to enter unless someone will lend him a
coat. The account continues:

Though there were several great coats about the coach, it was
not easy to get over this difficulty which Joseph had started. The
two gentlemen complained they were cold and could not spare
a rag; the man of wit saying, with a laugh, that charity began at
home; and the coachman, who had two great coats spread under
him refused to lend either, lest they should be made bloody; the

lady's footman desired to be excused for the same reason, which the lady herself, notwithstanding her abhorrence of a naked man, approved: and it is more than probable, poor Joseph, who obstinately adhered to his modest resolution, must have perished, unless the postilion, (a lad who hath been since transported for robbing a hen-roost) had voluntarily stript off a great coat, his only garment, at the same time swearing a great oath, (for which he was rebuked by the passengers) "That he would rather ride in his shirt all his life, than suffer a fellow-creature to lie in so miserable condition." [Bk. I, ch. 12]

Here is a world of casual encounters and ambiguous personal relations, one in which moral judgments are hard to make. Different moral precepts make conflicting demands; modesty, for example, gets in the way of charity. The courageous decision is made upon pusillanimous motives, and the same moral agent is capable of both virtuous and vicious acts. The postilion who alone obeys the Christian admonition to clothe the naked turns out to be a thief. And people are swayed by other motives than the ones they profess; the lady's fastidiousness, for example, proves fraudulent when we discover that the bottle which was supposed to contain Hungary water is in fact filled with brandy (Bk. I, ch. 12). In such a complicated and misleading world as this the moral judgment of a Parson Adams or a Pamela is ludicrously inadequate.

The world of *Joseph Andrews* exceeds that of *Pamela* in another way, too. It is not only infinitely more complex, it is much wider. The movement of the novel from London to Somerset offers a parallel to the movement in *Pamela* from Bedfordshire to Lincolnshire, but Fielding expands our horizon in other ways than by the mere change of scene. By far the greater part of the novel has a rural setting—the road, especially, with its alehouses and inns, but also an occasional country house, the seat of a squire or rural magistrate. But Fielding provides a fuller spectrum of life than the limited movement of the characters allows by introducing narratives which display other facets of life than those observable by the travelers. The Leonora story, though not particularized in time and place (the names of characters—Leonora, Horatio, Bellarmine—suggest a convention far removed from realism, reminiscent of the novellas in *Don Quixote*) obviously depicts a stylized, artificial, and therefore urban, pattern of life, and Wilson's own autobiographical narrative deals in concrete and Hogarthian terms with the life of a London rake. One inference to be drawn from all this is that vanity and hypocrisy are not specifically rural affectations, but that the whole of society is similarly afflicted.[11] A more important point, however, is that the dimensions of Fielding's world constitute our most convincing proof that the moral life is a difficult and demanding one because we see something of the magnitude both of the forces arrayed against it and of the sheer inertia that all moral activity must combat.

Confronted by the manifold evil and duplicity of this world, simple idealism, even so sturdy a variety as Adams's, is bound to fail. Still, "failure" is a relative term, and we may well inquire in what way Adams may be said to fail. Certainly he does not fail in any purely spiritual sense; his simple Christian morality receives no taint from the evil which surrounds him (this is part of what I meant when I said he was as "virginal" as Pamela), and he remains as committed as before to the Christian life. But Richardson himself provides the license for judging the success or failure of any ethical system by its temporal consequences, and it is clear that Adams derives no benefit of this kind from his constancy to his principles.[12] His goodness, in fact, has exactly the contrary effect of involving him in difficulties of all kinds, and of condemning him to be as often misunderstood by others as they are misunderstood by him. His virtue and his absent-mindedness between them relegate him to the position of the perennial butt.

But though Adams is quite clearly ludicrous as a virtuous man in a wicked world, he is just as clearly an admirable and lovable person, perhaps even more so than his literary prototype, Don Quixote. In this respect, however, he differs more or less conspicuously from Pamela, perhaps because by his very failure to live successfully he acquires the regard which Pamela forfeits by her worldly success. But if Adams's moral stance is to function as a burlesque of Pamela's, the difference must be explored. It is clear, I think, that whatever admiration or affection we may feel toward Adams rests not so much upon his moral perfection as upon his imperfection. The human quality in him that we respond to is, ironically, his very hypocrisy. The parson who has written a sermon against vanity arouses neither liking nor antipathy, but the parson who is proud of his sermon on vanity wins us at once. And the case is the same with Adams's "hypocrisy" toward the end of the novel when he completely disregards his own injunctions to Joseph to bear affliction with fortitude and then breaks down at the news of his own misfortune. Mrs. Adams's comment is revealing, too, when she interrupts her husband as he inveighs against excessive marital devotion:

I hope, my dear, you will never preach any such doctrine as that husbands can love their wives too well. If I knew you had such a sermon in the house, I am sure I should burn it; and I declare, if I had not been convinced you had loved me as well as you could, I can answer for myself I should have hated and despised you. Marry come up! Fine doctrine indeed! A wife hath a right to insist on her husband's loving her as much as ever he can; and he is a sinful villain who doth not. Doth he not promise to love her, and to comfort her, and to cherish her, and all that? I am sure I remember it all, as well as if I had repeated it over but yesterday, and shall never forget it. Besides, I am certain you do not preach as you practise; for you have been a loving and a cherishing husband to me, that's the truth on't. [Bk. IV, ch. 8]

The fact is that the natural man is stronger than the doctrinaire Christian, and the natural man proves to be entirely unself-conscious about asserting his humanity, either by his innocent vanity or by his love for his wife and child. Yet even in its differences Adams's character reflects upon Pamela's, for what is most repulsive in her is not her virtue but the self-consciousness and complacency with which she regards it.

It will be objected, I suppose, that having declared Adams sympathetic for his failure to live up to his own principles and Pamela contemptible for her fidelity to hers, I have aligned Fielding on the side of sin. But Fielding, it need hardly be said, is not opposed to virtue as such; he objects only to a concept of virtue which makes it wholly self-regarding, and he objects to the comfortable assumptions that virtue is an easy choice or that providence rewards the virtuous in some very simple and material way. Pamela's ideal falls considerably below Adams's, because it is self-regarding. Like the lady in the coach whose modesty prevented her from being charitable, Pamela allows her virtue to become a form of self-indulgence. Adams, on the other hand, though he cannot heed his own stoical adjurations to Joseph, does really devote his life to the service of others. But that he himself falls short of the Christian ideal he would be the first to admit, and that he is imperfect—which is to say human—is not Fielding's way of saying that virtue is a lost cause, but that the moral life is hard. Morality for Fielding is much more than obedience to a set of perfectly simple prescriptive rules; it is a complex and precarious ordering of often conflicting obligations which is made more difficult by the fact that the world is so big and complicated and confusing.

In the final chapters of *Joseph Andrews* Fielding reverts to a more overt and explicit kind of parody of *Pamela*, a change signaled by Pamela's own appearance at Booby-Hall. The irony with which she advises Joseph against a union with Fanny because of Fanny's humble rank is obvious but effective:

"Brother," said Pamela, "Mr. Booby advises you as a friend; and, no doubt, my papa and mamma will be of his opinion, and will have great reason to be angry with you for destroying what his goodness hath done, and throwing down our family again, after he hath raised it. It would become you better, brother, to pray for the assistance of grace against such a passion, than to indulge it."—"Sure, sister, you are not in earnest; I am sure she is your equal at least."—"She was my equal," answered Pamela, "but I am no longer Pamela Andrews, I am now this gentleman's lady, and as such am above her—I hope I shall never behave with an unbecoming pride; but at the same time, I shall always endeavour to know myself, and question not the assistance of grace to that purpose." [Bk. IV, ch. 7]

The satire here is directed not only against Pamela's social snobbery but, even more importantly, against the moral egotism that enables her to see herself as the recipient of divine grace. I do not believe that Fielding questions her sincerity, as he did in *Shamela*, but he offers a powerful rebuke to her spiritual pride, a pride which suggests the arrogance of the Calvinist divine proclaiming his own election. We see overtly displayed the spiritual pride which was satirized implicitly by Adams's selflessness and humility.

But a good many scenes and events in the fourth book which do not include Pamela or her husband recall Richardson's novel and take on satiric pungency when they are referred to events or situations in that novel. The main business of *Pamela*, of course, is the often riotous assault on Pamela's virtue by Mr. B., an archetypal situation which is mirrored frequently, though in miniature, in the concluding chapters of *Joseph Andrews*. I shall pass over the hilarious episode in which Adams mistakes Fanny's bed for his own, a staple device of farce,[13] and consider here only the ludicrous attempts of Beau Didapper to ravish Fanny, which lead up to Adams's comedy of errors. The language of the beau's first encounter with Fanny is very much like that of countless such scenes in *Pamela*:

He stopt his horse, and swore she was the most beautiful creature he ever beheld. Then instantly alighting, and delivering his horse to his servant, he rapt out half a dozen oaths that he would kiss her; to which she at first submitted, begging he would not be rude: but he was not satisfied with the civility of a salute, nor even the rudest attack he could make on her lips, but caught her in his arms, and endeavoured to kiss her breasts, which with all her strength she resisted, and, as our spark was not of the Herculean race, with some difficulty prevented. [Bk. IV, ch. 7]

That Beau Didapper is not "of the Herculean race" (he is, Fielding tells us, "about four foot five inches in height") is crucial to the effect here, for it not only explains why Adams, entering the fracas between Beau Didapper and Mrs. Slipslop in the dark, mistakes Didapper for the female in distress and Mrs. Slipslop for the would-be ravisher, it enables us to see Fanny's successful defense of her virtue as a *reductio ad absurdum* very much like the inversion of the first book, when Joseph was called upon to defend his virtue against Lady Booby. And Fanny's conduct throughout contrasts sharply with the absurdities of Pamela's in a similar situation. Fanny is less "nice" than Pamela, readily admitting the beau's salute, and the inference is that Pamela's scruples are absurd and excessive. In any case we have no doubts of Fanny's essential dignity and wholesomeness; as Digeon acutely observed, she is to be opposed to Pamela as an example of "authentic" chastity.[14] And in the second place, Fanny responds to the assault on her chastity by vigorously (and successfully) defending herself instead of resorting to the passive technique of fainting, as Pamela habitually does. The contest is also significant in that it pits the health and high spirits of the country girl against the degenerate and impotent passions which we have already (in Mr. Wilson's tale, for example) learned to associate with the town beau.

The denouement, which Fielding effects with a magnificently absurd double discovery, has generally been regarded as owing more to the traditions of theater or of romance than to a sentimental moral fable like *Pamela*, but even here I think we can discern the hand of the parodist.[15] The whole point of Richardson's novel was that virtue was to be rewarded, that providence, moving in its own mysterious ways, sought out and bestowed its blessing upon the virtuous. Ehrenpreis attributes much the same view of providence and the law of compensation to Fielding by declaring that "it is well known that Fielding's profuse employment of coincidence is his deliberate way of teaching us to trust in Providence." [16] All right. But does Fielding expect Providence to operate according to a prearranged timetable or to put a price on virtue in pounds, shillings, and pence? It would seem to me far more likely that he uses the absurd piling up of coincidence at the end of *Joseph Andrews* to ridicule the notion that the cosmos so patly rewards virtue and punishes vice. The contrived ending of this novel—the opportune arrival of the peddler and of Mr. Wilson, their sensationally improbable disclosures, the stale device of the birthmark—is a final ironic commentary on the world of *Pamela*, a world which suffers no injustice to triumph, where patient merit, though it must take for a while the spurns of the unworthy, is always rewarded in the end. But the satiric effect of the ending depends on its relation to the rest of the novel, for if we had been made to regard such events as commonplace we could hardly respond to them as violations of the cause and effect sequence that the first part of the novel had taught us to regard as normal. Every novel establishes, most often implicitly, its own canons of probability, so that an event which appears wildly improbable in one tale will be perfectly ordinary in another. The ending of *Joseph Andrews*, as I have suggested, would offend no one who was conditioned to the normal artifices either of stage comedy or of sentimental fiction, but because it is superimposed on a story in which the moral

assumptions are realistic and the ordering of events as chaotic
as life itself, the improbability is magnified to the point of
ludicrousness. Fielding has turned his story inside out, as it
were, by grossly violating the sense of probability he has
instilled in us. *The Threepenny Opera* illustrates exactly the
same technique, turned to a somewhat different purpose, for
where Brecht bitterly assails the sentimental complacency of
the public, Fielding directs the main thrust of his satire against
the naïve and unrealistic assumptions of Richardson's novel.

There can be no quarrel with the judgment that *Joseph
Andrews* is a more nearly self-contained, as well as a richer,
novel than *Shamela*. *Joseph Andrews* is, as Fielding's preface
proclaims, an experiment in the comic, and as such its humor
is largely independent of its relation to *Pamela*, but grows
instead out of the universalized attributes of its characters.
Reading *Pamela* is not a prerequisite to the enjoyment of
Joseph Andrews. *Shamela*, on the other hand, can pretend to no
autonomy at all; the reader who has not also read *Pamela* will
miss the whole point, for the joke depends on the closeness with
which Fielding has imitated Richardson. The technique, as we
have seen, is an absurdly simple one; by altering a single
assumption, the assumption of Pamela's moral naïveté, Fielding
succeeds in charging Richardson's book with a new significance,
in realizing a layer of meaning which is only latent in *Pamela*.
It is nevertheless true that the incongruity, the likeness in difference, can only be perceived by the reader who is simultaneously aware of the motives assigned by Richardson and of
their perversion at the hand of Fielding. As comedy, which
deals at least in part with universals, *Shamela* does not work; as
parody it does all that can be done with the technique of close
imitation.

Yet it seems to me fruitful to regard *Joseph Andrews* as
parody too, of a different, less pointed, but more comprehensive, kind. *Shamela* is a work which never transcends the

limitations imposed on it by the book it is attacking; Fielding's assault comes from within, so to speak, and the weight of his animus falls wholly on Pamela, the character. *Joseph Andrews*, however, establishes its own vantage point from which to observe the world of *Pamela*, and the absurdities that Fielding finds there are laid to the charge of Richardson himself. Furthermore, parody is not simply one of a number of ingredients which make up the novel *Joseph Andrews*, for in Fielding's irrepressible impulse to ridicule *Pamela* and Richardson, I believe, can be found the novel's unifying perspective or inner form. If we fail to recognize that impulse the novel becomes fragmented and incomplete, and the best evidence of this is that the critics who ignore or undervalue the element of parody most often find fault with the novel's structure. The suggestions most frequently offered as unifying principles—the spectrum of town and country life, or the journey from London into Somersetshire—are not really principles at all, but arbitrary patterns, which themselves derive point and emphasis from Fielding's persistent, if not altogether systematic, efforts to subject to ridicule the proposition at the heart of *Pamela*, that the choice between good and evil is simple. I have no concern here with the positive implications of this point, although it is essential to recognize that Fielding is doing more than sweeping away the rubbish of Richardson's morality; he is expounding his own morality. That the novel is Christian and moralizing in its tendency, however, has been ably and fully argued,[17] and I do not intend to trace Fielding's principles to their source, or even to characterize his religious and moral position. My concern is rather with the negative proposition that I take to be, if not the most important idea, at any rate the shaping idea of *Joseph Andrews*, that the morality which Richardson offers is worthless as an ideal and fraudulent as a policy.

To argue that *Joseph Andrews* is given form by Fielding's

impulse to parody is not to diminish its claims to greatness. On the contrary, to assert, as I have done, that the novel is a consistent parody of *Pamela* is to establish an additional claim. Parody and comedy are doubtless to be regarded as distinct modes, but they do not get in each other's way at all. The characters and incidents of *Joseph Andrews*, which are richly comic in their own right, simply take on satirical point by being referred always to Richardson's simple-minded assumptions about the world. And it can scarcely amount to a derogation of Fielding's genius to defend him from the imputation that he found no adequate form to contain his comic matter, or that he started out to do one thing, then twice changed his mind. The most remarkable thing about *Joseph Andrews*, I believe, is that it should be simultaneously a coherent parody of another work and an authentic comic masterpiece in its own right.

‡ CHAPTER V ‡

Sterne and the Logos

"I would have avenged myself, if I had been able," said Sancho, "whether I had been dubbed a knight or not; although it is my opinion that those who had such sport with me were not phantoms or human beings under a spell as your Grace says, but flesh-and-blood men like us. They all had names, for I heard them calling one another by them as they were tossing me. There was one who was called Pedro Martinez, and another Tenorio Hernandez, and the innkeeper's name was Juan Palomeque the Left-Handed."
—CERVANTES, *Don Quixote*, trans.
Samuel Putnam

The novel had been invented so often by 1759, when the first two volumes of *Tristram Shandy* appeared, that Sterne was under no compulsion to invent it again. *Moll Flanders, Tom Jones, Roderick Random*, and to a lesser extent Richardson's three novels had established a biographical format, and Sterne took from them virtually nothing else. Indeed, in important ways, Sterne stands outside the main tradition of English fiction, for not only did he systematically violate all the expectations that Defoe, Richardson, Fielding, and Smollett had taught novel-readers to form, his magnum opus has remained stubbornly indigestible ever since. This is not to say that Sterne ignored or was indifferent to tradition. He systematically and shamelessly pillaged every writer who had anything to offer him, especially Rabelais, Cervantes, Burton, and Locke,[1] and of course his arsenal of comic effects depends on the existence of a recognizable novel tradition. But in the most important sense *Tristram Shandy* is unique, and this uniqueness raises a number of problems for criticism. The familiar categories of plot and character, and even of diction and thought, are of little use in attempting to understand the nature and the form of the novel. Nevertheless, though *Tristram Shandy* resists conventional critical distinctions, I believe it has an identifiable substance and form, and my attempt, in what follows, is to give an account of them.

Literary criticism, obviously, must begin with the linguistic surface of any work it proposes to examine, but in dealing with most novels, the critic can, indeed must, pass very quickly to the things which language signifies, specifically, thought, character, events. Even the most mannered novelists generally expect us to look through their words to the "realities" they convey. But with Sterne the case is different. We always have the sense, in reading *Tristram Shandy*, that Sterne is deliberately holding our attention on the surface of the novel so to speak, on the words which compose it. We are continuously made conscious of the ways in which words (or other signs) impinge on what Sterne would call the "sensorium," and the devices by which this is accomplished are worth noting.

One of Sterne's—or rather Tristram's—most conspicuous mannerisms is his trick of making the reader a full and active partner in the process of communication. The frequent apostrophes, "Sir," "Madam," "Your Worships," constantly solicit the reader's attention, or make even greater demands upon him, asking him to read more carefully, to consult his prior reading, or even to reread a chapter in order to recover a subtlety that Tristram is particularly proud of and does not want his lady reader to miss. The reader feels talked at as well as to, and the result is an effect of participating in a conversation with the author. This effect is further reinforced by the deliberate attempt to make the act of writing and the act of reading seem to occur simultaneously. Tristram writes with a clock at his elbow, and the time-sense is acute. "It is about an hour and a half's tolerable good reading since my uncle Toby rung the bell" (Vol. II, ch. 8), he writes, or "I write in such a hurry, I have no time to recollect or look for it" (Vol. I, ch. 21), and the reading time is equivalent to and superimposed upon the writing time. At one point Tristram rebukes his inattentive lady reader for missing the implication that prenatal baptism was a specifically Roman Catholic doctrine; a passage of actual dialogue with the reader ensues, ending with his sending the lady back to reread the last chapter, and then he proceeds to while away the "interim" by chatting inconsequentially with his masculine readers. "But here comes my fair Lady," he concludes, and the narrative moves forward again (Vol. I, ch. 20). The effect of simultaneity is further enhanced by the suggestions that at any given moment Tristram is as innocent as his reader as to what lies ahead, that he can speak only what the Lord has put in his mouth:

Is it not a shame to make two chapters of what passed in going down one pair of stairs? for we are got no farther yet than to the first landing, and there are fifteen more steps down to the bottom; and for aught I know, as my father and my uncle Toby are in a talking humour, there may be as many chapters as steps;— let that be as it will, Sir, I can no more help it than my destiny:— A sudden impulse comes across me—drop the curtain, Shandy—I drop it—Strike a line here across the paper, Tristram—I strike it—and hey for a new chapter! [Vol. IV, ch. 10]

And Tristram furthers the illusion of perfect spontaneity by confiding to the reader his present difficulties in writing.

"When a man sits down to write a history," he complains, "tho'
it be but the history of Jack Hickathrift or Tom Thumb, he
knows no more than his heels what lets and confounded
hinderances he is to meet with in his way,—or what a dance he
may be led, by one excursion or another, before all is over"
(Vol. I, ch. 14). His triumph at a successful coup turns into
despair when he thinks of the difficulties which lie ahead:

What a lucky chapter of chances has this turned out! for it has
saved me the trouble of writing one express, and in truth I have
anew already upon my hands without it—Have not I promised
the world a chapter of knots, two chapters upon the right and
the wrong end of a woman? a chapter upon whiskers? a chapter
upon wishes?—a chapter of noses?—No, I have done that—a
chapter upon my uncle Toby's modesty: to say nothing of a chapter upon chapters, which I will finish before I sleep—by my great
grandfather's whiskers, I shall never get half of 'em through this
year. [Vol. IV, ch. 9]

Such frequent asides to the reader make him a collaborator in
the difficult art of the writer, for he is invited to share the
triumphs and the perplexities of novel-writing. The technique
leads to, among other things, a sharpened awareness of the
verbal surface of the novel.

Another resource which Tristram taps to the same purpose
is a closet full of curious and recondite documents, which he is
fond of reproducing in full. He offers us, among others, the
texts of a marriage settlement, a disputation by the doctors of
the Sorbonne, a sermon, an instrument of excommunication,
and a *fabella* by the fictitious Hafen Slawkenbergius. Setting
aside for a moment the satirical or purely comic purposes which
these documents serve, I think it is apparent that an important
reason for their inclusion is their variety of styles and forms of
discourse. Two of the documents are in Latin, one in French,
one in the distinctive style of pulpit oratory, and one in the

abstruse language of the law. After quoting two and a half pages of this last text, the marriage settlement of his parents, Tristram abruptly breaks off the involuted legal terminology to declare: "In three words,—'My mother was to lay in, (if she chose it) in London'" (Vol. I, ch. 15). Since the substance can be so easily and tersely delivered, the only reason for quoting the document at all is to provide us with a sample of its curious language.

Throughout the novel, in fact, we are confronted by cant and jargon words and the special vocabularies of law, medicine, mathematics, rhetoric, and military science. And it is not only Dr. Slop who talks of consubstantials, impriments, and occludents; Tristram's own vocabulary is full of words like *buccinatory*, *orbicular*, and *oedematous*. We feel always that Tristram, and through him Sterne, is attempting to stretch the fabric of language to its utmost extent. Not content with ransacking the special lexicons of art and science, he coins words freely, not so much to render nuances beyond the reach of ordinary language, as to reveal his own virtuosity.[2] The usual pattern is to take an existing root and graft unusual suffixes upon it (*concupiscible*, *philosophating*, *parallelogramical*, *scientintically*), and the effect is not to alter meaning but to hold our attention upon the word.

A somewhat similar device is Sterne's extensive use of non-verbal means of communication. The Shandean quirks of typography—the black and marbled pages, the pointing fingers, the lines, diagrams, and rows of asterisks—are substitutes for words, commenting on the inadequacies of ordinary language, but more importantly, reminding us that words, too, are typographical devices. A similar effect arises within the novel, when the characters communicate with each other (whether by design or not) through inarticulate sounds, gestures, or expressions. Mr. Shandy's crossed arms or his posture on the bed are unintentionally eloquent, and Toby's "*argumentum fistula-*

torium," the whistling of "Lillabullero," is more expressive than his words. Toby, of course, relies more than his brother on nonverbal means of communication, and his "humph," on being told by Dr. Slop that the Roman Church has seven sacraments, is not only indicative of his feelings, it is a reasoned disquisition. The "humph," so Tristram tells us, was "not accented as a note of acquiescence,—but as an interjection of that particular species of surprize, when a man, in looking into a drawer, finds more of a thing than he expected.—Humph! replied my uncle Toby. Dr. Slop, who had an ear, understood my uncle Toby as well as if he had wrote a whole volume against the seven sacraments.—Humph! replied Dr. Slop, (stating my uncle Toby's argument over again to him)" and so on (Vol. II, ch. 17). When Corporal Trim throws his hat on the floor to express the finality of death, he is using gesture to extend the possibilities of language, but when he describes Tristram's accidental circumcision he uses gesture as a kind of euphemism, to avoid the necessity of indelicate language: "Trim, by the help of his forefinger, laid flat upon the table, and the edge of his hand striking a-cross it at right angles, made a shift to tell his story so, that priests and virgins might have listened to it" (Vol. V, ch. 20).

By the very frequency of their employment, the nonverbal means of communication become incorporated into the fabric of language; gestures acquire a full range of connotative and denotative meaning, and questions of propriety and decorum are raised by expressions or gestures or "meaningless" sounds just as they are by words. Walter Shandy, the most verbal character in the book, understands the language of gesture better than anyone: "There are a thousand unnoticed openings, continued my father, which let a penetrating eye at once into a man's soul" (Vol. VI, ch. 5), and he goes on to enumerate the gestures which he finds offensive for this reason, concluding that the tutor whom he employs for Tristram "shall neither

strike, or pinch, or tickle,—or bite, or cut his nails, or hawk, or
spit, or snift, or drum with his feet or fingers in company;—nor
(according to Erasmus) shall he speak to any one in making
water,—nor shall he point to carrion or excrement." Nothing
that a man says or does, no gesture or expression, is void of
meaning in the Shandean world, and this intense preoccupation
with the process of communication helps to focus our attention
upon the word.

One final characteristic of the novel's language must be
noted; the sheer exuberance of verbal fancy, which, like the
cant and jargon words and the coinages, carries us back to
Rabelais. The Rabelaisian catalogue, the long, pedantic, inevitably redundant series (I shall not reproduce any of these; the
curious reader is referred to the lists of wearing apparel [Vol.
VI, ch. 19] or of the branches of knowledge [Vol. I, ch. 21]
for examples), overpowers the reader with the weight of
verbiage. And the outrageous puns and *double-entendres*,
usually obscene, are Rabelaisian, too, reflecting the same almost
infantile delight in the tricks which language can be bent to.

It is easy to be misled, as I think F. R. Leavis is, into taking
all this wordplay as "nasty trifling." It is play, but play may be
of a very serious kind. In *Tristram Shandy* Sterne seems to me
to be anything but frivolous (though he may be facetious), for
his linguistic jugglery tells us a good deal about the properties
of words. The novel's deepest meaning, perhaps, as well as its
principle of organization, may be sought in the commentary it
offers on its own medium.[3] Language (Sterne seems to be
saying) mediates, often inadequately, often unnecessarily, between mind and mind, and between mind and things. Words
are double in nature; sometimes they may be regarded as pure
exfoliations of mind, at other times they are substitutes for
things. This distinction is analogous to, but not identical with,
the distinction between connotation and denotation. As what
I have called exfoliations of mind, words (and gestures or other

nonverbal signs) are the openings into the soul; they signify no existing reality, only the ideas or the emotions which are themselves products of the conceiving mind. They express the person who gives them utterance, but no other thing. Words as substitutes for things, on the other hand, "mean" the thing they denote, and in fact are often confused with it. The interchangeability of words and things is a recurrent motif in *Tristram Shandy*. Tristram refers nostalgically to the school of eloquence which flourished, by his account, in Rome, whose greatest effects were produced by substituting the thing for its name, in the manner of Swift's Laputan projector (Vol. III, ch. 14), and of course Toby's researches lead him inevitably from the terms of fortification to the models of counterscarps, ravelins, and curtins.

Corresponding to the two natures of language are two functions. Language operates either as expression or as evocation. It may be used, that is, to objectify what is in the mind, either thoughts or feelings, and its use in this way is not dependent on an audience. Toby's whistling of "Lillabullero," for example, generally does communicate, but it is not intended to do so. On the other hand language may be used evocatively, or what amounts to the same thing, magically. By signifying things, words come to have power over things, and the operation of naming acquires an almost mystical significance, as when Tristram congratulates himself on the coining of the rhetorical term, *argumentum fistulatorium* (Vol. I, ch. 21). Neither of these functions of language can be said to have been invented or discovered by Sterne, but his fictional application of them is, so far as I know, unique. Nearly all the misunderstandings in the novel can be said to arise because of the confusion between the two kinds or uses of words, and the misunderstandings clearly impel and sustain the motion of the narrative.

The confusion typically arises when one mode of discourse is mistaken for the other. "Zounds!" cries Phutatorius when the hot chestnut drops into his breeches, but his hearers, unaware of the accident, are at a loss to interpret his utterance:

> One or two who had very nice ears, and could distinguish the expression and mixture of the two tones as plainly as a *third* or a *fifth*, or any other chord in musick—were the most puzzled and perplexed with it—the *concord* was good in itself—but then 'twas quite out of the key, and no way applicable to the subject started;—so that with all their knowledge, they could not tell what in the world to make of it.
>
> Others who knew nothing of musical expression, and merely lent their ears to the plain import of the *word,* imagined that Phutatorius, who was somewhat of a cholerick spirit, was just going to snatch the cudgels out of Didius's hands, in order to be-mawl Yorick to some purpose—and that the desperate mono-syllable Z—ds was the exordium to an oration. [Vol. IV, ch. 27]

Allied to the confusions which arise from mistaking the mode of discourse are the divagations which begin when one mode substitutes inappropriately for another. When Dr. Slop attempts to untie the knots with which Obadiah has secured his bag of medical instruments and in the process accidentally cuts his thumb, he begins to curse Obadiah: "Curse the fellow . . . I wish the scoundrel hang'd—I wish he was shot—I wish all the devils in hell had him for a blockhead—" (Vol. III, ch. 10). Now, of course Dr. Slop is using language expressively here to relieve his own feelings of exasperation, but Mr. Shandy, a most literal-minded man, takes him quite seriously, that is, he assumes that Dr. Slop's words are used evocatively, and he makes him a present of the famous curse of Ernulphus, a horrifying, cold-blooded, and comprehensive anathema. The purpose of this document, whose very comprehensiveness and orderliness drain it of all passion, is quite literally to bring damnation upon its ob-ject, and it is therefore not only far more extreme than the case calls for, its intention is altogether inappropriate.

Perhaps the most striking instance of the confusion of the

two modes, however, is in the varied response to the death of
Tristram's brother Bobby. Instead of giving way to conventional expressions of sorrow, Mr. Shandy launches into a stylized, pedantic oration on death, full of the traditional platitudes.
Toby, attending only to the sense, is bewildered, for the cathar-
tic effect of the language is not in its meaning but in the act of
speaking itself. A parallel scene takes place in the kitchen, where
Trim discourses eloquently of death, but he fails utterly to
communicate with his hearers because the expressive character
of his language is submerged entirely in the denotative. They
hear the words, but not the tune. Death suggests to Susannah
only the clothes she will receive when her mistress goes into
mourning; to the scullion it conveys no meaning at all, except
that he is himself alive; to Obadiah it means that he will have "a
terrible piece of work in stubbing the ox-moor" (for Mr.
Shandy had been debating whether to use a legacy to allow
Bobby to travel or to improve his property). Only momen-
tarily, when Trim drops his hat to the floor as a gesture expressive of the inevitability of death, do his hearers emerge from
their self-absorption long enough to realize the full import of
Trim's speech (Vol. V, ch. 2–7).

But even when the two modes of discourse do not interfere
with each other or substitute for each other inappropriately,
they remain curiously ineffectual. The language of expression
does not work, at least as communication, because, as we have
seen, people insist on interpreting it in another sense than the
one intended. Tristram's own attempts to express his feelings
are either ludicrous or sentimental (that is, exaggerated), or
both. When he adjures his uncle Toby to avoid that "bewitch-
ing phantom, KNOWLEDGE," he is overcome by emotion
and ends with a tender apostrophe, "O my uncle! my uncle
Toby!" which is incomprehensible to the reader because the
feeling expressed is incommensurate with the occasion (Vol. II,
ch. 3). Tristram is aware of this, and he allows "the apostrophe

[to] cool" by an irrelevant (and not very convincing) analogy between writing and painting. Tristram has attempted, so to speak, to express feeling without any objective correlative, and the attempt is a failure, for any such effort to express mind without reference to things (as in the *Tristrapaedia*) is futile.

The language of expression does, however, work for the speaker, especially when its import is least understood by the hearer. Wit is the most convenient and efficacious avenue for the discharge of spleen. When Mr. Shandy entrusts Obadiah with the breeding of his mare, the unlooked for result is a mule, and everyone expects the direst consequences for Obadiah: "My mother and my uncle Toby expected my father would be the death of Obadiah—and that there never would be an end of the disaster.—See here! you rascal, cried my father, pointing to the mule, what you have done!—It was not me, said Obadiah. —How do I know that? replied my father. Triumph swam in my father's eyes, at the repartee—the Attic salt brought water into them—and so Obadiah heard no more about it" (Vol. V, ch. 3). And when Tristram himself is called upon to pay what he regards as an unjustified impost during his travels in France he repays himself by discharging his wit at the commissary: "I was sensible I had said as many clever things to the commissary as came to six livres four sous" (Vol. VII, ch. 36). But it remains true that expressive language is regularly misunderstood by its auditors, and its effectiveness as expression is paradoxically a consequence of its being so misunderstood.

The language of evocation generally turns out to be still less effective, because its power resides in its communicative efficiency. Toby finds himself unable to explain how and where he has received his wound because of his ignorance of the nomenclature of fortification. But even after he has made himself expert (his expertise is itself an indication of the latent power of words over things), the ambiguities of the technical vocabulary of fortification impede communication. Dr. Slop insists on taking words like "curtin" and "horn-works" in their nontechnical (or indecent) sense, but even a literal-minded man like Mr. Shandy has difficulties with the shifting terminology, and Toby tries vainly to explain:

The common men, who know very little of fortification, confound the ravelin and the half-moon together,—tho' they are very different things;—not in their figure or construction, for we make them exactly alike in all points;—for they always consist of two faces, making a salient angle, with the gorges, not straight, but in form of a crescent.—Where then lies the difference? (quoth my father, a little testily.)—In their situations, answered my uncle Toby:—For when a ravelin, brother, stands before the curtin, it is a ravelin; and when a ravelin stands before a bastion, then the ravelin is not a ravelin;—it is a half-moon;—a half-moon likewise is a half-moon, and no more, so long as it stands before its bastion;—but was it to change place, and get before the curtin,— 'twould be no longer a half-moon; a half-moon, in that case, is not a half-moon;—'tis no more than a ravelin.—I think, quoth my father, that the noble science of defence has its weak sides. [Vol. II, ch. 12]

The ambiguities are not finally resolved until Toby has replaced the words with things, and takes to discoursing of battles and sieges by re-enacting them. But the "language" of the bowling green is as incomprehensible and esoteric as the ordinary language it replaces. Toby and the faithful Trim live in a private world that others cannot enter. Tristram conveys his own sense of this by telling the story of the bowling green campaigns out of its chronological sequence, a fact which serves to stress the inaccessibility of the bowling green campaigns.

The power of words to control matter is implied by the discussion of baptism and by Walter's elaborate theory of names (for he holds that the associations of a name govern the thing named, not the contrary), as well as by the story of the Abbess of Andouillets, who tries to make the mule go by the use of the mule-driver's obscenities (at the same time that she avoids the sin of the language by dividing the syllables of the words with the novice who accompanies her) (Vol. VII, ch. 25). Sterne in fact develops, chiefly through the agency of Mr. Shandy, an ontology which holds that reality is constituted by naming it. Whatever has or can be given a name must really exist (as Sancho Panza naïvely assumes), exactly as though every word spoken by man is a finite repetition of the infinite logos, the mystical word of creation. Tristram certainly regards the exfoliations of his own brain with a certain amount of awe; he coins an aphorism and then remarks, "That observation is my own;—and was struck out by me this very rainy day, March 26, 1759, and betwixt the hours of nine and ten in the morning" (Vol. I, ch. 21), as though the act of creation, even purely verbal creation, is somehow mysterious and irrevocable. That the act or process of naming should be regarded as irreversible is itself an indication of its magical nature. Tristram, having told us that Toby "was a man of courage," feels as committed to the word that has passed his lips as any Quaker (Vol. II, ch. 12), and Trim encounters a similar difficulty after having declared that the King of Bohemia was unfortunate, for he must invent reasons to justify the adjective (Vol. VIII, ch. 19). Naming is a sacred, even a sacramental rite, because it brings something into being that cannot later be denied or annihilated. It doesn't really matter that this extreme realism is denied by events: people are misnamed, the mule does not go.

The difficulties in communication which beset all the characters in this novel, the reverential but wholly absurd attitude toward language and the act of naming, suggest that Sterne's primary intention is satiric, that he is making fun of the abuses and inadequacies of language. *Tristram Shandy* is in fact an extraordinarily rich catalogue of the possibilities of misunderstanding and confusion that are inherent in language, but it is clear, at the same time, that Sterne's feeling about language is ambivalent. He understands the idols of the marketplace for what they are, but he also loves words and enjoys luxuriating in them. We sense, I believe, that while he sees all the absurdities of the lawyer's language in the Shandean marriage contract, he still enjoys rolling words like *messuage, escheats, deodands,* and *hereditaments* off his tongue, that he is himself strongly affected by the incantatory qualities of language.

Sterne is interested in the logos in another sense. The logos is not only the mystic word of creation; it is also the rational principle governing the universe, and Sterne is as much preoccupied with speculative thought as he is with the language that expresses it. No sooner, in fact, do we penetrate the verbal surface of the novel, than we become aware of a bewildering profusion of ideas, theories, and hobby-horsical notions of the world. It may be said that the book at this level of significance is made up of a series of antitheses, between theory and practice, between the abstract and the concrete, between the deductive and the inductive motions of the mind, between learning and common sense, between authoritative and empirical knowledge, and so on.

Walter Shandy is of course the most prolific of theory, which is to say that he possesses the most stubborn faith in the power of the logos. His various theories of the making and rearing of children, together with their successive refutations, furnish, in the most literal sense, the substance and form of the first five and a half volumes. He has formed wholly a priori and deductive theories of the influence of animal spirits on the homunculi, of the influence of noses on family fortunes, of the influence of names on the thing named, and of the influence of circumcision, education, and sartorial correctness on the well-being of the child. The satiric thrust of all this is unmistakable, and one is reminded at once of Rabelais and Swift. Mr. Shandy's theories of education are not unlike those of Master Tubal Holophernes, who succeeded in teaching Gargantua the alphabet so well that he could say it backwards after five years and three months of intense application. Gargantua also spent eighteen years and eleven months in the study of the *Tractatus de modis signifi-candi* with its commentary, and confounded his adversaries in debate by reciting the *Tractatus* backwards.[4] The argumenta-tive use of the permutations of this medieval treatise of specula-tive grammar is clearly reflected in the *Tristrapaedia* and the method of disputation inculated by it. Sterne, like Rabelais, is interested in making fun of the rigid logical system that we associate with scholasticism, a satiric point that is also made by presenting the schoolmen's arguments on the possibility and legality of prenatal baptism. Mr. Shandy, furthermore, bears certain striking affinities with the projectors in the academy at Lagado, chiefly in his distrust of, and lack of concern for, the practical consequences of speculative thought. It is important to observe, however, that Walter's theories are not all ridiculous in the same way, or for the same reason. Insofar as its purpose is satiric, the theory of the homunculi is directed against the scientific theories, and still more at the a priori methods of reasoning, illustrated by Descartes and Leibniz. The theory of noses, on the other hand, is not really satiric at all. By insisting that *nose* means only *nose*, Sterne has in effect invited us to make the obvious substitution of *penis* for *nose*, and the theory which at the literal level is speculative and absurd is, at the occult and indecent level, quite irrefutable. The theory of names, unlike the theory of the homunculi, is not pseudo-scientific. Whatever satire is implied is directed against the superstitious use of language, including the sacrament of baptism, rather than against the absurd fabrication of so-called scientific laws. The theory of education which finds its expression in the *Tristra-paedia* does not attack the reasoning processes of the scientific mind but the propensity (a scholastic one) to accept explana-tions of natural phenomena which are purely verbal. Finally, Walter's theoretical statements about circumcision (Vol. V, ch.

27) and trousers (Vol. VI, ch. 19) illustrate the absurdity of relying on authority for matters which ought to be decided by reference to convenience or utility, and which therefore lie within the province of common sense.

Walter's theories are invariably refuted by experience, but in a rather curious way. The parallel with *Don Quixote* is suggestive. Don Quixote's vision of life is rudely denied by every contact with reality, but the refutation comes as a consequence of his actually living according to the theory of life he has formed. When the knight assumes that the windmills are giants, the sheep an army, or the barber's basin a helmet, he acts in accordance with his assumptions, but his assumptions are generally refuted by the brutal nature of the reality that his imagination has transformed. Walter Shandy's theories do not work either, but they are never, or rarely, tested; they never really come to the point of application, or else they are misapplied. His frustration therefore stems, not from the intractability of matter, but from the perverseness and stupidity of other people or from his own impractical nature. He believes, for example, that the posture and disposition of the "animal spirits" during the act of coitus have important consequences for the homunculus, or sperm, and that the child to be formed will take his nature from the conditions of his conception. It therefore behooves parents to "mind what they are about" when they make a child, and the sexual act must be performed with composure and even with gravity (Vol. I, ch. 1). It must not be forgotten that Walter's bull endeared himself to his owner by going "through the business with a grave face" (Vol. IX, ch. 33). Whether this theory is sound or not we are never to know, because Mrs. Shandy interrupts her husband at the crucial moment by inquiring whether he has forgotten to wind the clock, an irrelevance which destroys not only the purposive sequence of Mr. Shandy's actions, but that of the narrative as well, for we are immediately launched into a world apparently governed by the capricious associations of the mind. It ought to be pointed out, furthermore, that the bull's gravity is of no consequence to his get, because he turns out to be sterile.

In a similar manner Walter's other hypotheses never have a chance of being tested by experience. The nose, which is to prove so infallible an augur of the newborn child's character and fortunes, is marred by Dr. Slop's ineptitude (Vol. III, ch. 27); the name *Trismegistus*, which is to provide a powerful magic to compensate for the disaster of the nose, is transformed by Susannah's stupidity and the curate's impatience into *Tristram*, the most ominous of all names (Vol. IV, ch. 14). *Trismegistus* ("thrice great") probably owes its beneficent power in Mr. Shandy's eyes less to its literal meaning than to the associations it derives from Hermes Trismegistus, regarded by the Neoplatonists as the author of all mystical and "hermetic" doctrines. The theory of circumcision is entirely *post hoc*, because Mr. Shandy is led to formulate it only after the event has been brought about by Trim's and Toby's thoughtlessness (Vol. V, ch. 19), and the admirable and ingenious scheme of education summed up in the *Tristrapaedia* is never actually applied, because Tristram grows faster than Mr. Shandy can evolve his method (Vol. V, ch. 16). Finally, Mr. Shandy's intention of breeching Tristram on principle (that is, by consulting ancient authorities to discover the correct method of fastening breeches) is never in fact realized, because no sooner does he arrive at the conviction that *latus clavus* means hooks and eyes than the narrative breaks off never to return (Vol. VI, ch. 19).

The disparity between theory and practice is one of the most insistent ideas suggested in *Tristram Shandy* and supplies a fundamental insight into Mr. Shandy's character. Unlike the active, unreflective Quixote, Mr. Shandy is the perfect type of the contemplative man. He believes that life should be presided over by theory, but he never takes the trouble to see that life actually is so ordered, and he makes it plain that life is less important than the idea of it. "What is the character of a family to an hypothesis?" asks Mr. Shandy, "Nay, if you come to that— what is the life of a family" (Vol. I, ch. 21). There is abundant evidence, furthermore, that Mr. Shandy is as impractical a man as ever lived; Shandy Hall must be one of the worst-managed estates in the province of literature, for not to recapitulate the series of disastrous accidents which mar Tristram's birth and upbringing, every plan that Mr. Shandy forms goes awry, every department of his household is mismanaged. The hinges on the parlor door squeak intolerably, but Mr. Shandy makes no attempt to set things right, even though his nerves are continually abraded: "There was not a subject in the world upon which my father was so eloquent, as upon that of door-hinges.—And yet at the same time, he was certainly one of the greatest bubbles to them, I think, that history can produce: his rhetoric and conduct were at perpetual handy-cuffs.—Never did the parlour-door open—but his philosophy or his principles fell a victim to it;—three drops of oyl with a feather, and a smart stroke of a hammer, had saved his honour for ever" (Vol. III, ch. 21). "His whole life," Tristram goes on, was "a contradiction to his knowledge." Mr. Shandy has elaborate ideas for improving the ox-moor, but they come to nothing; he tries horse breeding and gets a mule, or cattle breeding and his bull proves a fraud.

Sterne's attitude toward speculative reason, like his attitude toward language, is ambivalent. He makes Tristram simultaneously logophobe and logophile. "I hate set dissertations," Tristram remarks (Vol. III, ch. 20) and immediately proceeds to make one. Certainly there is a strong element of satire in the treatment of speculative thought, and we feel that once again Sterne is bringing his sights to bear on scholasticism and, closer to home, neoclassicism. One of Tristram's stoutest aversions is rhetoric, the rules of eloquence. He not only rejects these rules in his own practice as a writer, he constantly burlesques them. "I . . . beg Mr. Horace's pardon," he declares, "for in writing what I have set about, I shall confine myself neither to his rules, nor to any man's rules that ever lived" (Vol. I, ch. 4). By describing Trim's posture and attitude, as he reads the sermon, with exaggerated precision, Tristram makes fun of the rules of eloquence (Vol. II, ch. 17), and he is scornful of the critic who operates by rule: "And what of this new book the whole world makes such a rout about?—Oh! 'tis out of all plumb, my Lord,—quite an irregular thing!—not one of the angles at the four corners was a right angle.—I had my rule and compasses, &c. my Lord, in my pocket.—Excellent critic!" (Vol. III, ch. 12). Tristram's logophobia is also revealed in his frequent burlesques of the pedantic appeal to authority. Sometimes he does this by a perfectly straight-faced *reductio ad absurdum* of the pedant's citations; more often by an affectation of bumbling incompetence in bolstering a perfectly trite or platitudinous remark with the weight of ancient learning:

'Tis either Plato, or Plutarch, or Seneca, or Xenophon, or Epictetus, or Theophrastus, or Lucian—or some one perhaps of later date —either Cardan, or Budaeus, or Petrarch, or Stella—or possibly it may be some divine or father of the church, St. Austin, or St. Cyprian, or Barnard, who affirms that it is an irresistable and natural passion to weep for the loss of our friends or children— and Seneca (I'm positive) tells us somewhere, that such griefs evacuate themselves best by that particular channel. [Vol. V, ch. 3]

At times, in fact, Tristram seems to bear a closer resemblance to his uncle Toby than to his father, and nowhere is this more apparent than in the evidences of his own extreme sensibility. Toby's elaborate and absurd gesture of tenderness toward the fly which buzzes about his nose at dinner has an extraordinary effect on Tristram, who traces his own philanthropy to the profound impression made on him by this trivial incident (Vol. II, ch. 12).

Sterne reveals his own impatience with the abstract and theoretical chiefly by means of another of his masks, Parson Yorick, whose pet hate is the polemic divine: "One ounce of practical divinity," he declares, "is worth a painted ship load of all their reverences have imported these fifty years" (Vol. V, ch. 28). And it is Yorick who is overcome by Trim's eloquence when the corporal glosses the tenth commandment with the statement that "honouring thy father and thy mother" means allowing them three halfpence a day out of his pay (Vol. V, ch. 32). But Tristram himself can remark upon the "commonplace infirmity of the greatest mathematicians! working with might and main at the demonstration, and so wasting all their strength upon it, that they have none left in them to draw the corollary, to do good with" (Vol. II, ch. 10).

Still, there is no reason to suspect Tristram of illegitimacy, for he is undoubtedly his father's son, a relation betrayed by his fondness for digressions, his inveterate habit of lecturing his readers, and his pride in the manipulation of the narrative. Tristram makes no apology for his digressions, and in fact seizes the opportunity of the epigraph to the seventh and eighth volumes to declare overtly that "this is not an excursion, but the work itself." He loves the pedagogic posture, and at the slightest provocation will surrender his cap and bells—the insignia of his ordinary role—to deliver a reasoned disquisition on any matter of theoretical interest that arises. "Now if you will venture to go along with me," he says, "and look down into the bottom of this matter, it will be found that the cause of obscurity and confusion, in the mind of man, is threefold," and so on (Vol. II, ch. 2). But the best example of Tristram's logophilia is the all-purpose travel book, of which we get a generous sample in the fifth chapter of the seventh volume. "Calais, Calatium, Calusium, Calesium," he begins, and proceeds to erect a purely speculative description of the city of which he knows no more, by his own admission, than he does of Grand Cairo. The point

Tristram is presumably making here is that one can talk about subjects he is totally ignorant of, provided he understands the forms of discourse. Tristram has obviously profited from the *Tristrapaedia*, and taken its main lesson to heart.

Questions of the speculative versus the empirical, or the theoretical versus the practical, which obviously involve Mr. Shandy and Sterne himself in his various personae, seem to leave no room at all for uncle Toby. Toby, the perfect example of the eighteenth-century *âme sensible*, seems to stand in a kind of rigid opposition to Mr. Shandy, the man whose whole being is expressed through his reason, however impotent his reason may be to determine the course of his own or any life dependent upon him. The very neatness of the opposition, however, suggests its sterility as a formulation that will help to further our understanding of the novel. Though reason is his god, Mr. Shandy is very far from being a reasonable man, and it is perhaps his passionate nature that does the most to make him interesting, to humanize him. His emotional responses are characteristically violent or extreme, as a single example amply demonstrates. Mr. Shandy has been discoursing airily of learned men and their "solutions of noses," whereupon Toby's innocent query, "Can noses be dissolved?" produces the most striking results:

My father thrust back his chair,—rose up,—put on his hat,—took four long strides to the door,—jerked it open,—thrust his head half way out,—shut the door again,—took no notice of the bad hinge,—returned to the table,—plucked my mother's thread-paper out of Slawkenbergius's book,—went hastily to his bureau,— walk'd slowly back, twisting my mother's thread-paper about his thumb,—unbutton'd his waistcoat,—threw my mother's thread-paper into the fire,—bit her sattin pin-cushion in two, fill'd his mouth with bran,—confounded it;—but mark!—the oath of confusion was levell'd at my uncle Toby's brain,—which was e'en confused enough already,—the curse came charged only with the bran,—the bran, may it please your honours,—was no more than powder to the ball. [Vol. III, ch. 41]

In a somewhat analogous fashion Toby's sensibility is colored by his Shandean proclivities. Occasionally, in fact, Toby can meet his brother on Mr. Shandy's own ground, as when he delivers a closely reasoned "apologetical oration" in defense of the profession of arms (Vol. VI, ch. 32), or when he takes the wind out of Mr. Shandy's sails by anticipating his allusion to Locke (Vol. III, ch. 18). But Toby reveals his own love of the speculative and hypothetical most clearly by his preoccupation with the simulated sieges of the bowling green, where theory plainly has lost contact with practice. Toby has in effect been cast in the same role of speculative *raisonneur* as his brother, and partly by the very quality in him that seems most antithetical to the rational faculty—his sensibility. Toby uses sentiment in much the same way that Mr. Shandy uses speculative reason—to re-shape experience to something nearer the heart's desire, and sentiment in Toby is as remote from actuality as reason in his brother. Toby maintains a fund of emotion, as it were, which he seems not only willing but eager to expend when any remotely suitable occasion presents itself, in much the same manner as Mr. Shandy seizes any opportunity to fashion or confirm a hypothesis. I do not mean to suggest that Toby's sentiment is either meretricious or insincere, but it is in a sense its own justification and need not, we feel, be proportioned to its object. Out come the tears on cue, whether the cue be supplied by the death of an old soldier, by the sufferings of Corporal Trim's brother Tom (of whose real existence we never quite become convinced), or by the misfortunes of the wholly imaginary King of Bohemia. Tristram and his father, Toby and Trim, have this much in common, that they all have their most intense existence in a world of their own making.

Mr. Shandy's real antitype is not Toby, who is as Shandean

as he is, but Mrs. Shandy, who, like Obadiah and Susannah and Dr. Slop and the Widow Wadman, never rises above actuality. She is, as Tristram says, the "truest of all the Poco-curante's of her sex" (Vol. VI, ch. 20), unmoved by any passion, indifferent to the realm of speculative thought which her husband so continuously inhabits, incurious about what she does not understand. "She had a way . . . and that was never to refuse her assent and consent to any proposition my father laid before her, merely because she did not understand it. . . . She contented herself with doing all that her godfathers and godmothers promised for her—but no more" (Vol. IX, ch. 11). As a character she is wholly devoid of interest, for unlike her volatile husband she is completely inert and passive, content to live her life without regarding it.

Mrs. Shandy's inability to kindle one spark of interest is itself indicative of the kinds of things in the novel that can arouse our interest and engage our feelings. Clearly the brute facts of existence—conception, birth, circumcision, and so on—are not the materials out of which this novel is made, nor are they the incidents which determine its structure, except in a very limited sense. The term "incidents" may perhaps be taken in a special sense to designate the whole complex of thought and feeling under which the characters submerge actualities like birth and death. There is a progression, usually beginning with the actuality, or the naming of it, and continuing its seemingly erratic course [5] until life throws up another fact that must be dealt with and responded to. Life which meets with no response, either intellectual or emotional, is not worth bothering about; what really matters is that life should engender some human attitude toward it. It follows, then, that human potentiality can never be realized in action—man is born, he spawns and dies—it can only be realized in talking about action. As Sterne declares in his epigraph to the first volumes, "It is not actions (pragmata) which disturb men, but opinions (dogmata) about actions."

Nothing could more clearly indicate what Sterne has taken for his province, and nothing could supply a more effective hint as to the way in which he organizes his material.

Again we must confront the possibility that Sterne's intention may be satiric, for his attitude toward Mr. Shandy's theoretical absurdities and Toby's sentimental excesses, like his attitude toward language itself, is by no means simple. The novel obviously contains incidents which can only be read as an attack on reason, either under the guise of neoclassicism, or under that of scholasticism. I have already alluded to Tristram's frequent strictures against criticism and the rules of eloquence as evidence of his hostility toward neoclassicism, and the inherent absurdity of the theological and legal disputes about prenatal baptism or whether a mother is related to her child are manifest even without Toby's rejoinder, after it has been proved that a certain noble lady is not of kin to her child, "And what said the duchess of Suffolk to it?" (Vol. IV, ch. 29). There is undoubtedly a rich vein of anti-intellectual satire in the novel, but to stop there is a little like classifying *Don Quixote* as an attack on romance. Mr. Shandy's towering hypotheses may be ridiculous, but they are better than no hypotheses at all, because in the world of *Tristram Shandy* to reason about life is to live. That life constantly refutes reason is not an argument for doing away with reason; it is only an affirmation of the essential incongruity and pathos of the human condition. Mr. Shandy's hypotheses are formed or rejected not according to any pragmatic test whatever, but solely according to their intrinsic beauty or ugliness. In speculating about the seat of the rational soul, for example, Mr. Shandy rejects out of hand the theory of Joseph Borri, "the great Milaneze physician," who held that the soul inhabits a "very thin, subtle, and very fragrant juice . . . in the cellulae of the occipital parts of the cerebellum." "My father could never subscribe to it by any means; the very idea of so noble, so refined, so immaterial, and so exalted a being as the *Anima*, or even the *Animus*, taking up her residence, and sitting dabbling, like a tad-pole, all day long, both summer and winter, in a puddle,— or in a liquid of any kind, how thick or thin soever, he would say, shock'd his imagination; he would scarce give the doctrine a hearing" (Vol. II, ch. 19). It is true that life can never be contained in the vessels Mr. Shandy prepares for it, but his idea of life has more of order, symmetry, and proportion than life itself, which always seems to take him unawares.

Toby's quixotism provides an even closer parallel to the original than Mr. Shandy's, for the warlike nature of his hobby-horse suggests the form of Don Quixote's principal delusion, and his eloquence on behalf of the military virtues recalls Don Quixote's demonstration that the profession of arms is superior to the profession of letters. The bowling green is Toby's Sierra Morena, the scene of his heroic—and altogether imaginary—exploits, but he reveals his quixotic nature most clearly, perhaps, in his habit of translating the harsher realities of his experience into the terms of a sentimental romance, and like Quixote he becomes so enchanted by his own vision that he seeks the harsher realities where none exists. Both Toby and Trim, in fact, have lost the capacity to discriminate between real occasions for sorrow and those which are wholly illusory. Toby shares with his brother, and with Don Quixote, the happy faculty of refashioning in thought the intractable and unsatisfactory stuff of ordinary existence.

But if Sterne owes much to Cervantes in the substance of his novel, he owes little or nothing to the form of *Don Quixote*, for *Tristram Shandy* has nothing of the picaresque. The question of structure in *Tristram Shandy* may be discussed, I think, without reference to the question of whether the novel is a finished whole,[6] for what we need to know is not whether the book might have been continued, or even whether it reaches a stable point of rest, but what principle, if any, controls its seemingly erratic and aimless progression. Chronology has only a very limited influence upon this progression, for though events occur in chronological order (up to a point), they serve chiefly to provide the starting points for Mr. Shandy's flights of reason or for Toby's flights of sentiment.[7] The Widow Wadman section reverts to an earlier period of time, and its justification, I think, lies in the use Sterne makes of it to defy the tyranny of chronology. The early series of events in Tristram's life serves to develop the expectation of a prolongation of the series, but Sterne's greatest delight is in the violation of "normal" expectations. This in itself does not, of course, supply an intelligible principle of development, for the ways of violating the reader's expectations are infinite, and Sterne must avoid obvious pattern even here; hence the more spectacular devices can be used only once. Whatever positive principle of organization is to be found in the novel is not in the relationship of events to each other, for events themselves are relatively unimportant. The principle is to be sought rather in the connections among the ideas or feelings which constitute Sterne's real subject matter.

One obvious possibility is to find in Sterne's frequent allusions to the Lockean psychology a law for the novel's development, but to draw on Locke is to avoid the problem altogether, for to admit "free" association amounts to a denial of any order at all. It is tempting to attribute to *Tristram Shandy* the origin of the stream of consciousness technique,[8] but if this is true at all, it is true only with important reservations. Two, at least, of the distinguishing characteristics of the stream of consciousness technique are clearly present in *Tristram Shandy* —the superior prominence given to "psychological" time (that is, duration as measured by human awareness of it) as distinct from "actual" time, and the articulations of the narrative brought about by association. But there are important distinctions to be drawn between Sterne's technique and that of modern exponents of the method. The associations which constantly distort and redirect the narrative do not usually occur within Tristram's consciousness, but are made by characters whom we never really penetrate. Mr. Shandy's crossed arms suggest to Toby the zigzag approaches of the fortifications at Namur, and he breaks out, quite irrelevantly, with the remark, "I wish you had seen what prodigious armies we had in Flanders" (Vol. II, ch. 18). We are made aware of this capricious association entirely through the conventional means of conversation and gesture, for we remain outside of the consciousness in which the association occurs. A still more important qualification is that the associations which are characteristically made in the stream of consciousness technique without transition or explanation are invariably explained to us by Tristram himself, and the explanation, occurring after the event, necessitates the interruption of the flow of psychological time. The technique of *Tristram Shandy*, therefore, while it bears certain resemblances to the stream of consciousness, is actually quite different.

The structure of the novel is not supplied by the configuration of any single consciousness, not even Tristram's own, though obviously his own thought processes and emotional responses have a good deal to do with the style of his narration. Too much of what goes on in the book lies outside his power to direct it, as he is often petulantly willing to admit. The individual consciousness, whether Tristram's or Mr. Shandy's or Toby's, operates not on events or things, but on the words which communicate or designate them, so that the inner form of the novel may be said to be objectified in the most public of all intellectual systems—language. Even a word which has no correspondent reality—*animal spirits*, for example—will serve as the starting point for one of Mr. Shandy's or Toby's flights. Characteristically, the naming of an event, whether the event has actually occurred or not, prompts the expenditure of thought and feeling, but thought and feeling are expressed by words or other signs, and so the process continues until the whole complex progression is dissolved, or superseded by another. The narrative is in effect self-sustaining, for it feeds on its own medium.

In one sense, of course, actuality, or more precisely the characters' awareness of actuality, determines the structure and order of incidents. The winding of a clock, a creaking hinge, a knotted string, can send the whole mechanism jolting ahead, but it would be perverse to say that the actuality causes the motion or supplies its direction. The cause lies rather in the total sensibility revealed in the response to experience, and in the system of language governing the expression of the response. The ontological order is curiously reversed. We would expect the response to produce the appropriate language. Actually the resources of language limit and control the response, and may even be said to cause it. And what we may term the secondary response is still further removed from the actuality by the intervention of language, for characters are constantly responding to unintended and secondary meanings. Mr. Shandy's error over the mortars (Vol. III, ch. 22), Toby's mistaking the sense of *auxiliaries* (Vol. V, ch. 42), and the multiple ambiguities lurking in the word *plan* (Vol. VIII, ch. 23) are all illustrative. In their defiance of the inert order of things, Mr. Shandy and the other characters have insensibly submitted to the control of the logos. Words, not things, are the masters in the world of *Tristram Shandy*. The forms of discourse themselves determine what can be said, and hence what can be thought or felt, exactly as in the *Tristrapaedia*. This lends an irony which is both devastating and comic to the elaborate display of rhetorical terminology, for the terms of rhetoric imply that man controls the effects of language, instead of the reverse.

The order that results is not, perhaps, "logical" in the ordinary sense. It is certainly not empirical, for virtually any series of events could produce it. It does, however, reflect a genuinely imaginative vision of life, for it submits to no limits except those which are inherent in its own medium. Don Quixote's delusion consisted in his taking the products of his own fancy for realities; Mr. Shandy's (and Toby's and Tristram's) consists in the belief that the mind's operations are autonomous; but both Quixote and the people of the Shandean world endear themselves to us by the splendor of their delusions, by their heroic and emphatic rejection of the tyranny of the commonplace.

‡ CHAPTER VI ‡

Humphry Clinker and
the Novelist's Imagination

But men must know, that in this theatre of
man's life it is reserved only for God and angels
to be lookers on.
—BACON, *The Advancement of Learning*

The Expedition of Humphry Clinker is by universal assent
Smollett's masterpiece, but the language in which it has been
extolled somehow seems less appropriate to a work standing in
the company of *Pamela*, *Tom Jones*, and *Tristram Shandy* than
it does to a work of the same kind as, say, *The Spectator* or
Boswell's *Journal of a Tour to the Hebrides*.[1] The peculiar
excellences of *Humphry Clinker* have generally been located,
that is to say, not in its imaginative structure, but in its qualities
of observation and reflection. Readers most struck by the
observation tend to place the book among the literature of
travel; those most struck by the reflection prefer to regard it
as in the nature of an essay. In either case the informing principle lies outside the book itself, either in the scenes which are
being described or in the writer's sensibility, revealed by his
response to those scenes. Though it would be foolish to deny
that *Humphry Clinker* does possess the qualities implied by
these ways of approaching it, it is also possible, I believe, to
read the book as a novel, to pursue, that is, the distinctively

imaginative power which differentiates the work of fiction from all the possible modes of nonfiction. The main question to be raised amounts to this: whether the various letter writers are to be thought of as so many masks for the author himself (permitting him various levels of ironic discourse), or whether the letter writers achieve autonomous existence to the point that their thoughts and feelings are important as belonging to them, rather than for their own sake.

Whatever may be said about the plot of *Humphry Clinker*, it is clear that the pattern of events supplies only a crude and adventitious formal principle. The triple marriage and the discovery of Humphry's true identity at the end of the novel supply a thoroughly conventional denouement and affect significantly the destinies of three of the five characters whose letters comprise the novel, but the two most prolific correspondents, and for that reason the two characters into whose minds and hearts we most frequently penetrate, undergo no change of fortune at all, so that the conclusion is singularly inconclusive in disposing of whatever it is that provides the central concern of the novel. Furthermore, the story line proves inadequate to organize or explain the manifold ingredients of this book, if only because it intrudes itself upon our notice so rarely, and in spite of the fact that the Wilson-Lydia affair is introduced very early, the whole thing savors of afterthought. It is not plot, then, that lends imaginative wholeness to *Humphry Clinker*.

One of the most suggestive, as well as one of the most original features of *Humphry Clinker* is its employment of the multiple epistolary point of view.[2] This device has the effect of enriching and complicating the narrative texture, but at some cost in pace and movement. Each letter writer, naturally enough, approaches the common body of experience from a different point of view, and in reporting on that experience the writer is more likely to indulge his own special interests and prejudices than to promote the coherence and terseness of the story. The story, in fact, is not something that comes into being because the narrators tell it; the relation is curiously reversed. They come into being because of their efforts to communicate a fragment of the story that is, so to speak, already there. The "story" we infer from their collective efforts, but more important, more immediately present to consciousness, are the personalities of the various narrators. One important ingredient in each characterization, it may be pertinent to insert here, is the selection of a correspondent. Thus the valetudinarian Matthew Bramble corresponds with his doctor; Jery Melford, the nascent man of the world, writes to his titled university friend; the frugal, not to say grasping, Tabitha writes to her housekeeper at Brambleton Hall; Lydia, who is truly a languishing character, entrusts the secrets of her heart to her schoolgirl confidante; and Win Jenkins writes to the fellow servant who is ultimately to become the index of her own social progress. The epistolary method yields not only an efficient technique of characterization, it permits complicated, many-leveled ironies, or alternatively, when we can discern no ironic thrust, it affords an enriched perspective on the experience that the novel records. Its varied implications supply a much richer subject of inquiry than the narrative structure of the novel.

Of the five "speaking" parts the most important is obviously that of Matthew Bramble, the irascible Welsh hypochondriac who is leading his dependents on a tour of England and Scotland, partly as an educational enterprise, but chiefly as a therapeutic venture that takes him to one watering place after another. It is his keen observation and salty commentary that provide the highest flavored part of the whole narration, and his own character is as interesting as any that he reports for us. As a literary type Matthew Bramble represents a median stage in the development that leads from Sir Roger De Coverley to Mr. Pickwick. All three are, in an important sense, spectators of life, and they have all emerged from retirement in middle or late years to learn something of life that their more restricted earlier experiences have withheld from them. They are all men of highly developed sensibility, with quick and ready sympathies for other human beings (though in Mr. Bramble's case these are concealed by an unpleasant manner). Mr. Bramble, who is given the first letter in *Humphry Clinker*, opens on a suggestive and characteristic note:

Doctor,
The pills are good for nothing—I might as well swallow snow-balls to cool my reins—I have told you over and over, how hard I am to move; and at this time of day, I ought to know something of my own constitution. Why will you be so positive? Prithee send me another prescription—I am as lame and as much tortured in all my limbs as if I was broke upon the wheel: indeed, I am equally distressed in mind and body—As if I had not plagues enough of my own, those children of my sister are left me for a perpetual source of vexation—what business have people to get children to plague their neighbours? [3]

Mr. Bramble's concern with the state of his bowels is to be a kind of leitmotiv, and it is appropriate that the first sentence of the novel introduces it. But the bowels, in addition to being the locus of Mr. Bramble's bodily complaint, are also traditionally the seat of pity, and the implied connection between his somatic and psychic ills is also to assume considerable thematic importance in the novel.

It is tempting to say that the churlishness revealed by the tone of this letter is to be supplanted by something much more agreeable, and that the course of the novel is to mark the mellowing of Mr. Bramble's character, but to do so would be to simplify both his character and the design of the novel. The abruptness of his salutation (later he will begin, "Dear Doctor," or "Dear Lewis," or even "Dear Dick") and the testiness of his complaints are merely the reflection of a temporary mood, one that he will revert to many times again in the course of his journey, and they are here (as elsewhere) in incongruous juxtaposition with the shamefaced tenderness brought to light later in the same letter: "Let Morgan's widow have the Alderney cow, and forty shillings to clothe her children: but don't say a syllable of the matter to any living soul—I'll make her pay when she is able" (I, 8). It is perhaps too easy to regard his character as conforming to that overworked literary stereotype, the-rough-exterior-that-hides-a-heart-of-gold, but he is much more finely drawn.[4] There is nothing of the sentimentalist in Matthew Bramble, even when he is most intent on pursuing his furtive charities; he is a true scion of the eighteenth century in making reason his guiding light, and he is nowhere more vehement than in rebuking Humphry Clinker as a "wrong-headed enthusiast" (I, 195). It is perhaps true that he is easily moved by the various "pathetic recognition" scenes which are scattered so liberally and so gratuitously throughout the novel, but even in these cases the reason approves the motions of the heart: one should be moved by extraordinary merit or by extraordinary patience in affliction. At the other extreme, Mr. Bramble is quick to anger, but again his passions are not irrational; they are merely the inevitable responses of a hyperaesthetic person to whatever disturbs his notions of what is decent and right. Their violence confirms Jery Melford in his early diagnosis of his uncle's character: "Mr. Bramble is extravagantly delicate in all his sensations, both of soul and body" (I, 195), but their occasions testify to the loftiness and disinterestedness of his principles. When, exasperated by Lord Oxmington's rudeness, Mr. Bramble sends his lordship a challenge, it is less the affront to his own dignity that irritates him than it is the nobleman's failure to behave with nobility and hence with decorum.

The misanthropy that Mr. Bramble confesses to is to be distinguished carefully from the cynicism of Mr. Quin and the

contumaciousness of Lieutenant Lismahago. Mr. Bramble professes to be in agreement with Quin about life, "which, Quin
says, would stink in his nostrils, if he did not steep it in claret"
(I, 72), but the fact is that Quin's acid wit reveals a temperament quite unlike Mr. Bramble's thin-skinned but stubbornly
optimistic relation to life. When the ladies of Bath reveal their
lack of breeding at Mr. Holder's teaparty, Mr. Quin's characteristic response is a cynical laugh, but Mr. Bramble's delicacy, as
Jery Melford reports, was hurt. "He hung his head in manifest
chagrin, and seemed to repine at the triumph of his judgment"
(I, 75). The truth is that though Mr. Bramble's fastidiousness
is shocked again and again by the bestiality of other human
beings, his indignation never fails him; his "misanthropy"
(which, like Swift's, is really only a frustrated idealism) never
hardens into cynicism. By the same token it is something more
immediate, more fundamental to his character than Lismahago's
controversial propensities, which never destroy his composure
or shock his principles, whichever side of a question he may
assume.

There is a depth to Matthew Bramble's character which is
not immediately apparent. It requires a considerable period of
intimacy before Jery can come to an understanding of the
strength and tenacity of other people's regard for his uncle. At
the outset he confides to his college friend a strong dislike:
"My uncle is an odd kind of humorist, always on the fret, and
so unpleasant in his manner, that rather than be obliged to keep
him company, I'd resign all claim to the inheritance of his
estate" (I, 12). As the acquaintance ripens, however, Jery
arrives at a feeling not only of respect but of affection for his
crotchety old uncle, a transformation that belongs rather to
Jery than to Matthew. It is certainly true, as Jery remarks, that
Mr. Bramble's health and spirits are wonderfully improved by
his travels, particularly his visit to Scotland, but there is no
reason to suppose that the change is evolutionary or permanent.

To the end Mr. Bramble is capable of living up to his name by revealing that unpleasantness of manner that Jery had complained of, and we are not allowed to suppose that his access of good spirits is anything more than the refreshment which might normally be expected to accompany such diversions and changes of scene as he has enjoyed. Any fresh sample of human absurdity or bestiality, we feel, will immediately cancel Mr. Bramble's "cure." For this reason, it is difficult to regard the character development of its central personage as supplying the organizing principle of the novel, though it is still possible to regard the exposition of that character as the shaping purpose. To the exposition of Mr. Bramble's character many of the resources of the novel are indeed turned; he is himself one of the "originals" whose contemplation gives him so much pleasure (and pain), but it is important to note that his character is in large part defined by his relations with his traveling companions, and that we cannot very well ignore their importance in the design of the novel.

The largest number of letters (28) and the greatest portion of space (almost half) are given to Jery Melford, Mr. Bramble's nephew, but since he has virtually no story of his own, his function in the novel is primarily that of recording the events which affect everyone else more than himself. In the general knotting of fortunes at the end of the book, Jery is very nearly caught by Liddy's charming friend and correspondent Laetitia Willis, but though he recognizes that his "destiny must one day be fulfilled," he significantly postpones that fulfillment (II, 222). Jery remains outside the events he describes; hence his utility as the principal narrator. Still, though he has no story of his own, he does undergo some change, one index of which is his change of heart about his uncle. His letters at the beginning of the tour reveal more than a touch of undergraduate snobbishness and arrogance, along with some affectation. His first letter to Sir Watkin Phillips, Baronet, of Jesus College, Oxford, opens with a ponderous period, of which I quote less than half: "As I have nothing more at heart than to convince you I am incapable of forgetting, or neglecting the friendship I made at college, I now begin that correspondence by letters, which you and I agreed, at parting, to cultivate . . ." (I, 10–11). Both the matter and the manner of this letter convey the impression of a conceited, intolerant, and somewhat pompous young man, but in the course of the novel the impression yields to something quite different and more favorable. Here is Jery again, at the end of his journey, but though the style has not improved much, the personality it reveals has changed considerably:

George Dennison is, without all question, one of the most accomplished young fellows in England. His person is at once elegant and manly, and his understanding highly cultivated. Tho' his spirit is lofty, his heart is kind; and his manner so engaging, as to command veneration and love, even from malice and indifference. When I weigh my own character with his, I am ashamed to find myself so light in the balance; but the comparison excites no envy—I propose him as a model for imitation—I have endeavoured to recommend myself to his friendship, and hope I have already found a place in his affection. I am, however, mortified to reflect what flagrant injustice we every day commit, and what absurd judgment we form, in viewing objects through the falsifying medium of prejudice and passion. Had you asked me a few days ago, the picture of Wilson the player, I should have drawn a portrait very unlike the real person and character of George Dennison—Without all doubt, the greatest advantage acquired in travelling and perusing mankind in the original, is that of dispelling those shameful clouds that darken the faculties of the mind, preventing it from judging with candour and precision. [II, 202–203]

There is enough left of Jery's earlier sententiousness for us to recognize the same hand here, and he seems as self-centered as before, but the earlier arrogance is missing. Nevertheless, in spite of the considerable change we may discern in him, Jery's own affairs are given too little prominence, his letters too much taken up with the concerns of others, for us to take his development as a significant enough motive in the novel to control and organize everything else. Jery's principal function is manifestly to contribute facts and valuations about his traveling companions that they themselves cannot give us. The three women are so taken up with their own personal expectations that they can rarely spare a thought for anyone else, and Mr. Bramble's point of view is so jaundiced by his bodily ills that it falls to Jery to provide the disinterested and impersonal commentary which will enable us to see the other characters in perspective.

One index of Jery's importance as narrator is that so many of the quotations supporting my analysis of Mr. Bramble's character are taken from Jery's letters. There are a number of facets of Mr. Bramble's character which we cannot very well expect him to reveal to us through his own letters. Most of the softer, more agreeable traits—his kindness, his generosity, his sympathy—he tries to conceal or to disguise, and it remains for Jery to give us the evidence that his uncle either does not mention at all or else puts in a misleading light. At the same time, some of the more palpable facets of Mr. Bramble's character—the surliness of his temper and the delicacy of his physical sensations—need to be given the perspective of a more or less disinterested, uncommitted point of view. For both of these reasons Jery Melford assumes the narrative responsibility for most of the significant episodes of the novel, particularly when they affect Mr. Bramble as central figure. Thus it is Jery who describes for us the developing relations between Mr. Bramble and the titular hero, Humphry Clinker, culminating in the recognition scene in which Humphry and Matthew discover their kinship; it is Jery who serves us up the debates between Mr. Bramble and Lieutenant Lismahago; and it is Jery who is called upon whenever Mr. Bramble is involved beyond his customary role as sightseer—in the episodes of Martin the highwayman, the lawyer Micklewhimmen, and Lord Oxmington. Mr. Bramble's own letters, on the other hand, tend to be expository rather than narrative; it is he who indulges us with accounts of the therapeutic facilities at Bath, Harrogate, and Scarborough, of such London attractions as the British Museum, Blackfriars Bridge, and Vauxhall, and of the typical diets of London and the Scottish highlands.

The three women who, with Humphry Clinker, complete Mr. Bramble's entourage, are given much less space than the two men; their letters comprise only a third of the total, and since these letters scarcely ever run to more than a page or two, they account for only about an eighth of the book's length. It seems likely, however, that they form a significant portion of Smollett's design. For one thing, the letters of Liddy, Tabitha, and Win tend to be concentrated at the more important foci, notably at the beginning and end of the novel; in the central reaches they occur more sparingly and offer only occasional punctuation to the narrative that is being sustained principally by Jery with commentary by Mr. Bramble. Furthermore all three women are to undergo a significant change of fortune in that each is to find a husband in the course of the journey.

Lydia Melford, Jery's sister and Matthew's niece and ward, is cast in the role of the ingenue, and since the burden of nearly all her letters is her inextinguishable passion for Wilson, she would become something of a bore if we were given too much of her. She does, however, suggest another way by which the other characters are to be measured. Her brother, by giving us what is for all practical purposes an omniscient point of view, leads us to a more or less objective judgment of the characters and events he tells us about. Lydia, by personifying a relentlessly romantic point of view and standard of valuation, provides a useful foil to her uncle, though here, too, she must be used with restraint. The closeness with which her statements

about Vauxhall parallel (though to opposite effect) those of
Mr. Bramble suggests not only that Smollett is consciously
manipulating the device, but that the focus of his imaginative
vision in *Humphry Clinker* is the differing modes of perception
of the various characters as these are related to significant
individual differences. Here is Mr. Bramble's description:

Vauxhall is a composition of baubles, overcharged with paltry
ornaments, ill conceived, and poorly executed; without any unity
of design, or propriety of disposition. It is an unnatural assembly
of objects, fantastically illuminated in broken masses; seemingly
contrived to dazzle the eyes and divert the imagination of the
vulgar—Here a wooden lion, there a stone statue; in one place, a
range of things like coffee-house boxes, covered a-top; in another,
a parcel of ale-house benches; in a third, a puppet-show representation of a tin cascade; in a fourth, a gloomy cave of a circular
form, like a sepulchral vault half lighted; in a fifth, a scanty slip of
grass-plat, that would not afford pasture sufficient for an ass's
colt. The walks, which nature seems to have intended for solitude,
shade, and silence, are filled with crowds of noisy people, suck-
ing up the nocturnal rheums of an aguish climate; and through
these gay scenes, a few lamps glimmer like so many farthing can-
dles.

When I see a number of well-dressed people, of both sexes,
sitting on the covered benches, exposed to the eyes of the mob;
and, which is worse, to the cold, raw, night-air, devouring sliced
beef, and swilling port, and punch, and cyder, I can't help com-
passionating their temerity, while I despise their want of taste and
decorum; but, when they course along those damp and gloomy
walks, or crowd together upon the wet gravel, without any other
cover than the cope of Heaven, listening to a song, which one
half of them cannot possibly hear, how can I help supposing they
are actually possessed by a spirit, more absurd and pernicious than
any thing we meet with in the precincts of Bedlam? [I, 126–27]

A page or two later, in the very next letter, we get Liddy's
response to the same scene:

I was dazzled and confounded with the variety of beauties that rushed all at once upon my eye. Image to yourself, my dear Letty, a spacious garden, part laid out in delightful walks, bounded with high hedges and trees, and paved with gravel; part exhibiting a wonderful assemblage of the most picturesque and striking objects, pavilions, lodges, groves, grottoes, lawns, temples, and cascades; porticoes, colonades, and rotundos; adorned with pillars, statues and painting: the whole illuminated with an infinite number of lamps, disposed in different figures of suns, stars, and constellations; the place crowded with the gayest company, ranging through those blissful shades, or supping in different lodges on cold collations, enlivened with mirth, freedom, and good humour, and animated by an excellent band of musick. Among the vocal performers I had the happiness to hear the celebrated Mrs. ——, whose voice was loud and so shrill, that it made my head ake through excess of pleasure. [I, 131–32]

The most striking feature of these two passages is their close parallelism. For every detail, even for every phrase of Mr. Bramble's description there is a corresponding detail or phrase in Lydia's. Matthew's "crowds of noisy people," for example, are for Lydia "the gayest company," and their occupation, rendered by Matthew as "devouring sliced beef, and swilling port, and punch, and cyder," is described by his niece as "supping in different lodges on cold collations." Even without Lydia's account, we can recognize in Mr. Bramble's many of the consequences of attitudes and prejudices already known to us, and Lydia's description is perfectly consistent with her monolithic sensibility, but it is in the juxtaposition of the two that their chief significance lies. There is comic irony, no doubt, in the fact that neither of the two characters is aware of the neatness with which their responses to a single experience are opposed to each other, but more important is the way in which the contrast deepens our knowledge of the two characters. Mr. Bramble professes himself offended by the spectacle of Vauxhall, and yet his observation is by far the keener and more detailed of the two, suggesting that his disapprobation of Vauxhall and the people who frequent it is consistent with an interest in and concern for humanity that Lydia does not approach. The most convincing testimony is not the "compassion" that Mr. Bramble admits to, but the specificity with which he renders the scene, and the accuracy of his nouns (which Lydia's account permits us to judge) are more important and suggestive indices of his character than the splenetic quality of his adjectives. On the other hand, the looseness and vagueness of Lydia's description, though it suggests something of the sweetness of her temper (as well as her taste for romances noted by her uncle), testifies to the flaccidity of her mind and the relative coarseness of her perceptions. Whatever inferences we may draw from the two letters, it is clear that what matters is the response of the two characters, not the thing which elicits the response. It is not Vauxhall that we are concerned about, but the insight it gives us into Mr. Bramble and his niece.

The other two women, Tabitha Bramble and Win Jenkins, are the merest sketches, by comparison with the portrait of Mr. Bramble or even that of Lydia, and they have none of Jery's powers of detachment and observation. They are, I believe, subtly discriminated, but Saintsbury's assertion, that "the malapropisms and the heterography of mistress and maid are differentiated with a just and masterly precision," [5] is questionable. The malapropisms and misspellings seem to me, in fact, to make up no very important part of the characterization of the two women, if only because their strong tropism toward the indecent is perfectly unconscious and is explicable only insofar as it serves Smollett's own private purposes. Mistakes in the use of language, even unwittingly indecent ones, provide a severely limited fund of comedy, hardly sufficient to sustain even the relatively few and short letters of Tabitha and Win. The comedy that derives from the fact that Tabitha is old and ugly and cannot find a husband is scarcely more durable (though the old maid is still a familiar comic type); what deepens and humanizes her (as Saintsbury observed) is the strength and genuineness of her affection for her brother, an affection usually concealed effectively by her single-minded pursuit of her own ends, but which occasionally appears with a kind of majestic dignity at moments of tension. Win Jenkins owes more to her butchery of the English language than Tabitha, but chiefly because of Win's pretensions to a higher place in the world than fortune has allotted her. She imitates her betters in everything, not least in her writing of letters, which serves less to exchange information than to confer on the writer the cachet of gentility. She rarely fails to draw attention to this mark of status by referring to the chance of a frank or other mode of conveyance. More purely than any other character she embodies the comic spirit of the novel, for unlike Matthew, or Tabitha, or even Jery and Lydia, her experience is never touched by the tragic or pathetic, not even the potentially tragic or pathetic, and she is allowed the final word in the novel as she extends her magnificent offer of patronage to her erstwhile peer, assuring the reader more convincingly than Mr. Bramble's confidence in his "cure," that all's right with the world.

If one wanted to talk, as a good many of Smollett's most ardent admirers do, of Smollett's powers of characterization and his lengthy gallery of "originals," it would now be obligatory to go on to a discussion of Lieutenant Lismahago and perhaps also of certain other characters whose portraiture occupies the attention of one or the other of the letter-writers. I am not particularly concerned, however, with the eccentricity, or even with the picturesqueness of Smollett's characters; I am much more interested in a somewhat rarer quality—their independence, not of each other or of the world they pass through, for I have endeavored to show some of the ways in which they reveal themselves through their interaction with others, but of the author's purposes (apart, that is, from the one overriding purpose of imaginative creation). To the extent that the characters are independent, that they serve no merely rhetorical aim, the novel can be regarded as an imaginative construct with an internal principle of organization, rather than as a work whose structural integrity comes from without, whether we regard it as a satire, an autobiography, a political treatise, or a travel book. What is conclusive here, I believe, is that the five characters so far considered derive their very existence from their attempts to render for their various correspondents a common body of experience, and it is inherent in Smollett's method that the body of experience being rendered should be subordinate to the characters and personalities of those who render it. At the focus of Smollett's imaginative vision in *Humphry Clinker* are the modes of perception by which the five main characters assert their individuality.

To say that the focus of the novel lies in the way that the several characters confront their common experience, however, does not supply us with an intelligible principle of the novel's development. It gives us, as it were, no more than a center of gravity, and it remains to show how the potentialities of this specific center are translated into an actual thematic development. That the structure of the novel is to be defined thematically is perhaps already implicit in the travel format with its virtually inexhaustible possibilities for thematic organization. Perhaps, as some critics maintain, Smollett is using the matrix of the "expedition" to vindicate his native Scotland and to answer the libels of some influential Englishmen of the period. Such was the view of Horace Walpole, who regarded *Humphry Clinker* as the rankest kind of Scottish nationalist propaganda, and in recent years a similar interpretation has been offered by Louis Martz.[6] Apart from the external evidence as to Smollett's intention, which is both inconclusive and irrelevant, the objections to such a reading of the novel are of two kinds. In the first place, the novel spends too little time and space recommending Scotland, and its judgments of both England and Scotland are so equivocal, so full of qualifications and exceptions, that they hardly serve the propaganda purposes imputed to them. Fewer than an eighth of the letters are dated from Scotland, and though the travelers find much to admire and to enjoy north of the Tweed, particularly Mr. Bramble, who is enchanted by Glasgow and the Loch Lomond region, they find so much to criticize that the effect of their admiration is considerably attenuated. On the other hand, though many of the English scenes evoke the travelers' contempt or ridicule, particularly in Bath and London, the satire is diluted by everything that excites their admiration or respect, as well as by the considerable portion of the book that is rhetorically neutral. It might be pointed out, too, that Lismahago is less than an ideal apologist for Scotland, for quite apart from the fact that he is fully alive to the disadvantages of Scotland, his own personal attributes would be more likely to confirm than to destroy prejudices about the disagreeableness of the Scots. In the second place, the very qualities that make for imaginative wholeness in the novel work against its value as propaganda. What is central to the novel as novel, as I have been arguing all along, is the way in which the raw materials of observation are transformed by the idiosyncrasies of the various observers into feelings, beliefs, and valuations which are of interest because of the special relation in which they stand to the persons who hold them. Smollett's choice of points of view is a device of characterization rather than of propaganda. Whatever rhetorical capital is to be made, for example, of Matthew Bramble's reflections on Vauxhall, quoted above, is immediately canceled by Lydia's exactly opposite response. We remain neutral toward Vauxhall, even though we tend to prefer Mr. Bramble's valuations to Lydia's, because the direction of our involvement in the novel is inward, from the things being observed to the characters who observe them.

M. A. Goldberg offers a more strictly thematic interpretation of the novel by suggesting that the central conflict, instead of being between England and Scotland, is between the ideas of primitivism and progress as the eighteenth century understood these terms, with Smollett taking up the position of mediator, along with the "Scottish Common-Sense School." [7] Insofar as this reading presents the novel less as a partisan tract than as an exploration of opposed intellectual systems it is less subject than the Scottish propaganda interpretation to the second objection specified above, but here, too, the interest in the characters as such is not perhaps altogether compatible with the interest in historical generalizations like "primitivism" and "progress." I do not think it necessary, at any rate, to inquire to what extent or how plausibly the novel does in fact provide the materials for such a study, since for reasons already considered I believe that the question of primitivism versus progress lies outside or rather on a different plane from what I have defined as the novel's imaginative center. Still, it ought to be possible to hit on some thematic formulation that will remain in novelistic terms, which will simultaneously preserve our awareness of the highly individualized characters and define the nature of their interrelation in the imaginative structure of the novel. I have already rejected the notion that the novel describes Mr. Bramble's journey from sickness to health on the ground that his relative euphoria at the end of the novel marks no real or permanent change in him, and for the same reason we may discard the analogous proposition that the journey records his transition from misanthropy to philanthropy, since his psychic nature is as volatile and changeable as his physical one. Moreover, though Mr. Bramble is clearly the main character in the novel, we cannot very well admit a structural principle that has no place for the other members of the party. I believe it is possible, however, to trace a change in the relation of all the characters to each other, a change which begins in the evolutions of plot, but which can be universalized as theme.

To document this change it is necessary to go back to the beginning of the novel, to glance briefly at some of the earliest letters. "Those children of my sister," Mr. Bramble complains, "are . . . a perpetual source of vexation—what business have people to get children to plague their neighbours?" (I, 7). Jery grumbles that his uncle is "always on the fret" and finds his company intolerable (I, 12), and Tabitha also suffers from the same cause: "What between his willfullness and his waste, his trumps, and his frenzy, I lead the life of an indented slave" (I, 63). The feeling is apparently reciprocal, for, Jery tells us, she "acts upon him as a perpetual grind-stone" (I, 40), and Matthew himself protests to Dr. Lewis, "I vow to God, she is sometimes so intolerable, that I almost think she's the devil incarnate come to torment me for my sins; and yet I am conscious of no sins that ought to entail such family-plagues upon me—why the devil should not I shake off these torments at once? I an't married to Tabby, thank Heaven! nor did I beget the other two" (I, 16). What is significant here is not that the characters get on each other's nerves; with the sole exception of Lydia they are all of a temperament that makes such clashes inevitable. The suggestive point is that none of the characters feels any burden of responsibility toward the rest; even Lydia is so preoccupied with her own bruised heart that she is not really a member of the family, and Mr. Bramble emphatically and repeatedly complains that he has done nothing to deserve the afflictions that attend his exercise of paternal authority. What takes place, then, in the course of the novel is not a fundamental change in the temperament or character of any of the principal personages but an important change in the relations among them. At the end of the novel the idiosyncrasies of the various characters remain as strong as ever, but now they come into play over a firm substructure of acknowledged responsibility and family unity. All of the characters, I believe, participate in this movement. The three marriages brought about at the end of the novel affect or clarify the relations of all six of the newlyweds to the family group. Lismahago and George Dennison, obviously, are outsiders who are brought within the family, but the change in Tabitha's and Lydia's status is somewhat more subtle. By their marriages they loosen their ties to Mr. Bramble and the others, but those ties are at the same time strengthened and clarified by the removal of conflict and ambiguity in their respective positions. Tabitha's energies, which have been altogether devoted to the search for a husband, are now free for the re-establishment of her relation to her brother on a more stable and agreeable foundation, and Lydia, who has been alienated from her uncle and brother by her faithfulness to an inadmissible suitor, is now restored to grace. Both Humphry and Win, finally, are transformed from servants into members of the family. Mr. Bramble and Jery are of course affected by the acquisition of relatives-in-law, and by the changed basis of the women's relation to them. Mr. Bramble, in particular, is doubly blessed in the enlargement of his family and in the loosening of their dependency upon him. The fact is, as he acknowledges himself, he enjoys the company of his new brother-in-law, but does not desire too much of it: "though an olla is a high-flavoured dish, I could not bear to dine upon it every day of my life" (II, 118).

The evolution of the change I have been describing is recorded not only in the incidents which make up the plot, but also in the permutations of the point of view. Whatever its disadvantages in rendering a continuous narrative, the multiple point of view lends itself perfectly to the chronicle of changed and growing awareness that we encounter in *Humphry Clinker*. Each character's contribution consists of a series of letters written over a considerable period of time, so that each letter in the series affords a discrete portion of the character's consciousness. There is no coloring of attitudes revealed to us in early letters by the knowledge of what is to be disclosed in later ones, so that wherever a character's attitudes appear to be changing or developing, each of his letters displays a more or less definite and determinate state in the process. The fact, too, that the letters are by different hands helps to point up the changing relations among the characters because they so often present us the same matter seen from different perspectives.

One of the perennial problems in the interpretation of the novel—what we are to make of the title and the importance it confers upon the character of Humphry Clinker—is illuminated, I believe, by regarding the growth of the acceptance of the family relation as the animating principle of the novel. Mr. Bramble's discovery that Humphry is his own illegitimate son throws a strongly ironic light on his earlier declarations that people have no business to get children to plague their neighbors or that he is conscious of no sins that ought to entail such family plagues upon him. His acknowledgment of Clinker at the end of the novel, therefore, is not just another instance of the generosity he has displayed, often by stealth, from the very beginning; it is a declaration that he has changed from the role of observer or spectator to that of participant, that he has moved from a position of detachment to one of responsibility, consciously and even cheerfully elected. Humphry is a living reminder that Matthew is involved in mankind by his own sin, and Humphry's presence deprives him of the right to despise the follies and absurdities of other men, or to draw credit from the disinterestedness of his own benevolence. Clinker's own function in the novel becomes by this means a little clearer, and the otherwise inexplicable series of events which he enters into are seen as normal consequences of his thematic function. Nearly all of his actions toward his patron, for example, achieve significance as a commentary upon the father-son relation that he and Mr. Bramble are ultimately discovered to occupy. The spiritual presumption of his Methodist teaching, his humility and his almost aggressive loyalty toward Mr. Bramble, above all his repeated endeavors (sometimes ill-considered) to rescue his master are not adventitious incidents in the novel but motives in a clearly ordered thematic development. The relation of mutual dependency and obligation is one that begins to develop from the moment of Clinker's first appearance in the novel and culminates fittingly in the overt recognition of the ultimate basis of the relation. It was not a wayward impulse that led Smollett to title his novel *The Expedition of Humphry Clinker*, for though the title character may have only a minor part in the novel's action, he is at the center of its thematic development.

Nearly all of Smollett's critics have preferred *Humphry Clinker* to the earlier novels, and they have endeavored to fix its characteristic flavor and tone. A "pleasant, gossiping novel," Hazlitt calls it, and Saintsbury's adjectives are "kindly and genial." [8] I think every sensitive reader must feel the qualities referred to here, but the pleasantness and geniality of the novel are rather elusive properties when one tries to pin them down, for the pervasive humor of the novel is both coarse and violent, and though Matthew Bramble superficially prefigures a sentimental archetype who is to emerge in the novels of Dickens, *Humphry Clinker* owes virtually nothing to the cult of sensibility that influenced Sterne and the Gothic writers. The pleasantness, the geniality, and perhaps one might add the serenity, of *Humphry Clinker* are a product, not of the sentimental impulse to distort or reshape an unpleasant reality, but of a mature realism that recognizes the stupidity, the brutality, the essential shabbiness of the world, and yet accepts it and goes out into it. The "expedition" of Humphry and his family is just such an adventure. For Mr. Bramble it represents an excursion from the security of Brambleton Hall into a world that for all its ugliness presents a crucial challenge, not to the fastidious tourist who looks and remains aloof, but to the man who is prepared to acknowledge his membership in the human race.

CHAPTER VII

Mansfield Park and Jane Austen's Moral Universe

> What is character but the determination of incident? what is incident but the illustration of character?
> —HENRY JAMES, "The Art of Fiction"

Admirers of *Pride and Prejudice* and *Emma* always have trouble with *Mansfield Park*. Anyone who has learned to appreciate the brilliant and multifaceted social comedy of the former novels is likely to be put off by the tough-minded but simple didacticism of the latter, and Fanny Price seems remarkably insipid alongside Elizabeth Bennet or Emma Woodhouse. If only someone else had written *Mansfield Park*—say Mrs. Gaskell, or even George Eliot [1]—there would be no problem, but the uncompromising fact is that *Mansfield Park* is as inevitably a product of Jane Austen's artistic vision as either *Pride and Prejudice* or *Emma*, even though it seems to offer a concern with a somewhat different set of human values, and even though it is written in a flatter tone. [2] The differences, real or alleged, between *Mansfield Park* and the other novels may be conveniently dealt with, in fact, under the headings of differences in substance and differences in manner.

It is easy to mistake the central moral issue of *Mansfield Park*. A careless reading yields the impression that the novel is recommending an ideal of simple repression, or (since Jane Austen characteristically presents moral ideas in the form of dichotomies, like Sense and Sensibility) an ideal of propriety, of Chesterfieldian decorum, defined by reference to an opposite ideal of spontaneity and self-expression. The assumption that an antithesis of this kind is at the moral center of *Mansfield Park* is cognate with the awareness that Fanny Price and Mary Crawford typify the two ideals, and that Mary Crawford is much more like Elizabeth Bennet than either is like Fanny. It is apparent, therefore, that *Pride and Prejudice* (to limit the comparison, for the moment, to this single novel) and *Mansfield Park* differ radically in their moral assumptions and in the kinds of people they ask us to admire. And it is apparent, moreover, that in the face of such an obvious and strongly marked antithesis the modern reader must give his allegiance to Elizabeth, and therefore also to Mary.[3] To put the case in its strongest terms, Fanny is a stick, whom we cannot even believe in, let alone admire, while Mary is as vivacious, charming, and witty as the most fastidious taste can demand.

It is a nice, though possibly superfluous, question whether the moral antithesis generates the character opposition or vice versa, but I believe it is apparent that the foregoing analysis does violence to both, principally by rendering them too simply. At any rate it seems to me profitable to examine them more closely, not by looking at the author's judgments about them, but by looking at characters and events, speeches and actions, to see if our sense of the moral issue and of the characters who embody it may not be somewhat sharpened. When we begin to examine the moral antithesis we are confronted by a curious inconsistency. If we take the opposition to be between repression and spontaneity, that is to say, between a confining ideal of decorum and a liberating ideal of self-expression, we cannot be sure of the proper alignment of characters. In the matter of the theatricals at Mansfield Park it would seem to be Edmund

and Fanny who are on the side of repression, while all the
other characters are on the side of spontaneity. But when we
come to the final showdown with Mary, in which Edmund is
shocked by her response to Henry's elopement with Maria, we
must readjust our views:

"We must persuade Henry to marry her," said she, "and what
with honour, and the certainty of having shut himself out for ever
from Fanny, I do not despair of it. Fanny he must give up. I do
not think that even *he* could now hope to succeed with one of her
stamp, and therefore I hope we may find no insuperable difficulty.
My influence, which is not small, shall all go that way; and, when
once married, and properly supported by her own family, people
of respectability as they are, she may recover her footing in society
to a certain degree." [4]

Edmund's own feelings are revolted by Mary's attitude, because she is attempting only to hush the matter up, not to
pronounce the moral condemnation which seems to him called
for. At any rate, it is clear that if anyone has Chesterfieldian
notions of decorum here it is Mary, not Edmund, and that my
earlier formulation of the moral issue of the novel must be
revised. A still more striking reversal of moral attitudes is disclosed in the scene where Mary wonders whether Fanny is
"out" or not. The question is wholly one of propriety of conduct, and it is Mary who proves expert:

"A girl not out, has always the same sort of dress; a close bonnet
for instance, looks very demure, and never says a word. You may
smile—but it is so I assure you—and except that it is sometimes
carried a little too far, it is all very proper. Girls should be quiet
and modest. The most objectionable part is, that the alteration of
manners on being introduced into company is frequently too
sudden. They sometimes pass in such very little time from reserve
to quite the opposite—to confidence! *That* is the faulty part of
the present system. One does not like to see a girl of eighteen or

nineteen so immediately up to every thing—and perhaps when one has seen her hardly able to speak the year before." [ch. 5]

Mary's tone is playful, as usual with her, but there is no reason to doubt her concurrence in the proprieties of maidenly behavior. Significantly, it is only Edmund who seems wanting in a proper sense of the importance of the outs and not outs.

The play is the real moral crux, and it is perhaps the play which will permit us to catch the conscience of Edmund and Fanny. It is important to discern accurately the grounds of judgment in this episode, for it is just here that it is easiest to mistake the moral drift of the novel, and it is here that the author's insistent comments seem to depart most strikingly from the judgments which the reader is likely to form of events and characters.[5] Up to this point the author has apparently committed only the venial sin of telling us what we are going to feel anyway, and her commentary is nothing worse than redundant, but beginning with the play episode we are likely to feel that she is attempting vainly to distort our "correct" judgment by inserting irrelevant or downright wrong valuations. I shall reserve for the moment the question of a possible disparity between the author's valuations and the reader's, looking instead only at the scene itself in an effort to understand why Edmund and Fanny reach the conclusions they do.

To begin with, I think we must dismiss the convenient but specious idea that Edmund and Fanny object to private theatricals out of simple prudishness. A hyper-Victorian moral consciousness might conceivably find something to object to, either in subject or treatment, in Mrs. Inchbald's *Lovers' Vows*, but any such cavil would be irrelevant, because all the objections are voiced before that play is decided upon and have nothing, therefore, to do with any real or fancied indelicacy in the play. They are directed wholly against the idea of doing any sort of dramatic representation at all. Lionel Trilling thinks that the objections are rooted in the idea that assuming a role, pretending to be someone else, undermines the integrity of the self, but the subtlety of this notion is plainly out of reach of Sir Thomas's mental powers, even his subliminal ones (for it is obviously Sir Thomas's own strongly felt antipathy that moves Edmund and Fanny, and therefore his objections which ultimately matter). A still stronger reason for doubting this interpretation is the abundant evidence that neither puritanical nor Hebraic ideas of dramatic representation are current at Mansfield Park. Shakespearean plays are commonly read aloud in the drawing room after dinner (ch. 34), and Sir Thomas himself has encouraged the boys in dramatic reading. If we can believe Julia, Edmund himself has gone as far as anyone to see a play (ch. 13), and to clinch the matter, Fanny, the most pertinacious foe of the dramatic venture, "believed herself to derive as much innocent enjoyment from the play as any of them;—Henry Crawford acted well, and it was a pleasure to *her* to creep into the theatre, and attend the rehearsal of the first act" (ch. 18).

Edmund's view is that whatever one may think of private theatricals ordinarily, the family's present circumstances make their propriety questionable. The circumstances he alludes to are, first, the absence of Sir Thomas, together with the un-certainty as to his safety, the implications being that it would be culpable to do anything in his absence which could not be done in his presence, and that his danger increases the impro-priety of their levity, and second, the "delicacy" of Maria's situation as the fiancée of Rushworth. We can smile at such fastidious ideas of propriety, but they are acknowledged as binding by the very people who here flout them. Jane Austen is at some pains to show us Mary Crawford's views on the conduct of young ladies who are "not out," in a passage already quoted, and generally speaking there is no disposition on any side to challenge the reign of decorum at Mansfield

Park. It is true, of course, that Tom Bertram attempts to refute Edmund's strictures, but that his argument is no more than an attempt to rationalize his own selfish impulses, and that the whole company, except for the unperceptive Yates, shares his feelings, is made perfectly clear by their palpable sense of guilt at the unexpected news of Sir Thomas's return (ch. 19). The curious thing is that Edmund should feel the demands of propriety so strongly in this instance, and yet be so indifferent to the outs and the not outs, or so careless of Maria's reputation after she has eloped with Crawford.

But what appears to be an inconsistency in Edmund's values is only a deeper kind of consistency. We are expected to make as clear a distinction as he does between the manners which are enforced only by the capricious fiat of society, and the manners which are an expression of character. The Bertram girls have only the first kind of discipline. During the visit to Sotherton, when Julia finds herself doomed to the company of Mrs. Norris and Mrs. Rushworth, her purely superficial politeness is strained to the limit: "The politeness which she had been brought up to practise as a duty, made it impossible for her to escape; while the want of that higher species of self-command, that just consideration of others, that knowledge of her own heart, that principle of right which had not formed any essential part of her education, made her miserable under it" (ch. 9). We can disregard the pedagogic tone, but we cannot very well discount the insight we are given into Julia's mind and character. In what can only be a deliberate attempt to supply a contrast, Jane Austen makes Edmund, speaking of the clerical office only two pages after the passage just quoted, distinguish pointedly between manners as the superficial adornment of life and manners as the expression of an inward condition of mind and spirit: "Miss Crawford must not misunderstand me, or suppose I mean to call [the clergy] the arbiters of good breeding, the regulators of refinement and courtesy, the masters of the ceremonies of life. The *manners* I speak of, might rather be called *conduct*, perhaps, the result of good principles; the effect, in short, of those doctrines which it is their duty to teach and recommend." This is the real moral antithesis of *Mansfield Park*, between manners which are only manners—a kind of outward concession to good form —and manners which are firmly rooted in moral principle and therefore constant and unchanging. It is not really necessary to ask *what* principle, because the novel does not concern itself with opposing moral systems. Presumably since Edmund is entering the ministry the moral values implied are those of orthodox protestant Christianity. The central issue, to borrow Joseph Duffy's convenient terms, is between "moral integrity" and "moral anarchy," between the life of principle and the life without principle.[6]

What troubles Edmund about the theatricals at Mansfield Park is not the moral quality of the act itself, for he and Fanny both consent to participate, but the absence of moral sentiment in the agents. For the first time Edmund's eyes are opened to the differences which separate his brother and sisters from himself; he sees them for the first time as the character-less beings they are. The only thing which prevents him from seeing Mary Crawford in the same light is that his infatuation enables him to look upon her want of delicacy as an act of complaisance toward his own family. Edmund's judgment is confirmed pragmatically, not by the return of his father, but by the fact that the transitory impulse which gave rise to the whole affair proves almost immediately self-defeating. Except for Yates, whose vanity requires the simplest kind of nourish-ment, and Henry and Maria, lost in their flirtation, the mem-bers of the cast find the enterprise disappointing. To Tom it brings boredom; to Mary, embarrassment; to Julia and Rush-worth, outright disgust. Ironically, it is only Fanny who derives real enjoyment from the play.

The moral antithesis which is first rendered dramatically in the episode of the play is reflected in (or takes its rise from) certain key oppositions of character, of which the opposition between Mary Crawford and Fanny Price is the most important. Of course there are a number of characters who lie outside this basic opposition, but they are not necessarily irrelevant to it, because they may, like Lady Bertram, help us to understand better the terms of the opposition. The life of principle clearly comprehends the ideal of rationality, and it therefore excludes those whose judgment is weak or whose power of discernment is lacking. Lady Bertram, whose disposition and "temper" are unexceptionable, proves to be a moral imbecile; she inhabits a plane of existence where moral choice is unnecessary, where choice of any kind is rarely demanded of her. Henry Crawford manages her cards for her, making all the decisions under the pretext of teaching her the game (ch. 25). Her one unaided decision in the entire novel, to send her maid to help Fanny dress for the ball, is so wholly extrarational and charismatic that it continues to excite her own wonder and admiration throughout the rest of the book. That the maid arrives at Fanny's door just as Fanny emerges fully dressed is an incidental irony which only confirms how ineffectual Lady Bertram is (ch. 27).

The important figures, the ones whose characters make themselves felt in the crucial events of the novel, are Maria, the two Crawfords, Edmund, and Fanny. Edmund, whose moral stance I have already examined, is besotted by his love for Mary, so that his powers of judgment are distorted, and Maria, with sufficient powers of judgment and strength of character to lead the moral life, is betrayed by her vanity into permitting a fatal discontinuity between her judgment and her actions. She is clever enough to see how stupid Rushworth is, but willful enough to marry him to spite Crawford, who has wounded her vanity. The freest, and therefore most significant expression of the basic opposition of character, is provided by Henry and Mary Crawford and Fanny Price.

The contrast between the Crawfords and Fanny is weighted in every possible way to the advantage of the former. They have fortune, physical health and vitality, good looks (*pace* Rushworth), intelligence, talent, charm, wit—everything that Lionel Trilling has summed up in the expression "grace of ease." They are the kind of people for whom life is easy, whose triumphs are never gained at the price of pain and frustration. Poor, pathetic little Fanny, on the other hand, has everything against her. She is a poor relation with none of the advantages of wealth (she cannot even play the piano, an accomplishment which is regarded as the *sine qua non* of fashion for young ladies); she is without poise or spirit; she has demure good looks, but none of the Crawfords' glowing health or vitality. And her claims even on our pity are weakened by her vapors, her timorousness, her sententious moralizing, and her jejune appreciation of what she insists on calling "verdure." The contrast is so striking, and the reader's response to it so predictable, that I cannot help feeling that it is perfectly under the author's control. I cannot believe, that is, that Jane Austen allowed the Crawfords to "get away from her," and that to point her moral at the end she had to do them in the eye to prevent them from catching our sympathy entirely.

If we look more closely at Mary and Henry Crawford we cannot very well escape the conclusion that their behavior is all of a piece, that they are betrayed, in a sense, by the very qualities which constitute their charm—their quickness of apprehension and their natural volatility of temperament. Henry's mercurial quality is perhaps the more readily apparent of the two, but chiefly because of his masculine prerogative of following his own inclination. "From Bath, Norfolk, London, York—wherever I may be," he tells the Bertrams, "I will attend you from any place in England, at an hour's notice" (ch. 20). And his nostalgic feeling for the play-acting interlude at Mansfield suggests his temperament still more strongly: "I shall always look back on our theatricals with exquisite pleasure. There was such an interest, such an animation, such a spirit diffused! Every body felt it. We were all alive. There was employment, hope, solicitude, bustle, for every hour of the day. Always some little objection, some little doubt, some little anxiety to be got over. I never was happier" (ch. 23). But even Henry, attractive as he is for his vitality, senses his own lack of constancy. The clerical profession, so despised by his sister, he can see as a challenge to his own eloquence at the same time that he recognizes his own want of the requisite steadiness for such a profession: "I never listened to a distinguished preacher in my life, without a sort of envy. But then, I must have a London audience. I could not preach, but to the educated; to those who were capable of estimating my composition. And, I do not know that I should be fond of preaching often; now and then, perhaps, once or twice in the spring, after being anxiously expected for half a dozen Sundays together; but not for a constancy; it would not do for a constancy" (ch. 34).

Mary's restlessness finds expression less easily in overt actions, because she is a woman, subject to all the restraints on her freedom of conduct that her own sense of propriety demands. But her own volatility of temperament does find expression in her restlessness on Edmund's behalf. She repeatedly assails the clergy, particularly after she learns that Edmund, the younger son, is destined for that profession, and it must be said in her favor that she has been confronted with no very shining example in the person of her brother-in-law, Dr. Grant, who lives for the joys of his over-sized dining table, and who is ultimately taken off by "three great institutionary dinners in one week." But what she resents in the clergy is the deficiency, not the excess, of worldliness. A clergyman, she is fond of repeating, is "nothing," and she praises by contrast the profession of arms: "The profession, either navy or army, is its own justification. It has every thing in its favour; heroism, danger, bustle, fashion" (ch. 11). Mary's restlessness appears not only in her expressions of vicarious ambition but in response to any trial of her patience. When Edmund goes off for a period of meditation before taking orders, Mary's own temperament leads her to suppose him infatuated with the young ladies of the house where he is in retirement, and her agitation at his prolonged absence forces her to seek comfort from Fanny, whose patience is equal to the demands put upon it by Edmund's absence—an absence which is as trying to her as to Mary. Fanny's apparent placidity provides the needed solace, and Mary goes home again, as the author says with a flash of her old irony, "in spirits which might have defied almost another week of the same small party in the same bad weather" (ch. 30).

The Crawfords' fatal flaw is their want of constancy, their lack of moral ballast, which is itself an indication that they lack principle. In all other ways superior to Fanny Price, on this point alone they are over-matched. Jane Austen's characterization of Fanny is not accidental or haphazard. She has deliberately set herself the most difficult artistic challenge of all, to deprive her heroine of all the outward graces and to command our admiration for strength of character alone. The moral antithesis and the character opposition at the center of *Mansfield Park* are resolved by Fanny's act of moral heroism, a species of heroism which contrasts sharply with the Crawfords' ideal, in which heroism is associated with "bustle" and "fashion." Fanny had, Jane Austen tells us overtly in one of those quietly assertive statements which command assent, "all the heroism of principle" (ch. 27).

Fanny's heroism is accentuated, perhaps even made possible, by exactly those qualities which are most superficially repellent in her. To begin with, her physical slightness and frailty. Of course Jane Austen has no romantic or sentimental ideas about the attractiveness of female weakness. Emma Woodhouse and Elizabeth Bennet have abundant health and vitality, and Fanny's weakness can only be felt as detrimental to her attractiveness. Yet Jane Austen deals devastatingly with those characters who overvalue the purely physical advantages. Sir Walter Elliot, for example, preening himself on his complexion, is an egregious simpleton, and Rushworth betrays his stupidity most strikingly by his remarks on the despised Henry Crawford: "You should tell your father he is not above five feet eight, or he will be expecting a well-looking man" (ch. 19). Of course Crawford and Rushworth are contrasted in other ways than in physical appearance, a fact which Rushworth dimly apprehends but cannot articulate. Lady Bertram, surprised by Fanny's conquest of Crawford, can only attribute it to Fanny's fragile beauty, heightened by her blushes of embarrassment. "We certainly are a handsome family," Lady Bertram remarks complacently (ch. 33). Nevertheless, though she is severe on vanity, Jane Austen does not undervalue the physical advantages of health and beauty, and by bestowing these on Mary while withholding them (at least the former) from Fanny, she marks a contrast which serves to heighten the more significant contrast in steadiness and firmness of character.

Fanny's shyness and timidity are also important in the representation of her heroism. The crisis is her refusal of Crawford, for it is here that she must bring into play all the resilience of her character in withstanding Henry's persuasive arts, Mary's vivacious charm (Fanny has particularly dreaded this interview and sought to avoid it), and Sir Thomas's masculine and avuncular authority. Perhaps the truest index of Fanny's heroism is her ability to withstand Sir Thomas's displeasure, particularly when we remember his stateliness of speech and manner, his heavy pomposity, and Fanny's childish terror of him. It is clear that her victory must be entirely a victory of character, so she must be deprived of the weapons of wit, persuasiveness, physical vitality, and personal presence. All of these are arrayed against her, along with the weight of Sir Thomas's claims on her obedience and gratitude, and Edmund's claims on her love. Her successful resistance constitutes an authentic but little-regarded brand of heroism.

But even if the moral of the novel is a more interesting one than is generally allowed, there will still be plenty of people who will insist that the novel ought not to have a moral at all. That Jane Austen's novels are all morally tendentious seems to me a proposition that does not admit of much doubt, though a good deal depends on the use one makes of such a proposition. To declare, as Henry Austen does, that "she was thoroughly religious and devout," that she was "fearful of giving offense to God, and incapable of feeling it towards any fellow creature," and that "her opinions accorded strictly with those of our Established Church," is to endow her with a moral solemnity that is belied by the spirit and tone of her books.[7] On the other hand, to declare, as Marvin Mudrick does, that her ironic vision of life and her moral scrutiny of it are two distinct modes of apprehension that can never be made to coalesce is to ignore, I believe, the moralizing tendency of her creative imagination itself. Still, there is substantial agreement that in spite of varying degrees of sprightliness in the handling, Jane Austen's novels do invariably concern themselves with moral problems and moral values. Occasionally this concern is manifest in a title compounded of moral abstractions like "sense," "sensibility," "pride," "prejudice," or "persuasion"; often it is revealed in what many readers will regard as the intrusive commentary of the author; invariably it appears in the shape and direction of the novel's action. But if *Mansfield Park* does not differ from the rest of Jane Austen's fiction in its fidelity to a didactic impulse, perhaps its differences of subject may be located in the specific set of moral values that provide its central concern. Here, too, I find the differences exaggerated.

The occasion of Fanny's heroism, and the moral qualities which that occasion brings into play, are by no means unique in Jane Austen's fiction. Her books all deal, of course, with women, and it is therefore with the occasions and opportunities of feminine heroism that she is concerned. Women must play a passive role in the society Jane Austen pictures; they have no means of molding events except by their decisions upon any matter of choice that is presented to them. The constancy to an idea or an ideal of life which is so conspicuous a feature of Fanny's moral nature is equally conspicuous, I believe, as an attribute of Jane Austen's other heroines. Except for Elinor and Marianne in *Sense and Sensibility* (a novel which is, for a number of reasons, a special case) all of these women are confronted by an opportunity to compromise their ideals of life in the only significant way open to them—by accepting a proposal of marriage. No woman, at least in Jane Austen's world, chooses her mate, but she can always decline an offer and thereby refuse to compromise with social realities. Elizabeth Bennet refuses both Collins and Darcy; Emma refuses Elton; Catherine Morland refuses John Thorpe; Anne Elliot refuses Captain Wentworth. These refusals, except possibly Emma's, are perfectly disinterested. Only Emma is safe from the ultimate peril of spinsterhood, because only Emma has the fortune which can make a husband hers by right any time she chooses to admit the attentions of a suitor. All of these refusals are motivated by fidelity to a vision of life which cannot admit social or practical necessity (Charlotte Lucas is not of the stuff of the heroine, because her vision quickly yields to practical advantage). It may be, in fact, that Jane Austen most effectually subverts the values of the bourgeois society she depicts (as both D. W. Harding and Marvin Mudrick agree that she does) [8] by making her heroines incurably romantic. At any rate, I think it is undeniable that the dominant moral attribute of Jane Austen's heroines is their constancy to whatever ideal of conduct or character they profess (this is true even of Marianne, in spite of the "reformation" we are assured of by the author). Different as they are in temperament, intelligence, or other secondary qualities, their essential kinship with Fanny Price is manifest in their display of Fanny's own brand of heroism.

If *Mansfield Park* does not, after all, differ very sharply from the other novels, sharing with them a pre-eminently moral concern with character and incidents, it is still possible that it may differ from those other novels in being rather more austerely packaged. The reader is likely to feel—indeed many readers have felt—that the novel is not only didactic in purpose, it is explicitly (and therefore offensively) didactic in tone. Its moral truths, it might be said, are truisms and hence destructive of the novelist's art when they are proclaimed as unwearyingly as they seem to be in *Mansfield Park*. It is time to turn our attention to form, to take a look at the package.

The central question must be whether the moral truth is achieved at the expense of the novel's artistry, either by an artistically irrelevant commentary, or by the suspension of ordinary probabilities. It might be argued that Jane Austen's presence in the novel is constricting, that her seemingly irrepressible impulse to guide the reader's moral valuations is all but unforgivable.[9] While acknowledging a difference in tone between this and the other novels, I question whether the difference is really radical, between two mutually exclusive narrative modes (as Mudrick argues). The difference, it seems to me, may be adequately characterized as a muting, or still better, as a slowing down of the narrative. The tempo of *Mansfield Park* is *andante maestoso* in place of the *vivace* of *Pride and Prejudice* or the *allegretto* of *Emma*. The slowing down is perhaps itself a product of the didacticism in question; it is clear that many scenes in *Mansfield Park* which offer extraordinary possibilities of dramatic representation undergo a change in the middle. Jane Austen begins to dramatize an episode, then turns around and narrates it. The scene which is to culminate in Crawford's offer to Fanny, for example, begins with the dramatization of the harmless byplay in which the officious Mrs. Norris thinks Fanny is mistaken and that it is she herself who has been summoned by Sir Thomas, but after a chapter break, the real business of the episode is transacted at second hand, for we have Crawford's proposal only in indirect discourse (chs. 32, 33). Similarly, Jane Austen foregoes an opportunity to stage a brilliant comic scene when Sir Thomas surprises Mr. Yates in the midst of his declamations in the billiard room (ch. 19). Now of course there are some areas of experience which Jane Austen always declines to represent dramatically. "What did she say?" she asks coyly when she has brought Emma to listen to Mr. Knightley's proposal, "Just what she ought, of course. A lady always does" (*Emma*, ch. 49). So it would appear that the refusal to give us Mr. Crawford's own words when he proposes to Fanny is perfectly consonant with Jane Austen's usual practice. Still, a larger portion of the essential action of *Mansfield Park* is given in narration, a smaller portion in dialogue than in any other novel (with the possible exception of *Sense and Sensibility*), and the result is an inevitable slowing of its pulse.[10]

The verbal texture of *Mansfield Park* is curiously complicated and intricate. Jane Austen does not simply abandon the technique of irony in favor of a kind of bald didacticism; we find the two modes frequently interwoven. A point made with all the economy that the ironic method allows will frequently be hovered over by the narrator, who seems to wonder if we will miss the point. The characterization of Mrs. Norris is illustrative. Her character is a simple one; its salient attribute is officiousness, a desire to be in charge of things without any real commitment or sacrifice, especially of money. We learn all this about Mrs. Norris in a five-word clause in the first chapter: "Sir Thomas sent friendly advice and professions, Lady Bertram dispatched money and baby-linen, and Mrs. Norris wrote the letters." This is deft and perfect, yet Jane Austen must labor the point. "I am a woman of few words," she makes Mrs. Norris proclaim in a speech of 400 words to Sir Thomas, and we can still smile, though we cannot any longer admire the subtlety (or economy) of the technique. But the whole structure topples when the narrator confides to us, quite gratuitously, that "Mrs. Norris had not the least intention of being at any expense whatever. . . . As far as walking, talking, and contriving reached, she was thoroughly benevolent, and nobody knew better how to dictate liberality to others: but her love of money was equal to her love of directing, and she knew quite as well how to save her own as to spend that of her friends."

Neither the irony nor the didacticism is a new ingredient in Jane Austen's novels, but the heavy, measured tone produced by this involuted style is, in its degree at least, unique to *Mansfield Park*. Its justification is not to be sought in those attributes which Jane Austen's brilliant and facetious manner can achieve so easily, a deft representation of the thing to be rendered, together with a lively sense of all its possible absurdities. The style of *Mansfield Park* has a somewhat different function to perform. Marvin Mudrick speaks of it as a "committed" manner (indeed his whole distinction between the ironic and didactic ways of seeing is founded on the distinction between commitment and the lack of commitment), and the term is useful, but I think it is important to observe that the painful moral consciousness of the narrator is part of what is to be represented by this style. Every way of speaking tells us something about the speaker, of course (Buffon's aphorism is relevant), but here the speaker's mind is part of the *mundus representandi*. In *Mansfield Park*, alone among Jane Austen's novels, we are completely on the inside of the action. We cannot, of course, foretell the future, but we are never in doubt about character or motive. This is obviously a change from the almost wholly dramatic method of *Pride and Prejudice*, but almost equally so from the quasi-didactic method of *Emma*, for the presence of the narrator serves not so much to direct our judgments, as it does to condition us to the necessity of scrutinizing characters and incidents for their moral content. And the narrative persona, which remains as aloof and detached as possible in *Pride and Prejudice*, or helps us to look over the heroine's shoulder in *Emma*, here tends to merge with Fanny's own consciousness. The narrator's presence assists us to the continuous awareness that the smallest concerns of life have potential moral significance, that the life of principle or of moral heroism demands a constant vigilance. The narrator influences us less by making specific moral judgments for us, than by being continuously preoccupied with the necessity of moral valuation.

Irony is by no means necessarily destructive of this narrative function, as Mudrick would contend, because irony (as in Swift) may after all be morally committed. The quiet and apparently neutral observation that "the approach of September brought tidings of Mr. Bertram first in a letter to the game-keeper, and then in a letter to Edmund" (ch. 12) is an ironic commentary on Bertram's character and values, but its irony depends on the unspoken assumption that Tom's first thought should be of his family, not of his own pleasure. But the kind of irony which is morally uncommitted, which depends primarily upon the incongruity between a social attitude and the reality it conceals, is disruptive in the context of *Mansfield*

Park. I find, for example, that the passage which describes Fanny's embarrassment at having to introduce her father to Mr. Crawford is disturbingly out of key:

> She could not have a doubt of the manner in which Mr. Crawford must be struck. He must be ashamed and disgusted altogether. He must soon give her up, and cease to have the smallest inclination for the match; and yet, though she had been so much wanting his affection to be cured, this was a sort of cure that would be almost as bad as the complaint; and I believe, there is scarcely a young lady in the united kingdoms, who would not rather put up with the misfortune of being sought by a clever, agreeable man, than have him driven away by the vulgarity of her nearest relations. [ch. 41]

This is the kind of unattached or uncommitted irony we might expect in *Pride and Prejudice;* in *Mansfield Park* it is dissonant.

Tone and verbal texture, the qualities which make us aware of inner form, here seem to be in a purely mechanical alliance with structure. To decide whether this appearance is deceptive or not, we need to know whether the events of the novel are forced into the pattern which would make the narrator's moral valuations true and relevant, or whether they follow some logic of their own. Of course the logic of events is within the artist's power, just as the tone is; we do not demand that the novelist subscribe to historically valid theories of causation. We do, however, demand that events sustain their own motion, that the artist refrain from altering arbitrarily the "natural" sequence of events. But what is "natural" depends as much on the artist's way of viewing experience as it does on external reality, and we cannot therefore prescribe the course of events a priori. The important question, then, is not properly by what tone, what mode of representation, ironic or didactic or both, Jane Austen records her apprehension of experience, but the conditions under which that apprehension takes place, the qualities of the imaginative vision itself that determine what kinds of experience the writer is to deal with.

The charge that Jane Austen does in fact force events out of their probable sequence is most likely to be made about Henry Crawford's sudden abandonment of his suit for Fanny to run off with Maria Rushworth. Lord David Cecil is one of many critics who regard this turn of events as a blemish in the novel:

In *Mansfield Park* [Jane Austen] sacrifices form to fact. The original design of the book obviously intended Henry Crawford to fill the rôle of villain. But as she works Jane Austen's creative power gets out of control, Henry Crawford comes to life as a sympathetic character; and under the pressure of his personality the plot takes a turn, of which the only logical conclusion is his marriage with the heroine, Fanny. Jane Austen was not one to be put upon by her creatures in this way. In the last three chapters she violently wrenches the story back into its original course: but only at the cost of making Henry act in a manner wholly inconsistent with the rest of his character.[11]

I think there are several important errors here. I am inclined to treat with suspicion any critic who claims to be privy to an author's "original" (but unrealized) design. And if Jane Austen is clever enough to realize when she is off the rails (as Lord David graciously concedes), I think she is probably clever enough to avoid getting derailed in the first place. It is difficult to imagine that an experienced novelist (who had already written four novels and published two) could commit the double sin of making an egregious blunder and then publicly setting it right, particularly when we can assume that *Mansfield Park* was published only after careful revision. But the principal matter of concern here is the statement that Henry acts "in a manner wholly inconsistent with the rest of his character." I have already argued that in spite of his many attractive qualities Crawford's character is weakened by an extreme volatility of temperament and a consequent lack of steadiness or constancy that Jane Austen is at some pains to make clear to the most careless reader. It is in fact tacitly understood by the Mansfield Park family that Crawford's character is subject to just this objection and that his demonstration of real firmness of purpose is the essential condition of his successful courtship of Fanny: "Sir Thomas was most cordially anxious for the perfection of Mr. Crawford's character in that point. He wished him to be a model of constancy; and fancied the best means of effecting it would be by not trying him too long" (ch. 35). Now surely a probationary suitor cannot occasion very much surprise by failing in just the way that it was anticipated by everyone that he might, by demonstrating, that is, the propensity which had occasioned his probationary status in the first place. It is made quite clear, furthermore, that Crawford is attracted to Maria from his first meeting with her, and his choice of her as a partner in indiscretion is prefigured by the early conversation with his sister:

"I like your Miss Bertrams exceedingly, sister," said he, as he returned from attending them to their carriage after the . . . dinner visit; "they are very elegant, agreeable girls."

"So they are, indeed, and I am delighted to hear you say it. But you like Julia best."

"Oh! yes, I like Julia best."

"But do you really? for Miss Bertram is in general thought the handsomest."

"So I should suppose. She has the advantage in every feature, and I prefer her countenance—but I like Julia best. Miss Bertram is certainly the handsomest, and I have found her the most agreeable, but I shall always like Julia best, because you order me."

"I shall not talk to you, Henry, but I know you *will* like her best at last."

"Do not I tell you, that I like her best *at first?*"

"And besides, Miss Bertram is engaged. Remember that, my dear brother. Her choice is made."

"Yes, and I like her the better for it. An engaged woman is always more agreeable than a disengaged. She is satisfied with her-self. Her cares are over, and she feels that she may exert all her powers of pleasing without suspicion. All is safe with a lady en-gaged; no harm can be done." [ch. 5]

The signposts are in fact scattered liberally along the way, usually in the shape of prefigurative irony. "If Miss Bertram were not engaged," Fanny is made to remark at one point, "I could sometimes almost think that he admired her more than Julia" (ch. 12). Or Mrs. Norris is represented glorying in her match-making skill: "[She] was all joyous delight—for she had made the match—she had done every thing—and no one would have supposed, from her confident triumph, that she had ever heard of conjugal infelicity in her life, or could have the smallest insight into the disposition of the niece who had been brought up under her eye" (ch. 21). It must be remembered, too, that Maria's character is such as to help render the elope-ment plausible, for the woman who could marry Rushworth to spite Crawford is quite capable of running off with Crawford to display her contempt for Rushworth.

It is not so much the fundamental implausibility of the catastrophe as its suddenness that is likely to take the reader by surprise. Whatever shock the event occasions is made possible by the removal of Fanny (and therefore also of the narrative point of view) to Portsmouth, remote from the scene of events, even though Jane Austen apparently attempts to soften the shock, first by a hint in a letter from Mary Crawford, then in a pruriently reticent newspaper account which comes to Lieuten-ant Price's notice. But the surprise may be heightened, too, by the feeling that perhaps Crawford will remain true to his pur-pose. Edmund is convinced of Crawford's new-found steadi-ness, and he writes to Fanny: "I am more and more satisfied with all that I see and hear of him. There is not a shadow of wavering. He thoroughly knows his own mind, and acts up to his resolutions—an inestimable quality" (ch. 44). Even Fanny senses a "wonderful improvement" in his manners, though she cannot yet be sure of his constancy: "She thought him altogether improved since she had seen him; he was much more gentle, obliging, and attentive to other people's feelings than he had ever been at Mansfield; she had never seen him so agreeable—so *near* being agreeable; his behaviour to her father could not offend, and there was something particularly kind and proper in the notice he took of Susan. He was decidedly improved" (ch. 41). Thus the news, when it comes, may produce some sense of shock, and we are likely to feel that Jane Austen is treating our sensibilities somewhat cavalierly in that she has no apparent concern with the immediate causes of events, a knowledge of which might easily reconcile us to the inevitability of the elopement.

I can meet this objection only with a tentative answer. I said a moment ago that a novelist did not need to subscribe to historically valid theories of causation as long as he subscribed to some law of cause and effect that would enable the reader to judge of probability. It has always seemed to me that Jane Austen's world (and I am here speaking of all the novels) is ruled, not by a mechanistic conception of causality, but by a more or less deterministic one. Events do not occur as the necessary conclusion of a finely wrought chain of cause and effect; they are brought about primarily by character. It should be explained at once that I use this term to designate, not individuality, but moral nature. By "character" I mean two things: first, an aggregate of principles and values, but chiefly moral principles and values, and second, the tenacity with which these principles and values are held and the energy with which they are exercised as determinants of conduct, for it is possible to speak not only of good and bad characters, but also of strong and weak ones. Character in this sense excludes knowledge and sympathy or antipathy, which may determine conduct, but which are readily subject to change. Character is not innate, but certain qualities that help to determine it are generally thought of as innate: intelligence, for example, or temperament. That character in the sense here given to it is the primary determinant of action amounts to a theory of moral determinism, in which it is assumed that everyone ultimately and inevitably finds expression for his moral nature. In this view, a man is not a criminal because he commits a crime; he commits a crime because he is a criminal. Translated into novelistic terms, action is ruled by character, not character by action.[12] It would of course be impossible in a limited space to offer anything that would amount to a demonstration of this assumption, but it ought to be possible to glance briefly at the heuristic possibilities of its provisional adoption. It is important to remember, however, that such an abridged discussion courts the danger of simplifying a view which is in itself simplistic. Nevertheless, it seems to me important to establish, even in a provisional and tentative way, the discernible laws of behavior in Jane Austen's fictional world, if only because my aim is to establish the kinship of *Mansfield Park* to the other novels.

Jane Austen's villains (if so robust a term may be used to describe characters whose conduct never sinks below caddishness) have striking features in common, not the least of which is their apparent inability to will their own reformation. This seems to me far more important than the equally apparent fact that they are all sexually aggressive (particularly in comparison with the heroes, who are not), and that Jane Austen therefore disapproves of them too strongly to permit them a share in the fortunes of the "good" people. Whether as a result of her disapproval or not, they are singularly inflexible beings, circumscribed within the original bounds of their character. Willoughby's jilting of Marianne we feel to be entirely inevitable, and once Wickham's character is free from the mists of ambiguity his elopement with Lydia can scarcely take us by surprise. It is important to observe that this event is not the means of dispelling the ambiguity; the event serves less to illuminate the character than the character to justify the event. In Willoughby and Wickham we can recognize the prototypes of Henry Crawford (and ultimately of William Elliot), but Crawford is a much more fully realized character than either.

The least typical of Jane Austen's villains is John Thorpe of *Northanger Abbey*. He is not a gentleman, not even a specious one, and his manners, alongside those of Willoughby and the rest, are distinctly coarse. But he, too, is condemned always to act in accordance with the givens of his own character, the acquisitiveness, the egotism, and the small-mindedness, which are made clear even before he takes any decisive action in the novel. The whole plot of *Northanger Abbey*, for that matter, is a useful illustration of the way in which Jane Austen makes events dependent on character. The turning points of the action are Catherine's invitation to Northanger Abbey and her abrupt dismissal from it a few weeks later. Thorpe's vanity is responsible for both events, because it is his boastful statement of Catherine's worldly position that induces General Tilney to issue the invitation in the first place. And it is Thorpe's wounded vanity (because of Catherine's refusal of him) that later impels him to slander Catherine and her family to the General. Events grow quite naturally out of character here, but they are not felt as surprising, because the intermediate causes are also known. The result is a subtle and finely meshed plot that no critic seems to me to have adequately appreciated.

To attempt to document the influence of character on incident by reference only to Jane Austen's villains may appear to be begging the question, for her own strong moral disapprobation may dispose her to deny to these men the measure of flexibility and even of humanity that might otherwise be theirs. But the generalization does not rest solely, or even mainly, on the conspicuous instances supplied by Willoughby and his tribe. The heroes and heroines are as circumscribed by their characters as the villains are by theirs; the difference is that the consequences are not usually so striking or dramatic. The humor characters, who appear in all the novels, are quite obviously confined within their respective eccentricities or affectations. It is their own rigidity of character, as Bergson would say, that makes them comic. The examples are abundant: Mr. Collins and Mr. Elton, Miss Bates and Miss Steele, Sir Walter Elliot and Mr. Woodhouse, and of course many others. But it is the central figures, the ones who most nearly approximate three-dimensional reality, who supply the critical test.

The surprising thing is that the characters who seem most alive (for obvious reasons these are all women: Marianne Dashwood, Elizabeth Bennet, and Emma Woodhouse) are so limited in their capacity for change and growth. Marianne, the representative of sensibility in *Sense and Sensibility,* is an attractive figure (much more so than Elinor), but it is important to observe that the acuteness of her sensibility in no way interferes with the fundamental stability of her character, for she is a model of constancy. The "reformation" which we are told about (but not shown) at the end of the novel is not a change in her character so much as it is a modification of her outward demeanor, an acquired self-control which consists in curbing the expression of a temperament which is itself unchangeable. Elizabeth refuses Darcy near the beginning of *Pride and Prejudice,* and accepts him at the end, but the change of heart is no measure of the growth of her character, because both refusal and acceptance grow out of the same fundamental attitudes and values. The change is effected only by the growth of her knowledge of Darcy and of Wickham. The case is much the same with Emma, whose errors of judgment give her story its motion. But that her errors arise from insufficient knowledge, not from faulty principles, is an indication that her character remains essentially what it always was, for her judgment can be corrected by new knowledge. It can be argued, I suppose, that

Emma undergoes an important change at the end of the novel, when Knightley makes her see her errors, but as Mudrick acutely observes, her confession of guilt amounts really to an evasion of the responsibility of self-knowledge, in which case any apparent change is illusory. The plot of *Persuasion* is in one respect a duplicate of that of *Pride and Prejudice*, for both novels tell the story of a woman who accepts a man she has once rejected. The most striking difference in the pattern is that in *Persuasion* we enter *in medias res*, seven years after Anne's refusal of Captain Wentworth. But both stories demonstrate the inner consistency of the heroine (and of the hero), for both stories are resolved by the same traits of character which originally complicated them—in Elizabeth the pride of high principles; in Anne Elliot a sweet reasonableness, an amenability to persuasion, which superficially (as in the case of Fanny Price) belies her constancy and strength of character. Other examples could be brought forward, but even so brief and casual a survey as this strongly suggests, I believe, that Jane Austen's moral universe is largely populated by men and women trapped in their characters somewhat like crabs trapped in shells which (let us suppose) they can neither change nor outgrow.

If determinism is carried to the limits suggested by this metaphor, it might reasonably be asked what possible freedom of choice the personages enjoy which would enable them to act in morally significant ways, to be, in other words, either "heroes" or "villains." But faithfulness to (or confinement within) the givens of character does not necessarily destroy freedom of choice or action. The impulse to action arises out of character, but it is directed by circumstance, and even more importantly, by circumstance as it is appraised by a fallible intelligence. The people of Jane Austen's novels are free to make mistakes, not only in their judgment of external circumstance, but even in their judgment of their own feelings and desires. For this reason the response to life in this world is rarely simple or predictable, because people are constantly called upon to make difficult and complicated adjustments to life, even when the light of conscience remains steady. This is why the reader, even when he understands Elizabeth's or Emma's character better than she does herself, cannot predict her choices, though in retrospect they generally appear inevitable. I can see no inconsistency, therefore, in a view of life which treats people as morally free and at the same time as confined within their moral natures.

When we turn back to Mansfield Park, the implications of this deterministic view of life are obvious. Crawford acts as he does because it is in his character to do so; no other explanation is required, and accordingly none is offered. Crawford's elopement seems, in fact, far less improbable than his falling in love with Fanny in the first place, but even here Jane Austen reveals him as ensnared by a defect of his own character. His intention—openly declared to his sister—of carrying on a flirtation with Fanny (*faute de mieux*) is consonant with the volatility of his spirits already noted, and also with the egoism that must make itself admired. Fanny, who is in love with Edmund (that is her secret and her strength), is immune to Crawford's genuine charm, but he himself, acting the part of the lover, has not the wholeness of self which can keep him from becoming what he feigns, and he falls in love with Fanny. However, the question it not one of the relative plausibility of events, but of the very shape of the novelist's imaginative vision. If Crawford's—or Maria's—part in the final catastrophe is merely a conscious concession to a particular theory of morality, as a good many cynical readers view it, then the novel is badly flawed, but if Crawford's action, as I contend, is brought about by the way in which the novelist looks at experience and the causal relations uniting events, then I believe the artistry of the novel is vindicated. Jane Austen is not trying to superimpose her morality upon the story; the story follows what is for her the inescapable logic of a universe ruled by moral necessity. Jane Austen's determinism is quite unlike the sentimental world view of *Pamela*. She is not affirming a conviction that good people are rewarded and bad people punished; she is affirming, tacitly, that no one can escape his destiny, and, like Heraclitus, she holds that man's character is his destiny.

The most serious objection that such an interpretation of Jane Austen's imaginative vision must face is based upon the prominence she herself gives to education and environment as determinants of character, particularly in *Mansfield Park*. If character can be significantly altered by the exertion of human will, then obviously any theory of moral determinism will have to be discarded.

A number of commentators have pointed to the separate but interrelated "worlds" of *Mansfield Park*.[13] At the center, of course, is the aristocratic country house best exemplified by Mansfield Park itself, but also by the gloomy and pretentious Sotherton. Then there is the fashionable world of London, not directly represented in the novel, but seen through some of its more brilliant products, Mary and Henry Crawford. Finally, there is the plebeian world of Portsmouth, and the demonstration is complete. One's character, Jane Austen seems to be saying, will invariably take the impress of place; the same person will be differently affected by different environments. The light and frivolous Crawfords betray their worldly breeding, just as Sir Thomas reveals the qualities of solidity and permanence that are in the very air of Mansfield, just as Lieutenant Price's character matches the squalor and disorder of Portsmouth. Now this line of reasoning seems to me fallacious, though it is undeniable that characters must at some time be formed, and that environment must be one of the formative influences. But I can acknowledge the influence of place on character only in this rather special and limited sense. To insist on more than this is to reverse the actual operation of cause and effect in Jane Austen's world. Sir Thomas, for example, tries to change Fanny's mind by simply shipping her off to Portsmouth without reckoning that human personality and character are in important ways superior to their setting; the mind, after all, is its own place. The "worlds" of *Mansfield Park*, instead of imparting their qualities to the people who inhabit them, take their own character from the human figures. Furthermore, the worlds are not so homogeneous as they appear at first glance. The moral dichotomy between principle (or order) and anarchy which is at the center of the novel, appears in each of the locales. Mansfield Park, for example, is not simply the seat of order in the novel; it is also the seat of disorder, for it takes on the qualities of Lady Bertram and Mrs. Norris, of Tom, Edmund, Maria, Julia, and Fanny, as well as those of Sir Thomas himself. Sotherton is an uneasy compromise between the natural and the artificial, between freedom and restraint, anarchy and authority, but it is the human drama that takes place there that gives significance to the setting, not the setting which lends its character to the human agents. Portsmouth, too, as Fanny demonstrates, is amenable to order, can be acted upon, that is, by human agency. All of this makes clear, I believe, that the moral antithesis of order and disorder is independent of place.

The topic of education recurs so insistently in *Mansfield Park* that at least one critic has discovered in it the principle of the thematic development of the novel.[14] In a sense, I suppose, *Mansfield Park* can be said to be about education, but if so what it reveals is the failure of education as an effective determinant of character. Education, like environment, has a certain unmistakable but necessarily limited effect upon a child. The effect is limited, in the first place, because there are some ingredients of character beyond its reach, like tem-

per (what we should now call temperament), for example,
or disposition, both of which attributes are predetermined.
But the effect is also limited by a kind of natural variation
in children's susceptibility to it. In this respect it is a little
like vaccination for small-pox; no one can predict whether
it will "take" or not. All of this may be highly speculative,
but it accords with what the empirical evidence reveals. Everyone in the novel seems to have opinions on the subject, and
Jane Austen disposes of them all ironically. Sir Thomas's perfectly natural and commendable fears about admitting one of
the Price girls from Portsmouth into intimacy with his daughters are, in the event, not only wrong but ludicrously so.
"Should her disposition be really bad," Sir Thomas prudently
remarks to his lady, "we must not, for our own children's
sake, continue her in the family," and he concludes, "I hope
there can be nothing to fear for *them*, and every thing to hope
for *her*, from the association" (ch. 1). The irony is still more
pointed when the Bertram girls comment on Fanny's "stupidity" to Mrs. Norris and revel in the superiority of their own
educational advantages: "How long ago it is, aunt, since we
used to repeat the chronological order of the kings of England,
with the dates of their accession, and most of the principal
events of their reigns!" (ch. 2). Mrs. Norris is so far in agreement that the educational advantages of Mansfield are inestimable that when she later offers reluctant praise of Fanny
she tries to secure the credit for the Bertrams and herself:
"What would she have been if we had not taken her by the
hand?" (ch. 28). Mary Crawford complains that "Mothers
certainly have not yet got quite the right way of managing
their daughters" (ch. 5), and Lieutenant Price has the same
complaint against fathers: "But by G— if she belonged to
me, I'd give her the rope's end as long as I could stand over
her. A little flogging for man and woman too, would be the
best way of preventing such things" (ch. 46). Finally, Edmund

locates the causes of Mary's "corrupted, vitiated mind" in the fact that she was raised by an uncle who kept a mistress. This deep and pervasive interest in education never seems to lead to any very constructive proposals or any consistent theory. What it leads to, in fact, is nothing more than an ironic commentary on the fallibility of education. Neither we nor Jane Austen can believe for a moment that a regimen of Mansfield shrubbery and Edmund's homiletics would work any change in Mary or Henry Crawford. Certainly the same diet has produced no appreciable influence on Maria or Julia. On the other hand, Fanny's character is and always has been immune to any moral contagion whatever. She is what she is in spite of early training and environment, and in spite of the morally stultifying atmosphere of Mansfield Park. If education supplies the principal thematic development of *Mansfield Park*, then we must regard the novel as a satire, for Jane Austen's fundamental insight into the springs of human action remains her perception that character (as opposed to manners, which are superficial and at most a reflection of character) does not follow a "normal" or predictable course of change and development, and that character is the primary determinant of human action.

I began with the intention of demonstrating only that *Mansfield Park* is not essentially different in subject, inspiration, or technique from Jane Austen's other novels, that it is the inevitable product of the same artistic (that is, moral) vision which shaped the other books, but I find that this conclusion, however tentatively established, leads me to certain value judgments. *Mansfield Park* is not the most attractive of Jane Austen's novels—that distinction must still be reserved, I think, for *Pride and Prejudice* or *Emma*—but it is unique in that its artistic success is achieved in the face of the greatest risk of failure, giving it the special brilliance which belongs to victory snatched from defeat. The quality that is most impressive in *Mansfield Park* is its honesty. I don't mean that its honesty is a consequence of her having put irony aside (she hasn't), or of her speaking to us with her real voice and delivering her moral sentiments directly. The honesty I am speaking of is revealed by her selection of the most intractable material, by her refusal to allow other interests to divert our attention from it, and by her uncompromising fidelity to her idea of the world.

CHAPTER VIII

Redgauntlet, Henry Esmond, and

the Modes of Historical Fiction

. . . imaginary gardens with real toads in them.
—MARIANNE MOORE, "Poetry"

The convergence of fact and fancy in the historical novel creates some special problems for criticism. History and fiction are different literary modes and are in an obvious and elementary sense opposite to each other, for history deals with what actually existed, while fiction deals with imaginary people and events. History is thus "true," and fiction is not. A more important distinction is in the limits of the universe of discourse. A particular history is always surrounded by a larger circle of events than the one explicitly recorded, and it constantly refers to these events without mentioning them. The fictional world, on the other hand, is sharply limited. It may, and usually does, have important and complicated connections with reality, but its distinguishing attribute is its autonomy, its removal from the world of actuality. We never read history without bringing to bear whatever other knowledge we can summon to our aid; if our history book mentions the founding of Alexandria, it is appropriate to recall what Alexander imbibed of Greek culture at the feet of Aristotle, even though the book does not overtly allude to it. The fact takes part of its meaning from what the author assumes that we already know about the past. When we read a work of fiction, however, we know nothing except what we are told or directed to infer, and inquiries about Lady Macbeth's children or Hamlet's course of study at Wittenberg, as we are often reminded, are not only irrelevant but meaningless. If the two modes thus require radically different techniques of reading, how are we to come to terms with a work that professes to be both history and fiction?

It is some help, but not much, to remember that the historical novel is primarily a novel, and only secondarily a work of history. A distinction is to be drawn between the historical novel and fictionalized history, in which historical events are embroidered with imaginary detail. But the question remains, how are real people to be naturalized in the country of the mind? The very word "real" develops an ambiguity, for characters may be real in that they derive existence from the self-coherence of the imaginary world in which they are placed, or they may be real in that they existed historically. The problem is analogous to the one posed by those films which place animated cartoon characters alongside live actors; what are we to take as the norm of reality?

To produce a seamless blend of truth and falsehood is less a matter of action than of character, but less a matter of either than of perspective. The plot presents few serious difficulties. Imaginary events can readily be made to intersect real ones, and both can be brought within a single scale of probability, because the imaginary event is made probable by its causal relation to what we know happened. Character is more difficult. Probability here depends, in the case of the fictitious personage, on internal consistency, in the case of the historical figure, on consistency with known facts. Clearly all the characters, the imaginary and the real, must be reduced to a common plane of existence before we can accept them without uneasiness as belonging to the same fictional world, and since the imaginary characters cannot very well be expected to assume historical reality, the historical figures must be given what might be called fictive reality. The materials of history, both events and persons, can be successfully integrated with the materials of fiction by a judicious handling of point of view. The historian writes always from an omniscient point of view, not because he knows everything, but because his province is what is known. His task is to present his subject in the full glare of historical scholarship, to leave no corners in shadow, no matters, not even his doubts, in doubt. The historical novelist must avoid the full light that the historian seeks; his province is not the known, but the thing in the act of being known, and he must prevent the specious and the actual from being seen in the same perspective. He deals in the very illusions that the historian tries to free himself from. The result is that the historical novelist most often keeps history in the background and allows the fiction to occupy the center of the reader's consciousness. Sometimes, indeed, he keeps his history tidily out of sight. Jane Austen wisely allows us to see only the secondary effects and to hear only the most distant rumbles of the war which occupies the same space of time as the action of her novels. The effect has often been noted, and attributed, usually, to the more prosaic concerns of her fictional world, but it might be argued with equal plausibility that the Napoleonic Wars offer a more effective frame to her novels by the very obliqueness of her references to them.

In his effort to relegate history to the background, to preserve some sense of its mystery and incompleteness, the historical novelist may be aiming at either of two quite different effects; he may be seeking the opposite of what I have described as the technique of fictionalized history by embellishing his imaginary story with real characters and events. Or he may be seeking to establish some important thematic relation between the public and private events he describes. For the novel which aims at the first of these objectives we may more or less arbitrarily appropriate the term *romance*, implying that historical events and

personages, precisely because they are "historical" and belong
to a now vanished past, add a touch of romance to the commonplace. To romanticize the past is to affirm tacitly that it has no
real connection with the present, and the past functions in the
novel, like the Gothic castle or abbey, to suffuse its own atmosphere over the events of the story. But the backdrop of history
can function in another way, too, and make a contribution
more solid than atmosphere. For the novel which aims at this
second objective it might be convenient to employ the term
chronicle to suggest that history plays a somewhat more active
role in the purely imaginary course of events. Chronicle treats
the historic past not as picturesque and inert but as vibrant
and alive, influencing, even though from a distance, the attitudes
and values, as well as the actions, of the imaginary figures who
are involved in it. At the same time the imagined characters
and events serve to color our attitudes toward the historic past
in which they are embedded because of the dynamic nature of
their relation to it.

The differences between romance and chronicle are less a
matter of deliberate choice or consciously employed technique
than of the fundamental attitude toward history that is a part
of the novelist's imaginative vision. Accordingly it is both
easier and more rewarding to seek the evidences of this fundamental attitude in the minute details and surface texture of the
novel than in the broad outlines of its plot or formal structure.
Scott and Thackeray, in *Redgauntlet* and *Henry Esmond*, have
obligingly provided us with historical novels that are so similar
in plot that they afford an unusual opportunity to study a more
important variable (at least in the context of this discussion)—
the uses of the past. In both tales the hero, a young man of
doubtful parentage but aligned by heredity with the Stuart
interest, becomes involved in a fictitious Jacobite plot which
is abandoned at the last moment because of the willfulness of the
Pretender, who jeopardizes the enterprise by his attachment to

a woman. Although the Pretender is a different person in each case, and the events described are separated by more than fifty years, the situations are strikingly parallel and provide a firm basis for the comparison of the kinds of historical vision that the two novels reveal.

I

We tend to think of Scott as the author of robust, epic tales of adventure, but even the slightest acquaintance with his work ought to dispel that notion. The fact is that Scott's manner is anything but epic; [1] he is never bombastic (though his characters sometimes are) and rarely grandiose. The tone resembles that of the epic narrator less than that of the antiquarian researcher who is much more interested in precision than in heroism. Yet Scott's major concern is heroism, and the fact that he sought to define it by indirection is the best evidence that he understood the peculiar character of the historical novel, even if he did not always understand the way in which his words affect the reader.

In many ways *The Heart of Midlothian* is more typical of Scott's method than *Redgauntlet,* and the rambling diffuseness of its opening chapters actually conceals a considerable degree of subtlety and sophistication. Scott characteristically begins by peeling away the successive layers of external circumstance which enfold his story. The story itself comes from the recently freed debtor, Dunover, who tells it to the schoolmaster, Peter Pattieson, whose manuscript is presented to us with the pedantic scholia of Jedediah Cleishbotham, Scott's own alter ego. This device is a development from the old trick of claiming manuscript authority for a fictitious tale, but with a difference, for Scott has no intention of imposing on us, and unlike Defoe he does not use the device either to secure our credence or to provide himself with a recognizable outer form. His immediate aim is manifestly to secure distance from the historical events with

which the novel properly begins, and to this end he introduces
the distortions and irrelevancies that the transmission of the
story from mouth to mouth inevitably occasions. Later, when
fictitious characters and events become central, the distance
insensibly lessens, and the method becomes more dramatic as
the personality of the narrator fades. The novel begins with the
schoolmaster's reflections on the improvement in methods of
transportation, an apparently inconsequential topic which is
nevertheless important for three reasons: it serves to fix the antiquarian interests of Peter Pattieson and thus to characterize
him for his small but important role in transmitting the story to
come; it serves to introduce the accident which will bring
Pattieson into the company of the two lawyers and their
erstwhile client, Dunover; and most importantly, and most
subtly of all, it serves to announce the thematic conflict between
the past and the present and specifically to foreshadow Jeanie
Deans's ordeal in confronting the primitive difficulties of travel
which are the principal subject of the schoolmaster's reflections.
Scott's artistry here is considerable, and the best indication of
this is that inattentive readers are likely to miss the subtlety of
his contrivance even while they are affected by it.

It is perhaps needless to trace in detail the manner by which
Scott leads us into his narrative, for the principle which controls
his narrative technique is clear. Real events and persons are to
be approached obliquely, filtered through the consciousness of
people who stand at several removes from the actuality (it is
significant that we are never given Dunover's actual words).
What appears to be a violation of this principle, when we are
led along with Jeanie into the actual "presence" of Queen
Caroline, may be justified by recognizing that it is at this
climactic point in the novel that the "private" and "public" lines
of action converge, but even here the point of view is carefully
controlled. We approach the public and historical implications
of the event through the omniscient narrator's impersonal

account of the Duke of Argyle's address to the House of Lords, but we approach the private and fictitious implications through Jeanie's more limited point of view in what she thinks of simply as an interview with a great lady. Scott clearly recognizes that he cannot pass easily and at will from the fictional world of his novel into the sphere of historical reality, and he manipulates the necessary transitions skillfully so as to preserve always the primacy and the integrity of the fictional world.

The same principle is at work, though to somewhat different effect, in the later novel, *Redgauntlet*. Here again is a converging action; the apparently separate destinies of Darsie Latimer, Alan Fairford, and Redgauntlet himself are transformed at the climax of the action from matters of private and independent concern into matters touching the public destiny of Scotland and England. That the climactic event is itself fictitious (though involving more than one historic personage) does not alter the case at all, for there is the same subsumption of private concerns under matters of public policy already encountered in *The Heart of Midlothian*. In *Redgauntlet*, however, we find no analogue to the Porteous riots which are detailed so prominently at the beginning of the earlier novel, and consequently no necessity for the devices of distancing which Scott employed to put the Porteous affair into a manageable perspective. The novel opens, instead, with an exchange of letters between Darsie Latimer and Alan Fairford, the function of which is to provide exposition of their individual and personal situations, to narrate what is apparently a series of unconnected incidents, and above all to provide insight into the contrasting personalities of the two young men. Compared with the opening chapters of *The Heart of Midlothian*, the method is direct and straightforward, because in this case we are being ushered directly into a fictitious and imaginary world, although one that is connected in a number of ways with actual places and events.

Darsie Latimer is a young man of mysterious antecedents

who has grown up in the home of Saunders Fairford, an Edinburgh solicitor, and his son Alan, who is reading for the bar. By his own account, as well as in the opinion of his foster family, Darsie is of a volatile and restless temperament (Mr. Fairford, less flatteringly, calls him unsteady), a point on which Scott is at some pains to insist, and he does so, rather curiously, by having Darsie recall his schoolboy exploits with Alan:

If I became the pride of the Yards, and the dread of the hucksters in the High School Wynd, it was under thy patronage; and, but for thee, I had been contented with humbly passing through the Cowgate Port, without climbing over the top of it, and had never seen the *Kittle nine-steps* nearer than from Bareford's Parks.[2]

The passage from which this is taken is provided with copious annotations, identifying, among other things, the *Kittle nine-steps* as "a pass on the very brink of the Castle rock to the north, by which it is just possible for a goat, or a high-school boy, to turn the corner of the building where it rises from the edge of the precipice," and Scott goes on to reminisce about his own youthful escapades. The process of rooting Darsie's past in real places, charged with personal and historical associations, is a familiar technique in Scott; the same method is used in *The Heart of Midlothian*, where the whole story of the Deans sisters is made to grow out of the associations of "the heart of Midlothian," the Edinburgh Tolbooth, or jail. Part of the reason is that places fascinate Scott; they provide for him the tangible link between the past and the present, the symbols that enable him to breathe the atmosphere of history, but he is doing more here than indulging his own sentimental recollections. Darsie's connections with the Edinburgh of reality, though relatively unimportant at the moment, give him a historical dimension—a standing in real time and space—that will eventually smooth the transition from the fictitious world of his private and personal desires and frustrations to the "real" world in which his actions acquire public significance.

The plausible accomplishment of this transition is indeed the major technical problem of the novel, and it is achieved, as before, by the careful handling of point of view. Darsie's temperament (not to mention the financial independence which is conferred on him with the same mystery that surrounds his parentage) sends him adventuring into the border country along the Solway, while his friend Alan remains at home, somewhat reluctantly, to drudge away at the law. But adventure, not to be wooed, visits them both impartially in the form of cryptic encounters with people whose identities remain obscure and unsatisfying—Darsie's visit with the taciturn laird of the Solway Lochs, for example, or the visits which the Fairfords receive from the ill-mannered Herries of Birrenswork and the mysterious Greenmantle. These "adventures," of course, are made such entirely by the mystery that surrounds them, rather than by any real or fancied danger that attends them—even Darsie's predicament on the Solway sands does not represent any very imminent threat. The epistolary treatment, which limits knowledge to the writer's own unaided perceptions, and even prevents him, since the letter is written soon after the event, from correcting his misapprehensions by subsequent increments of knowledge, is not only effective, it is necessary, as long as the novel's substance is to be compounded of such events. But the mystery which surrounds these early episodes disappears when they come to be seen as coherent parts of a larger design, a design which is to submerge the private aspirations of both Darsie and Alan. Redgauntlet himself, who appeared to Darsie as the Laird of the Solway Lochs, and to Alan as Herries of Birrenswork, becomes the central and animating principle of the novel, but an indispensable part of his characterization is the half-light in which he first appears. As the concerns of Darsie and Alan are gradually superseded by Redgauntlet's design of restoring the Stuart dynasty in the person of the young Pretender, Charles Edward Stuart, the point of view moves outward, from the personal and intimate letters of the two young men, to Darsie's first-person journal, written while he is in his uncle's custody, to the alternating third-person narratives of Darsie and Alan, to the final chapters with their wholly omniscient, "historical" point of view.

But Scott's solution of the technical problem, admirable and interesting though it is, does not really explain why the problem exists to be solved—does not, that is, enable us to confront the prior question of the relation between the fictitious or personal, and the real or public, concerns of the novel. The fact that the two can be made to coalesce within a single, integrated view of experience does not by itself offer the hint that would enable us to understand or explain that experience. The problem remains, therefore, of determining the significance of Scott's peculiar blend of fact and fancy by inquiring into the thematic relationship, if any, between the two.

The main theme of *Redgauntlet*, as of many of the other Waverley novels, is heroism. David Daiches, one of the very small number of contemporary critics who take Scott's literary pretensions seriously, has argued that in Scott's best and most characteristic work (the Scottish novels of the seventeenth and eighteenth centuries) a dominant thematic contrast is developed between the outmoded and anachronistic heroic ideals associated with the old Scottish nationalism, finding expression, usually, in acts of rebellion or terrorism, and a newer conception of heroism which is conformable to civic order and remains within the law.[3] The first of these ideals is typically personified by representatives of the Jacobite cause, the second by all those who, whatever their sentiments toward the house of Hanover, disclaim rebellion and violence. At first (the succession implied has to do with the order of historical events, not with the order of composition of the novels) the conflicts between Scottish nationalism and English authority are seen as genuinely heroic, as in the struggle between the Covenanters and Claverhouse's

dragoons in *Old Mortality*, but as Scotland is transformed from
a primitive, feudal wilderness into a modern, civilized state, and
as the memory of the Stuart kings fades, the schemes of
fanatical Jacobites partake increasingly of the nature of melodrama or empty heroics, and the genuine modern heroes have all
come to terms with historical realities. *Redgauntlet*, in Daiches's
view, presents this typical conflict in its strongest terms, simply
because the date of the action is 1766,[4] and the claims of
Jacobitism, therefore, to represent the main stream of Scottish
thought and feeling are infinitely less tenable than they were
even in 1745, when the last historical uprising of the clans was
crushed. Redgauntlet himself has become a hero of pasteboard,
the representative of a thoroughly outmoded and discredited
movement, and the real heroes of the novel are the law-abiding
Whigs epitomized by the Edinburgh legal fraternity. The contrast, reduced to its plainest terms, is between the law and the
lawless. And yet Scott, for all his intellectual sympathy with
progress and the "new" Scotland, remains fundamentally ambivalent, so that even Redgauntlet's forlorn hope can stir his
blood with the recollections of Scotland's former glories.

I have summarized Daiches's arguments at such length partly
because I want to suggest certain qualifications, but mainly because I would like to build my own analysis upon what seems to
me a sound and fruitful conception. It is clear that the title character, Redgauntlet, is the "hero" of the novel, both because he
unites all the separate interests and because he is the real moving
force, whether he acts covertly, under an assumed identity, or
more openly, as he does at the end of the novel. Yet one wonders what heroic qualities he actually possesses, aside from his
unyielding determination and keen sense of his own dignity.
When we apply any pragmatic tests he does not come off very
well; the catalogue of his heroic deeds includes giving Darsie a
ride home on the back of his horse, destroying the fishing nets
of the unarmed and unresisting Quaker, kidnaping his nephew,

arresting Alan Fairford on a spurious warrant, and ineffectually attempting to get the conspirators to agree on some concerted action. The fact is that Redgauntlet's heroism is more a function of what he is than of what he does, and more a function of the way he is seen by other characters—particularly Darsie—than of either. To Darsie the Laird of the Solway Lochs appears as a forbidding yet commanding figure, one whose mere presence dominates any company he is in. Darsie, we know, has an active imagination, prone to exaggerate things. Alan writes, "Did I not once find thee gazing with respect at a lizard, in the attitude of one who looks upon a crocodile?" (I, 23). Yet Redgauntlet's powerful effect on Darsie's imagination cannot be wholly set down to the young man's predisposition to see every lizard as a crocodile; even Alan, when he first encounters Redgauntlet as Herries of Birrenswork, though he takes offense at the older man's arrogance, admits that "there was something . . . in the gentleman's appearance which commanded attention" (I, 63). Whatever that "something" is, however, we are never shown, but left to infer. As a fanatical Jacobite, the leading principle of Redgauntlet's character is loyalty, not to the state or its laws, but to the person of his king, the kind of loyalty that Carlyle would instantly have recognized and approved. Redgauntlet's conception of personal honor, in fact, gives him the utmost contempt for institutions and laws (even though he is capable of using the law for his own purposes, as he does in making Peter Peebles's preposterous warrant the excuse for detaining Alan), but it remains the center of gravity of his character and lends to his personality the force and intensity that other people find there.

If Scott's intention, as Daiches suggests, is to portray an anachronistic heroic type, he must not allow the ways in which he discredits Redgauntlet's heroism to interfere with our perception of its admirable qualities, or Redgauntlet becomes as

ludicrous as Mrs. Radcliffe's Gothic villains whose rantings
remind us of Lear's pathetic

> I will do such things,—
> What they are, yet I know not; but they shall be
> The terrors of the earth.

It is a danger that Scott cannot altogether meet or overcome
because of the very nature of the action he is rendering. The
main issue of the novel is to be solved in a way that gives no
scope to the kind of heroic qualities that Redgauntlet possesses;
he has no adversary of the same kind as himself, and the result is
that most of his "action" consists of shadow-boxing. Under this
strong disadvantage Scott labors in vain to convince us of his
heroism by detailing the strength of his impression on other
figures in the novel. We see clearly, I think, what Redgauntlet
is meant to be, and that, perhaps, is sufficient, but his character
does not produce real conviction. At the climax of the action,
the somewhat reluctant rebel chieftains are on the point of
abandoning the venture because of the Pretender's resentment
of their imposing the dismissal of his mistress (who is supposed
to have a confidante at the Hanoverian court) as a condition of
their support, but they rally to his defense at the arrival of
General Colin Campbell at Crackenthorp's Inn on the Solway,
the scene of their deliberations. Redgauntlet greets this arrival
almost with relief, since it appears to him to offer the kind of
threat which will unite the conspirators, and will put the sacred
cause to an immediate test of arms. He declares that the rebels
are prepared to meet Campbell's force, but the General's tone is
unexpectedly conciliatory:

"Pshaw! you take it too seriously—let me speak but one word
with you."

"No words can shake our purpose," said Redgauntlet, "were

your whole command, as I suppose is the case, drawn round the house."

"I am certainly not unsupported," said the General; "but if you would hear me"—

"Hear *me*, sir," said the Wanderer, stepping forward; "I suppose I am the mark you aim at—I surrender myself willingly, to save these gentlemen's danger—let this at least avail in their favour."

An exclamation of "Never, never!" broke from the little body of partisans, who threw themselves round the unfortunate Prince, and would have seized or struck down Campbell, had it not been that he remained with his arms folded, and a look rather indicating impatience because they would not hear him than the least apprehension of violence at their hand. . . .

"In one word, General Campbell," said Redgauntlet, "is it to be peace or war?—You are a man of honour, and we can trust you."
[II, 329]

All of Redgauntlet's most conspicuous traits of character are in evidence here: his preference for action over words, his reliance on a personal code of honor, his desire for the kind of solution to his dilemma which will test his courage and resolution. But he is not to be given the kind of test he wants; Campbell completely deflates him by extending the King's offer of amnesty. The rebels are to be permitted to depart in peace:

"What!—all?" exclaimed Sir Richard Glendale—"all, without exception?"

"ALL, without one single exception," said the General; "such are my orders. If you accept my terms, say so, and make haste; for things may happen to interfere with his Majesty's kind purposes towards you all." . . .

"Is this real?" said Redgauntlet. "Can you mean this?—Am I—are all, are any of these gentlemen at liberty, without interruption, to embark in yonder brig, which, I see, is now again approaching the shore?"

"You, sir—all—any of the gentlemen present," said the General,—"all whom the vessel can contain, are at liberty to embark uninterrupted by me; but I advise none to go off who have not powerful reasons unconnected with the present meeting, for this will be remembered against no one."

"Then, gentlemen," said Redgauntlet, clasping his hands together as the words burst from him, "the cause is lost for ever!" [II, 330–31]

The logic of Redgauntlet's "then" is perfectly clear; the movement he leads can survive the opposition of an enemy who takes its threat seriously and confronts it with the kind of violence that its adherents understand, but it cannot survive the opposition of an enemy who treats them as an indulgent parent treats wayward children. The conspiracy cannot remain intact, as the Pretender has already demonstrated, except in the face of opposition on their own romantic terms; by removing the opportunity for heroics, Campbell has shrewdly executed a bloodless coup, which is effective precisely because it is prosaic. Scott has clearly demonstrated in his denouement that the heroic ideal represented by the title figure is no longer viable, but in doing so he has not altogether avoided the danger of making Redgauntlet appear shallow and unconvincing.

Although Redgauntlet has no opponent he can cross swords with or otherwise meet on equal terms, it might still be fruitful to inquire whether the novel presents us with the embodiment of any opposing ideal of life. The central position of Darsie Latimer in the story suggests that he is conceived as at least a potential adversary to Redgauntlet, but Scott allows Darsie no heroics of any kind. Confronted with a choice between his loyalty to the House of Hanover (it will be remembered that Darsie's mother was a Whig, and that he has been raised in the staunch Whig household of the Fairfords) and the desperate enterprise of avenging his father that his uncle solicits him to, Darsie can only temporize, and he is not even permitted so ineffectual a heroic gesture as to declare for either side. He may be something more than that "sneaking piece of imbecility,"

Edward Waverley, but it is clear that Darsie has no story. The events of the novel could proceed without him; the excuse given for his kidnaping is scarcely convincing; and he effects nothing by his own will or action. Even his quest for a father is a gratuitous and inconclusive line of action. The fact is that like Edward Waverley (or Frank Osbaldistone in *Rob Roy*) he is less important for himself than for the perspective he provides on the action of others.

In Daiches's analysis the counterweight to the lawless violence of the Jacobites is the law itself, represented here by several characters with varying degrees of prominence. The national destiny of Scotland is not in the hands of the desperate men who attempt to restore the House of Stuart, but with the lawyers, who are the guardians of Scottish traditions as well as the preservers of the order which can alone ensure Scotland's peace, prosperity, and progress. Alan's father, a highly respected Writer to the Signet in Edinburgh, is the pattern of order and stability and loyalty to the Hanoverian succession, but his allegiance is not to the law as a social institution, the function of which is to preserve justice; it is to the law as a profession, a means of advancing the family fortunes, and in his way he is as self-willed and highhanded toward Alan as Redgauntlet is toward Darsie. It is certainly questionable whether Darsie's captivity at the hands of his uncle is more onerous than Alan's at the hands of his father. The crucial test is supplied by the information which arrives from Provost Crosbie, that Darsie has been kidnaped, just at the moment when Alan is to plead his first cause, in the interest of Peter Peebles. In spite of the fact that Mr. Fairford is indifferent to the justice at issue in Peebles vs. Plainstanes, and regards Peebles himself as a "degraded, worthless, drunken beast" (I, 209), he is more concerned that Alan advance his professional reputation than that he follow the dictates of friendship and personal loyalty by attempting to rescue Darsie, so he blandly conceals the knowledge of his friend's peril from Alan. Though Scott makes us understand the father's motives here, and refrains from condemning the act, he certainly does not put the legal profession in a light that will enable us to discern a set of values conspicuously preferable to those the novel is to discredit.

When we turn to the other representatives of the law in the novel, the case for law as an adequate counterweight to what Peter Peebles calls "your plaids, and your piping, and your nonsense" (II, 9) appears still weaker. Justice Foxley, for example, gives evidence not only of a stupidity reminiscent of Fielding's rural magistrates, but of corruption, and his clerk, Master Nicholas Faggot, although he possesses enough law to direct his principal, is both venal and cowardly. Both of these characters, however, are the merest caricatures; a more significant case is that of the worthy Provost Crosbie, the chief magistrate of Dumfries, who has supplied the first intelligence of Darsie's disappearance, and to whom Alan accordingly goes to inquire after his friend. Provost Crosbie's master passion is the dining table, and he desires nothing so much as to enjoy its pleasures in peace. He dislikes trouble of any kind, and asserts his conviction that Darsie's disappearance is only a temporary misunderstanding: "Rely on it, sir" (he assures Alan), "that if he has not returned to his friends in Scotland, he must have gone to his friends in England" (II, 53). In the matter of politics he is a skilled equivocator, and no one has ever been able to learn whether he is a Whig or a Tory. He is a non-juror, but he offers his failure to take the oaths to the House of Hanover as the merest act of negligence on his part, and lest the fact should give rise to any question of his loyalty to King George, he is quick to mention his losses in the 'Forty-five, most of them, however, in the form of food consumed by the Highlanders whom he had entertained. Whatever his real sympathies, he is chiefly concerned about avoiding a declaration of them, and in proposing a toast after dinner he is careful to say simply, "The King," with a glance at Alan which declares, "You can have no doubt whom I mean, and therefore there is no occasion to particularize the individual" (II, 72). Like his fellow magistrates and lawyers, Provost Crosbie uses the law, if not as an instrument for perverting justice, at least as a means of obfuscating the clear issues of right and wrong. This tendency of law is most forcefully presented in the fantastic lawsuit of the perennial litigant, Peter Peebles, whose complicated affairs and wildly eccentric character foreshadow Dickens's portrait of the Court of Chancery and the crazed Miss Flite.[5] Scott's whole treatment of the law and of lawyers in fact suggests that the legal fraternity can provide no acceptable substitute, as a principle of conduct, to fanatical Jacobitism.

The point is further emphasized by Scott's presentation of the Quaker, Joshua Geddes, and of Alan Fairford. Joshua, whose fishing nets are destroyed in the same wild adventure that is to prove so fateful for Darsie, is opposed simultaneously to the lawlessness of Redgauntlet and his followers and to the logic-chopping and equivocation of the law. As a Quaker he opposes the use of violence, even in self-defense, at the same time that he takes a simple, literal, most unlegalistic view of language. Darsie reports a very suggestive, though trivial, incident:

Miss Geddes had offered me some sweet-cake, which, at the moment, I declined; but presently afterwards, seeing it within my reach, I naturally enough helped myself to a slice, and had just deposited it beside my plate, when Joshua, mine host, not with the authoritative air of Sancho's doctor, Tirteafuera, but in a very calm and quiet manner, lifted it away and replaced it on the dish, observing only, "Thou didst refuse it before, friend Latimer." [I, 97–98]

And of course it is Joshua's refusal to swear a complaint that frees his attackers and alienates the magistrate. Joshua despises,

and is despised by, the legal fraternity because he does not hold
with swearing and verbal jugglery, and more than one lawyer
expresses doubts of the legality of his fishing nets and seems
willing to sanction their violent destruction. Joshua's own declaration of principle is as clear and straightforward as Provost
Crosbie's is equivocal:

> But I need say little on this subject to thee, friend Latimer, who,
> I doubt not, art trained to believe that courage is displayed and
> honour attained, not by doing and suffering, as becomes a man,
> that which fate calls us to suffer, and justice commands us to do,
> but because thou art ready to retort violence for violence, and
> considerest the lightest insult as a sufficient cause for the spilling
> of blood, nay, the taking of life. [I, 256]

Though he takes only a minor part in the action, Joshua, a
man of peace and a man of his word, provides the clearest
moral antithesis to Redgauntlet. Redgauntlet can, on occasion,
make common cause with the law, but he can establish no such
alliance with Joshua Geddes.

Alan Fairford, too, steers, a middle course between the
quibbles of the law and the ruthless opportunism of the Jacobites. Although trained in the law, Alan is quick to recognize
the law's limitations. It is suggestive that the first intimation
of Darsie's disappearance comes to him in the courtroom, and
without a word he sacrifices professional considerations to
personal ones as he obeys what is for him the moral imperative
of rescuing his friend. He arms himself both with his legal
knowledge (which avails little against Provost Crosbie's stubborn unwillingness to distinguish between right and wrong, or
even to admit that wrong might exist) and with the conventional weapons of violence, but neither is suited to his enterprise, and he must rely, finally, on "doing and suffering,
as becomes a man, that which fate calls us to suffer, and justice

commands us to do." Nevertheless, Alan is not to be allowed to become the hero of *Redgauntlet* in the sense that Jeanie Deans becomes the heroine of *The Heart of Midlothian*. Her adventure leads to decisive action, and an action which has repercussions far beyond the saving of Effie's life; it marks, in effect, the closing of the breach between England and Scotland occasioned by the lynching of Captain Porteous at the beginning of the novel. Alan's efforts, on the other hand, remain inconclusive, for the end he seeks, the freeing of Darsie, is accomplished without his intervention, though he does succeed, along with Joshua, in reaching Crackenthorp's Inn at the moment of crisis.

For the cause and effect relation between private and public events which Scott postulated in *The Heart of Midlothian*, he substitutes, in *Redgauntlet*, a more tenuous relation. Here private actions have no direct influence upon public events, but they do provide a commentary upon those events which directs our judgment and evaluation of them. Redgauntlet is defeated only indirectly by the moral heroism personified by Alan and Joshua. The immediate cause is a more impersonal force; perhaps it would be true to say the force of history itself. This is the real reason why Redgauntlet is drawn on a different scale, out of proportion with the other figures. The private, wholly fictitious line of action is ultimately submerged in the public, quasi-historical line which it elucidates and comments upon. This is not to say that the individual, personal concerns of Darsie and Alan and the rest are not important in the novel qua novel; in a real sense they are the novel, but Scott here as elsewhere conceives human events and values as existing in a vital and reciprocal relation with the events of history. Every human being, even an imaginary human being, occupies a place in history and derives a part of his significance from that particularization in time and space, at the same time that his values and purposes give substance and meaning to the life of the past.

II

Henry Esmond owes more to Clio than does *Redgauntlet*, but this general observation opens up a number of ironies and paradoxes. Scott chooses a period only five years before his own birth; Thackeray goes back more than a hundred years to the reigns of William III and Anne. And yet in spite of Thackeray's careful and profuse documentation and his often skillful imitation of eighteenth-century prose style, *Henry Esmond* clings stubbornly to the present. Thackeray's action covers a period of twenty-five years (compared with *Redgauntlet's* compression into a period measured in weeks), and yet there is scarcely any sense of the movement of time or the changes that accompany it. Henry Esmond is much more intimately involved with historical events and personages than Darsie Latimer or Alan Fairford, and yet Henry Esmond's personal destinies never quite come into focus with the historical events that surround them.

In the minuteness of his rendering of the historical past, Thackeray is rather the follower of Bulwer-Lytton (whom he detested) than of Scott (whom he admired). *Esmond* presents us, not only with detailed accounts of the chief actions of the War of the Spanish Succession: Blenheim, Ramillies, Malplaquet, but also with a dramatis personae that teems with historical figures, from Queen Anne to Trooper Dick Steele. Throughout Book Two, in fact, history may be said to occupy the foreground, and the private affairs of the nominal hero remain incidental. Though the entire book purports to be the third-person journal of Esmond himself, his own wounding at Blenheim is a parenthetical insertion in what is actually an omniscient account:

It was past mid day when the attack began on our left, where Lord Cutts commanded, the bravest and most beloved officer in the English army. And now, as if to make his experience in war complete, our young aide de camp having seen two great armies facing each other in line of battle, and had the honour of riding with orders from one end to other of the line, came in for a not uncommon accompaniment of military glory, and was knocked on the head, along with many hundred of brave fellows, almost at the very commencement of this famous day of Blenheim.[6]

Thackeray is profuse in his employment of historical personages. Some of these, like General Webb, or the Duke of Marlborough, are introduced for the unexceptionable reason that they were involved in the events Thackeray is narrating; unlike Scott, however, he makes no attempt to distance these figures, but seems rather to prefer to make us know them more fully than their function in the novel makes necessary. The portrait of Marlborough, though it reflects Esmond's own partisan loyalty to Webb, and is thus in a sense functional, goes far beyond its uses in the novel and becomes, in intention at least, a balanced historical judgment. Still more suggestive, however, are the actual persons introduced more or less gratuitously, not because they were involved in the events of the story, but because they conceivably might have been, and Thackeray seems to prefer to use the ready-made characters of history than to invent his own. Thus when Castlewood is occupied by soldiers, the party includes Corporal Dick Steele, who quickly forms an intimacy with Esmond; when a clergyman is required to comfort the Fourth Viscount's last moments, Francis Atterbury is called on; when a doctor of Jacobite sympathies and close discretion is needed to color the pretense that Frank Esmond is ill, Dr. Arbuthnot makes his appearance. And Thackeray goes out of his way to introduce such figures as Addison, to whom Esmond renders his assistance in the composition of "The Campaign," and Swift, whose unflattering portrait owes something to Esmond's own prejudices but perhaps still more to those of the author of *The English Humourists*. Here, as well as in such relatively sympathetic portrayals as that of Steele as a witty and kind-hearted, but irresponsible drunkard, the effect is rather to remind us of Thackeray's ventriloquial skill than to further the illusion of reality. Ironically it is the very insistence with which the historical or pseudo-historical intrudes into the novel that most plainly signals the artifice of a work of fiction.[7] Thackeray is much more subtle, and much more convincing, in that earlier "historical" novel of the Regency period, *Vanity Fair*. The scenes in Brussels at the time of Waterloo are among the most memorable and effective in the novel, but mainly because Thackeray carefully keeps the historical event in the background, on a scale that does not diminish his fictitious characters.

Thackeray's pastiche of eighteenth-century prose style, though sometimes brilliant, is uneven. Gordon Ray limits the conscious imitation of an earlier style to two passages, the mock *Spectator* paper and the Dowager's French letter,[8] remarking that for the rest Thackeray relies on an occasional archaism. Yet the most subtle and convincing passages are those in which Thackeray avoids archaisms of diction altogether and depends instead on the movement and rhythm of the sentence. Here, for example, is a short paragraph in which the use of the participle, the aggregating tendency of the sentences, and the rhythm of the prose are reminiscent of Swift:

The party stopped, and came to some parley or discussion, which presently ended, my lord putting his horse into a canter after taking off his hat and making a bow to the officer who rode alongside him step for step: the trooper accompanying him falling back, and riding with my lord's two men. They cantered over the Green, and behind the elms (my Lord waving his hand, Harry thought), and so they disappeared. [Bk. I, ch. 5]

When the principal device is simply archaism of diction or idiom the effect is not nearly so satisfying. The following passage, which seems to aim at a Fieldingesque facetiousness, rings quite false. Its facetiousness is thinly disguised sentimentality, and it altogether lacks the energy of Fielding's prose:

What is the meaning of fidelity in love, and whence the birth of it? 'Tis a state of mind that men fall into, and depending on the man rather than the woman. We love being in love, that's the truth on't. If we had not met Joan, we should have met Kate, and adored her. We know our mistresses are no better than many other women, nor no prettier, nor no wiser, nor no wittier. 'Tis not for these reasons we love a woman, or for any special quality or charm I know of; we might as well demand that a lady should be the tallest woman in the world, like the Shropshire giantess, as that she should be a paragon in any other character, before we began to love her. [Bk. II, ch. 15]

There are, finally, passages in which the sentimentality is not disguised at all, and which could never be taken for anything but pure Thackeray:

I took a little flower off the hillock, and kissed it, and went my way, like the bird that had just lighted on the cross by me, back into the world again. Silent receptacle of death! tranquil depth of calm, out of reach of tempest and trouble! I felt as one who had been walking below the sea, and treading amidst the bones of shipwrecks. [Bk. II, ch. 27]

Even when Thackeray is most successful in simulating eighteenth-century prose style, in fact because he is often so successful, he reminds us of the pastness of the past and therefore also of our present point of view toward the past.[9] The historical background and style of *Esmond* are devices which enable Thackeray to deal in the picturesque and the quaint. Where Scott attempts to lead us back into the past, Thackeray holds us in the present, and offers us the trappings of history to disguise the fact that *Esmond* is really a Victorian novel, perfectly of a piece with its predecessors, *Vanity Fair* and *Pendennis*.

It is not necessary to repeat the arguments of Geoffrey Tillotson, who derives "the Thackerayan oneness" from the author's constant relationship to his materials, which are themselves part of a single block,[10] or of Gordon Ray, who traces a clearly marked autobiographical thread through the first part of *Esmond*,[11] though they both tend to confirm the assertion that *Esmond* is, like Thackeray's earlier novels, contemporary in its most fundamental interests. Enough, too, has been made of the fact that Thackeray's fictional world is artificially unified by ties of blood (the Esmonds, Warringtons, Pendennises, Crawleys) as well as by common personages (Lord Steyne, Pendennis) or locales (Queens Crawley). My own concern at the moment is with the more limited observation that *Vanity Fair, Pendennis,* and *Esmond* present the same situation with the same emotional coloring. All three are essentially stories of contrasting types of womanhood, both of which are presented and commented upon by a single sensibility. On the one hand there are the clever, egotistical, volatile, and sexually attractive women like Becky Sharp, Blanche Amory, and Beatrix Esmond, whose worldliness and lightness is the closest Thackeray's reticence would permit him to approach the portrayal of sexual promiscuity (he takes pains to get Rawdon Crawley to the scene of Lord Steyne's attempted seduction of Becky in time, and of course the awful fears of Esmond and Frank remain unrealized when they find their runaway prince harmlessly concocting madrigals to Beatrix). The type appears also in a post-nubile or crone phase, the distinguishing characteristic of which is selfish vanity, and the chief function of which is to patronize young men. Beatrix Esmond is to mature into the Baroness Bernstein of *The Virginians,* but Thackeray permits us to see earlier examples in Miss Crawley and the Dowager Viscountess Castlewood. On the other hand there are the unintellectual, selfless, placid, and chastely beautiful women like Amelia Sedley, Helen Pendennis,

Laura Bell, and Rachel Esmond, all of whom represent the apotheosis of saintly purity. These women, too, have their distinguishable phases. As wives Amelia and Rachel lavish the same utterly selfless devotion on their husbands (neither of whom quite comes up to the feminine standards of purity, as a consequence of which they are both acutely uncomfortable) that as widows they confer upon their children. The two phases remain distinct in *Pendennis*, where Laura plays the role of wife and Helen that of mother. Thackeray's attitude toward the two types of women is ambivalent. Though he obviously disapproves of the first sort, he is himself attracted to it; and though he worships the second sort, he is sharply aware of the suffocating effect of its unselfish parasitism. His impatience with Amelia has often been noted, and he speaks, in *Pendennis*, of those "women in whose angelical natures there is something awful, as well as beautiful, to contemplate; at whose feet the wildest and fiercest of us must fall down and humble ourselves, in admiration of that adorable purity which never seems to do or to think wrong" (ch. 2). More suggestive still is the judgment of his wife put into the mouth of the ordinarily unperceptive Lord Castlewood: "Do you fancy I think that *she* would go astray? No, she hasn't passion enough for that. She neither sins nor forgives" (Bk. I, ch. 14). That Thackeray cynically sees through all these women does not, however, negate the fact that his cynicism is ultimately disarmed by his allegiance to conventional Victorian moral values; all three of the novels take their shape from the triumph of the second type of woman over the first.

What chiefly distinguishes *Esmond* from its two predecessors is not the pre-eminence given to the historical setting, but a new method of controlling structure and technique. *Vanity Fair* and *Pendennis* are shaped by the fundamental contrast itself, though in the latter novel the structural outline tends to be obscured by the gratuitous Dickensian intrigue. *Esmond* substitutes for this basically expository organization a narrative one. Esmond himself is the pivotal figure, the "hero" lacking in *Vanity Fair* (perhaps also in *Pendennis*), whose childhood attachment to his "mistress," giving way in the central portion of the novel to a hopeless love for her daughter, Beatrix, is supplanted (though not fundamentally changed) at the end of the novel by a new relation. The spatial organization of the two earlier novels yields to a chronological arrangement which would seem to offer fruitful opportunities for a significant parallel with historical events.

The trouble is that Thackeray's imaginative vision does not confront life as process, as a continuing movement of development and change; he sees life rather as a monstrous agglomeration of ironic incongruities which exist at any given moment, between what is and what ought to be, between what seems and what is.[12] His efforts to provide chronological coherence, not only in *Esmond*, but in his novels taken as a whole, merely attempt to conceal the fact that the chronological coherence is not there. Beatrix Esmond may be convincing as Baroness Bernstein, but she is not the necessary and inevitable product of her own past, or if she is, Thackeray can give no account of the aging process. Nor can Thackeray supply any convincing record of the dynamic stages of growth by which the scintillating young Becky Sharp is transformed into the slattern who tries to hide the gin bottle from her unexpected visitors. He is most effective, indeed, when he can give the old and the young version of the same character simultaneous existence, as he does with Helen Pendennis and Laura Bell. The time dimension is the one which most sharply reveals Thackeray's limitations as a novelist.

Esmond offers not only a new, more purely narrative structure, but new (to Thackeray) method of controlling point of view. The omniscient narrator who was allowed to comment freely on characters and events, oscillating between extreme cynicism and extreme sentimentality, gives way in *Esmond* to the explicit narrator, Esmond himself, who speaks sometimes in the first person, but more often in the third. Except for the chapter headings and the occasional "we" that distinguishes a party or a nation, it might be said that the uniform pattern is third person, but there are a number of passages where, under the stress of strong feeling, or for other reasons, Esmond lapses into the direct, first-person mode of narration:

Mr. Esmond had the fortune to serve at the head of his own company in his regiment, under the command of their own colonel as major-general; and it was his good luck to bring the regiment out of action as commander of it, the four senior officers above him being killed in the prodigious slaughter which happened on that day. I like to think that Jack Haythorn, who sneered at me for being a bastard and parasite of Webb's, as he chose to call me, and with whom I had had words, shook hands with me the day before the battle begun. [Bk. II, ch. 14]

At the opposite extreme, Esmond's limited point of view is occasionally made to give way to omniscience, usually, but not always, with an overt indication. Of many such instances, one will suffice: "that night when Father Holt arrived, and carried my lord away with him, was the last on which Harry ever saw his patron. What happened to my Lord may be briefly told here . . ." (Bk. I, ch. 6). In spite of these occasional variants, however, the main point of view in the novel is the limited one of Esmond himself.

Such a narrative technique has some built-in disadvantages when it is employed to survey the narrator's own past life, particularly when the period to be considered is long. The chief problem is to distinguish between what Wordsworth calls "the naked recollection of that time" and "what may rather have been called to life/By after meditation." It matters little whether the narration is in the first person or the third; if it is supplied by a consciousness which is simultaneously aware of the past and of the present, the two almost inevitably color each other. Even so skilled a portrayer of the childish consciousness as Dickens can scarcely ever give us what the child thought and felt, without also giving the effects of "after meditation." In *Great Expectations*, for example, the mature Pip is always looking over the young Pip's shoulder:

Conscience is a dreadful thing when it accuses man or boy; but when, in the case of a boy, that secret burden co-operates with another secret burden down the leg of his trousers, it is (as I can testify) a great punishment. The guilty knowledge that I was going to rob Mrs. Joe—I never thought I was going to rob Joe, for I never thought of any of the housekeeping property as his—united to the necessity of always keeping one hand on my bread-and-butter as I sat, or when I was ordered about the kitchen on any small errand, almost drove me out of my mind.[13]

Thackeray goes much further. In fact he seems to go out of his way to introduce overtly the reflections and emotions of the retired Virginia colonel who is nostalgically contemplating the most distant reaches of his own past:

. . . coming back to the lad, with a look of infinite pity and tenderness in her eyes, she took his hand again, placing her other fair hand on his head, and saying some words to him, which were so kind, and said in a voice so sweet, that the boy, who had never looked upon so much beauty before, felt as if the touch of a superior being or angel smote him down to the ground, and kissed the fair protecting hand as he knelt on one knee. To the very last hour of his life, Esmond remembered the lady as she then spoke and looked, the rings on her fair hands, the very scent of her robe, the beam of her eyes lighting up with surprise and kindness, her lips blooming in a smile, the sun making a golden halo round her hair. [Bk. I, ch. 1]

Dickens's vision renders two things which are quite distinct: the terror, the guilt, the distraction that the boy actually felt, and the older man's realization that the terror was unfounded, the

guilt disproportionate and misdirected, the distraction unnecessary but nonetheless painful. Thackeray's vision, on the other
hand, blurs the two things, is incapable of distinguishing what
the boy felt from what the man feels. This is true even when
Esmond's feelings differ from what he remembers them to have
been. As a young man Esmond had been a Tory and a Jacobite;
now, as he writes, he recognizes both the expediency and the
justice of the Revolution, but in writing about his youth he is
incapable of entering into himself as Jacobite or recreating the
enthusiasm he then felt. The past has lost its objective reality
for him and lives now only in his subjective response to it; the
naked recollection has been superseded by after meditation.
That Thackeray himself should speak of the novel as "grave
and sad" is itself a recognition of the pervasively elegiac tone
that results from the complete dominance of the retrospective
point of view. Whatever changes of fortune and attitude they
may undergo, Thackeray's characters are rarely seen as stages
in a progress toward something else; their existence in time
seems wholly a matter of convention and artifice. Doubtless the
mature Esmond (like the mature Pip) owes something to his
youthful follies, but the mature Esmond can never get out of
our way long enough for us to see those follies as dynamically
related to the process of growth:

These first passions of men and women are mostly abortive; and
are dead almost before they are born. Esmond could repeat, to
his last day, some of the doggerel lines in which his muse bewailed
his pretty lass; not without shame to remember how bad the verses
were, and how good he thought them; how false the grief, and yet
how he was rather proud of it. 'Tis an error, surely, to talk of
the simplicity of youth. I think no persons are more hypocritical,
and have a more affected behaviour to one another, than the
young. They deceive themselves and each other with artifices
that do not impose upon men of the world; and so we get to
understand truth better, and grow simpler as we grow older. [Bk.
I, ch. 9]

The past remains impenetrable; the event has been transformed by memory. There are at least two Pips, but there is only one Esmond.

For the reasons just given I cannot agree with those critics who see *Esmond* as essentially a *Bildungsroman*. Esmond does not become; he is. Though the novel is shaped by its narrative of events, the center of interest remains the more or less constant attitude of the mature narrator toward those events, so that the organizing principle of the novel remains external to it. The same can be said of the historical narrative which is superimposed upon and parallels the personal one. One critic says of the relation between the course of public and private events that Esmond "never fails to date happenings, or to mention his age at the time this or that befell him, or to place incidents in his personal life in relation to events of national history. Because he is an illegitimate son, because he does not even know the day of his birth, Esmond feels all the more strongly the need to identify himself with social and historical time." [14] Unfortunately the history does not succeed in vivifying the events of Esmond's life; it embalms them, perhaps for the psychological reasons which Talon describes, but I am inclined to suspect that history has become little more than a technical device for providing Esmond's character with the extension in time that the narrative method can only faintly suggest.

The relation between public and private events, between the world of historical realities and that of fictional possibilities, which is the central concern of Scott's best historical novels, is of secondary importance in *Henry Esmond*, but it would be a mistake to assume that Thackeray provides no thematic connection at all. Like *Redgauntlet* the novel depicts a convergence of public and private lines of action, though Esmond does not move toward the center of the intrigue in quite the same sense that Darsie and Alan do. For one thing *Esmond* substitutes a series of intrigues for the one central intrigue of *Redgauntlet,* and instead of moving from ignorance to knowledge, Esmond moves from the role of spectator (as, for example, in the plot which is to culminate in disaster on the banks of the Boyne) to that of participant and even of guiding intelligence. At the climax of the novel, as Esmond plans to bring forward the "Old" Pretender, James Edward Stuart, at the strategic moment when Queen Anne is on the point of death and the succession still in doubt, the prince puts himself *hors de combat* by "dangling after Trix" (as Frank so inelegantly puts it). The prince's failure to assert his hereditary right offers a suggestive parallel with Esmond's refusal to claim his own inheritance, a parallel which derives its significance from the fact that the motives are so different. The prince's withdrawal is an act of folly, if not of baseness; Esmond's sacrifice of his title in favor of his patron's family is his real patent of nobility. Even Frank is aware of the irony: "He [the Prince] is not like a king: somehow, Harry, I fancy you are like a king" (Bk. III, ch. 9). But there is a more important and a more fundamental connection than the one provided by the character relation of the two men. It is Beatrix's selfishness, her utter lack of feeling for others, displayed at the climactic moments, that throws her character into the sharpest contrast with that of her mother. Esmond's infatuation is finally cured (or so he says), and he turns from Beatrix to Rachel in a gesture that asserts the causal relation between public and private events. These thematic connections would be more effective than they are, however, if they disclosed anything we needed to be told. Since Esmond's character is implicit from the first in the very texture of his narration, the dramatic exposition of that character at the end of the novel is a trifle anticlimactic, and the real nature of his relation to Rachel should take no one by surprise either. Lord Mohun perceived it when Esmond was 22 years old: "By the Lord, I believe thou hast an eye to the pretty Puritan thyself, Master Harry," and Harry's indignant response is still more revealing: "I never had a mother, but I love this lady as one. I worship her as a devotee worships a saint" (Bk. I, ch. 13). Once again Thackeray's attempt to get at the truth of his characters narratively or historically is frustrated by his superior ability to get at that truth in other ways.

Esmond's claims to rank at the pinnacle of Thackeray's novels, a position that many of his most sympathetic critics, including Trollope, have given it, are not to be taken lightly. It contains some of his most firmly drawn, most autonomous and fully living characters. Beatrix Esmond is rivaled in this respect only by Becky Sharp, and Esmond himself is unique among Thackeray's male characters. Perhaps more important, the novel displays the most subtle and consistent control of tone among Thackeray's major works. Still, the qualities in *Esmond* that make for greatness owe nothing to the narrative and historical format. It is no more epic than *Redgauntlet*, but whereas *Redgauntlet*'s essential quality as a novel is conferred upon it by the success with which it integrates history and fiction, the essential quality of *Esmond* is something quite apart from the historical background, which remains external, decorative, and therefore, finally, unsatisfying. *Redgauntlet* is a less pretentious novel than *Esmond*—its appeal is to a more superficial level of feeling and a narrower range of human interest—but I think it must be judged a better novel than *Esmond* because in it Scott has found a structural form that is perfectly adapted both to the experience he has to render and to his mode of conceiving that experience.

‡ CHAPTER IX ‡

Structure and Idea in *Bleak House*

> I propose therefore that we enquire into the
> nature of justice and injustice, first as they ap-
> pear in the State, and secondly in the individual,
> proceeding from the greater to the lesser and
> comparing them.
> —PLATO, *The Republic*, trans. Jowett

If anything can supply an intelligible principle of Dickens's development as a novelist, it is the constant strengthening and focusing of his protest against social injustice. This pervasive concern with social justice is the link connecting the otherwise light-hearted and high-spirited meanderings of Pickwick in a world of coaching inns and manor farms to the sinister events which are preparing in the dark world of Chancery in *Bleak House* or of the Marshalsea in *Little Dorrit*. Speaking of this last novel, Shaw remarked in his often quoted preface to *Great Expectations* that it "is a more seditious book than *Das Kapital*. All over Europe men and women are in prison for pamphlets and speeches which are to *Little Dorrit* as red pepper to dynamite." [1] Shaw had, like Macaulay, his own heightened and telling way of putting things, but to a world which persisted in regarding Dickens as the great impresario of soap opera, Shaw's comments needed to be made. The indifference of society to the suffering of its members; the venality, brutishness, or sheer ineptitude of its public servants; its perverse substitution of the virtues of the head for those of the heart; the hopeless inadequacy of its political and philanthropic institutions: these are the recurring motifs of Dickens's novels, from the scenes in the Fleet Prison in *Pickwick* to the symbolic dust heap in *Our Mutual Friend.*

Dickens's aroused social conscience has of course led some of his critics into seeing his work as more doctrinaire, more rigorously ordered than it is. Thus T. A. Jackson and Jack Lindsay have tried in vain to assimilate Dickens's "line" to the orderly fabric of Marxism,[2] and Shaw, of course, tended to exaggerate the explosive force of the novels as propaganda. Nevertheless, in spite of Dickens's reluctance to make common cause with any philosophically grounded reform movement, it is possible to abstract from the novels a more or less consistent point of view toward society and its ills. This ground has been covered so often, and there is such substantial agreement on the articles of Dickens's creed, that I shall limit myself to the briefest summary.

The first point to be observed is that Dickens is not a radical who wants to tear society apart and rebuild it according to first principles. With all its anomalies and incidental absurdities, Dickens never really questioned the basic class structure of English society. It is certainly sounder to align him with the "conservative" tradition exemplified by Carlyle and Ruskin, for he shares with them a kind of perpetual and indignant astonishment that human beings should so far surrender their own nature as to consign their most fundamental interests to machines. The machines, of course, are the literal ones which were reshaping England into something brutal and ugly, but they are also the ones, figuratively speaking, represented by such doctrinaire systems of thought as Benthamism or the political economy of the Manchester School, or by the social or political institutions which assumed that human beings could be administered to by systematic processes in which the basic fact of man's spirituality might be conveniently ignored—democratic government, for example, or evangelical religion.

Dickens's distrust of institutions and of intellectual systems is not the product of experience, for this distrust is clearly evident in *Pickwick*, and though it accumulates emotional charge, it is not really deeper in the late novels. His anti-intellectualism is revealed, in part, by a kind of instinctive response to any attempt to stifle or destroy the irrational part of man's nature; hence Dickens's affectionate regard for the weak-minded, and the prominent symbolic role given to the nonrational entertainments of Sleary's Circus in *Hard Times* (the logical culmination of a series, beginning with Mr. Vincent Crummles and Mrs. Jarley). The only forces of social amelioration to which Dickens gives his unqualified assent are man's native impulses of benevolence and self-sacrifice. At first he is prepared to believe that these impulses are strong enough in normal human beings to combat the various evils of society. Pickwick's benevolence is irrepressible and unconquerable. But either because the evils have grown greater, or because Dickens's faith in the humanity of ordinary people has grown less, the early optimism fades and is replaced by a heavy and virtually impenetrable gloom, lightened only occasionally, and inadequately, by acts of private charity and self-sacrifice. The fierce indignation that breaks out in the early novels becomes a kind of brooding melancholy as Dickens looks at the world in the ripeness of his age.

Though Dickens's social criticism runs through all his novels, it gathers to its greatest clarity and intensity in the six novels which comprise the bulk of his later work: *Dombey and Son, Bleak House, Hard Times, Little Dorrit, Great Expectations,* and *Our Mutual Friend.* Of these *Bleak House* is the most comprehensive criticism of society and may fairly be taken to represent Dickens's mature diagnosis of, and prognosis for, his age. *Bleak House* is also one of his most artful books, and unlike *Hard Times*, another very artful book, it is quintessentially Dickensian in spirit and technique. In the present essay I propose to examine *Bleak House*, both as an embodiment of Dickens's social protest and as a narrative structure, in an effort to see how structure and idea engage each other.

I

The main theme of *Bleak House* is responsibility. The content of the book may most succinctly be described as a series of studies in society's exercise (more often the evasion or abuse) of responsibility for its dependents. In his earlier novels Dickens characteristically locates the source of evil in specific human beings, the villains in his typically melodramatic plots. Sometimes he makes evil grow out of sheer malignity (Quilp), but even when the evil represented is of a predominantly social character it is generally personified, in the acquisitiveness of a Ralph Nickleby, for example, or the officious cruelty of a Bumble. But *Bleak House* has no villain. It offers a jungle without predators, only scavengers. Evil is as impersonal as the fog which is its main symbol. The Court of Chancery, the main focus of evil in the novel and the mundane equivalent of hell, harbors no devil, only a rather mild and benevolent gentleman who is sincerely desirous of doing the best he can for the people who require his aid. Esther describes the Lord Chancellor's manner as "both courtly and kind," and remarks at the conclusion of her interview, "He dismissed us pleasantly, and we all went out, very much obliged to him for being so affable and polite; by which he had certainly lost no dignity, but seemed to us to have gained some." [3] This is not irony; by an inversion of Mephistopheles's paradox, the Lord Chancellor is "ein Teil von jener Kraft, die stets das Gute will und stets das Böse schafft."

Dickens found in the Court of Chancery specifically, and in

the law generally, the true embodiment of everything that was pernicious. The law touched Dickens often enough in his private life, and the actual cases of victims of legal proceedings always roused his indignation even when he was not personally involved. The result was a vein of legal satire beginning with the Bardell-Pickwick trial and running throughout the novels, but it is not Dickens's private grievance against the law that I am here concerned with. The law was to become for him a means by which as an artist he could most faithfully and effectively image a world gone wrong. Like Jeremy Bentham, Dickens was appalled by the chaos of the British law; its random accumulation of statute law, common law, and precedents in equity; its overlapping and conflicting jurisdictions; its antiquated and mysterious rituals and procedures. But Bentham was only appalled by the lack of intelligible system, not by the law itself, and he accordingly set out to put things right. Dickens, on the other hand, who shared with such other Victorian writers as Browning, Trollope, and W. S. Gilbert a profound misunderstanding and distrust of the legal mind, was as much disturbed by legal system as the lack thereof. It is perhaps suggestive that Dickens's satire does not merely attack abuses of the law, it attacks the fundamental postulates of the British legal system. Dodson and Fogg are contemptible less because they are lawyers than because they are grasping, mean, and hypocritical human beings. Dickens aims a subtler shaft at Perker, Mr. Pickwick's solicitor, an amiable and seemingly harmless man who cannot restrain his admiration for the acuity of Dodson and Fogg, and it is Perker, not his opponents, who is the prototype of the lawyers of *Bleak House:* Tulkinghorn, Vholes, and Conversation Kenge. None of these proves to be guilty of anything approaching sharp practice; on the contrary, they are all offered as examples of capable and conscientious legal practitioners, and the evil they give rise to is not a consequence of their abusing their functions but of their performing them as well as they do. Conversation Kenge may be taken as expressing the opinion of the legal fraternity at large when he holds up for Esther's admiration that "monument of Chancery practice," Jarndyce and Jarndyce, the case in which "every difficulty, every contingency, every masterly fiction, every form of procedure known in that court, is represented over and over again" (ch. 3). To Dickens this is a little like a surgeon's describing a newly sutured incision as "beautiful." He despised lawyers (and here Vholes is his principal example) because they drew their living from human misery without contributing significantly to alleviate it. But Dickens's feeling toward the cannibalistic Vholes is only incidental to the main point, which is the concept of the law implied by Kenge's rhapsody.

The law, especially British law, is an instrument of justice which often seems to the layman to put a higher value on consistency and orderly procedure than on justice itself. That in any given instance the law is capable of doing manifest injustice, no one would deny, but that the elaborate body of procedures, fictions, and precedents is the safest guarantee against capricious or arbitrary judgment, and in the long run, in the majority of cases, the most efficient mechanism of seeing justice done is the common ground for the defense of systems of jurisprudence. Justice becomes a by-product of law, and the law itself, by a kind of natural descent from the primitive trial by combat, assumes the character of an intellectual contest in which attack and counterattack, the play of knowledge, ingenuity, and skill, are of transcendent interest, even when the result is a matter of indifference. It amounts to no parodox, then, to say that the lawyer cares nothing for justice; he cares only for the law. Of the justice, that is to say, of the social utility, of his professional activity he is presumably convinced antecedently to his engaging in it, but he goes about his business secure in the knowledge that justice will best be served by his shrewdness in outwitting his adversary. To the lawyer the law is intellectual, abstract, and beautiful, like a game of chess, and it is just here that the fundamental ground of Dickens's quarrel with him lies. Justice for Dickens was generally open and palpable. He couldn't understand why man's natural emotional response to injustice wasn't a sufficient impetus to lead him to correct it if he could. With the abstract and intellectual approach to the evils of life Dickens had no sympathy and no patience at all, and the law, therefore, became for him a comprehensive symbol of an attitude toward life that seemed to him perverse and wrong. Dickens's anti-intellectualism is concentrated and brought to bear in his satire on the law.

But there is special point and relevance to the attack on Chancery in *Bleak House*. In the first place, Chancery exemplifies more perfectly than the law courts properly so-called the characteristically slow and circuitous processes of British jurisprudence. Its ritual was more intricate, its fictions more remote from actualities, its precedents more opaque, than those of the Queen's Bench, or the Exchequer, or the Court of Common Pleas. And of course the slowness of Chancery proceedings was legendary. Holdsworth emphasizes this point neatly by quoting Lord Bowen: "Whenever any death occurred, bills of review or supplemental suits became necessary to reconstitute the charmed circle of the litigants which had been broken. . . . It was satirically declared that a suit to which fifty defendants were necessary parties . . . could never hope to end at all, since the yearly average of deaths in England was one in fifty, and a death, as a rule, threw over the plaintiff's bill for at least a year." [4] The High Court of Chancery, then, provided a microcosm of the legal world of nineteenth-century England, magnifying the law's essential features and reducing its flaws to absurdity. In the second place, Chancery is specially appropriate as an image of the kind of responsibility that *Bleak House* is really about. The Lord Chancellor's legal responsibility is of a curious and distinctive character. The law courts, with their various ramifications and subdivisions, civil, criminal, and ecclesiastical, exist to provide a bar where anyone who believes himself injured according to the common or statute law may plead his case. But the law has many loopholes, and it is desirable that some provision be made to redress wrongs which are not covered by any existing law. Moreover a considerable body of potential litigants—chiefly widows and orphans—being unable to plead in their own behalf, must be protected against injustice. The Lord Chancellor's Court was devised for just such a purpose, to provide relief where the ordinary channels of legal procedure offered none. The origin of the Lord Chancellor's judicial function is described by Blackstone:

When the courts of law, proceeding merely upon the ground of the king's original writs, and confining themselves strictly to that bottom, gave a harsh or imperfect judgment, the application for redress used to be to the king in person assisted by his privy council . . . and they were wont to refer the matter either to the chancellor and a select committee, or by degrees to the chancellor only, who mitigated the severity or supplied the defects of the judgments pronounced in the courts of law, upon weighing the circumstances of the case.[5]

From a court of appeals the Chancellor's Court developed into an ordinary court of equity in which a plaintiff could sue for redress by the presentation of a bill, and which claimed, furthermore, exclusive jurisdiction in supervising the proper administration of trusts and wills. It must be remembered, too, that antecedent to his judicial responsibility the Lord Chancellor bore a responsibility which was ecclesiastical and eleemosynary. Let me quote Blackstone once more on the Chancellor's office:

Being formerly usually an ecclesiastic, (for none else were then capable of an office so conversant in writings,) and presiding over the royal chapel, he became keeper of the king's conscience; visitor, in right of the king, of all hospitals and colleges of the king's foundation; and patron of all the king's livings under the value of twenty marks *per annum* in the king's books. He is the general guardian of all infants, idiots, and lunatics; and has the general superintendance of all charitable uses in the kingdom. [III, 48]

Incorporating in his single office all the "charitable uses in the kingdom," the Lord Chancellor furnishes Dickens with a compendious symbol of all the ways in which one human being can be charged with the care of another: he is a father to the orphan, a husband to the widow, a protector to the weak and infirm, and an almoner to the destitute. What better focus of attention in a book about human responsibility could Dickens find than a suit in Chancery?

At one end of the scale is the Lord Chancellor in Lincoln's Inn Hall, at the other is Jo, society's outcast, with no proper place of his own, "moving on" through the atrocious slum of Tom-All-Alone's, itself a "monument of Chancery practice," for its dismal and neglected appearance proclaims its connection with Chancery. Who will take responsibility for Jo? Not government, engaged in an endless wrangle over the proper emolument for the party faithful; not religion, in the person of Mr. Chadband sermonizing over Jo's invincible ignorance; not law, concerned only with Jo's "moving on"; not organized charity, which finds the natives of Borrioboola-Gha or the Tockahoopo Indians a great deal more interesting than the dirty home-grown heathen. Jo subsists entirely on the spasmodic generosity of Snagsby, who relieves his own feelings by compulsively feeding half-crowns to Jo, or on the more selfless generosity of Nemo, who supplies Jo's only experience of human companionship until Esther and George and Allan Woodcourt come to his aid. Jo's function as an instrument of Dickens's social protest is clear. In his life and in his death he is a shattering rebuke to all those agencies of church and state which are charged with the care of the weak and the helpless and the poor, from the Lord Chancellor's court down to the Society for the Propagation of the Gospel in Foreign Parts. And Jo's experience throws a strong glare on the causes of their inadequacy; they fail conspicuously and utterly because they are nothing more than machines, because they are illuminated from the head, never from the heart, because, ultimately, they fail to acknowledge Dickens's most important moral and social maxim, that human beings can live together only on terms of mutual trust and love.

Between the Lord Chancellor and Jo, Dickens illustrates every relation of dependency which is possible in civilized society, in every one of which, as we have seen, the Lord Chancellor himself participates by a species of legal fiction. Consider, for example, the condition of parenthood. Every child begets a responsibility in his parents; in *Bleak House* Dickens examines a wide range of cases in order to trace the extent to which that responsibility is successfully discharged. Only a very few parents in the sick society of this novel manage to maintain a healthy and normal relation with their children; one must contrive to get as far from the shadow of Chancery as Elephant and Castle, to find a domestic happiness like the Bagnets'. The virtuous mean of parental devotion is the exception; more often we have the excess, like Mrs. Pardiggle's ferocious bullying of her children, or still oftener the deficiency, instanced by Mrs. Jellyby's total neglect of her family, or Harold Skimpole's similar behavior toward his. But the real symptom of disease is the frequency with which we find the normal relation between parent and child inverted. Skimpole is, as he frequently avers, a child, but the engaging qualities which this pose brings to the surface are quickly submerged again in his reckless self-indulgence, and his avocations, harmless or even commendable in themselves, the pursuit of art and beauty, become like the flush of fever, a sign of decay when we recognize that they are indulged at the expense of his responsibilities as the head of a family, and that his existence is so thoroughly parasitical. But just as there are parents who turn into children, a few children turn into parents. Charley Neckett, for example, at the death of her father is rudely thrust into maturity at the age of thirteen with a brother of five or six and a sister of eighteen months to care for. Esther describes her as "a very little girl, childish in figure but shrewd and older-looking in the face—pretty-faced too—wearing a womanly sort of bonnet much too large for her, and drying her bare arms on a womanly sort of apron. Her fingers were white and wrinkled with washing, and the soap-suds were yet smoking which she wiped off her arms. But for this, she might have been a child, playing at washing, and imitating a poor working-woman with a quick observation of the truth" (ch. 15). Even Esther herself exhibits a kind of reversal of roles. Like Charley (and a good many other characters in the story) she is an orphan, and her relations with the other inmates of Bleak House are curiously ambiguous and ill-defined. She is ostensibly the companion of Ada Clare and the ward of Mr. Jarndyce, both of which offices confer upon her a dependent status, yet in this household she assumes the moral leadership, a leadership which is explicitly recognized by the others' use of such nicknames as Little Old Woman, Mrs. Shipton, Mother Hubbard, and Dame Durden. Esther's relation with Mr. Jarndyce (whom she calls "Guardian") is further complicated by their betrothal; for as long as this lasts she stands toward him simultaneously as mother, daughter, and fiancée. In the Smallweed family the children all appear unnaturally old; only the senile display the attributes of childhood: "There has been only one child in the Smallweed family for several generations. Little old men and women there have been, but no child, until Mr. Smallweed's grandmother, now living, became weak in her intellect, and fell (for the first time) into a childish state" (ch. 21). The most complete and perfect inversion of all, however, is to be seen in the Turveydrop household, where young Prince labors unceasingly to maintain his father in the style to which he has become accustomed as an imitation Regency beau. The selfish old parasite, who sends his son off to his dancing school in Kensington while he goes himself to dine comfortably at the French House in the Opera Colonnade, is absolutely stunned by Prince's "ingratitude" at thinking of marriage with Caddy Jellyby, and the young couple must sue on their knees for Mr. Turveydrop's consent:

'My dear father,' returned Prince, 'we well know what little comforts you are accustomed to, and have a right to; and it will always be our study, and our pride, to provide those before anything. If you will bless us with your approval and consent, father, we shall not think of being married until it is quite agreeable to you; and when we *are* married, we shall always make you—of course—our first consideration. You must ever be the Head and Master here, father; and we feel how truly unnatural it would be in us, if we failed to know it, or if we failed to exert ourselves in every possible way to please you.'

Mr. Turveydrop underwent a severe internal struggle, and came upright on the sofa again, with his cheeks puffing over his stiff cravat; a perfect model of parental deportment.

'My son!' said Mr. Turveydrop. 'My children! I cannot resist your prayer. Be happy!' [ch. 23]

The irony is enforced by the fact that from this marriage can come only a stunted, malformed, deaf-mute child. Generally speaking, the society of *Bleak House* is one in which the normal responsibility of parent for child has most often been abused or shirked.

The pattern of inversion reasserts itself when we turn our attention to another relation of dependency—marriage. Of course there are obvious instances of the neglect of marital (as well as maternal) responsibility like Mrs. Jellyby's high-minded disregard of her family, and there are equally obvious instances

of abuse of the obedience enjoined by the marriage sacrament,
like the abject submission of the brick-makers' wives to their
husbands' brutality. Esther and Ada find one of these women
furtively bringing comfort to the bereaved mother of a dead
child, but with one eye always on the door of the public house:

> 'It's you, young ladies, is it?' she said, in a whisper. 'I'm
> a-watching for my master. My heart's in my mouth. If he was to
> catch me away from home he'd pretty near murder me.'
> 'Do you mean your husband?' said I.
> 'Yes, miss, my master.' [ch. 8]

But setting these instances aside, we are confronted in *Bleak
House* by a stereotype of marriage in which the normal economic and social functions of husband and wife are reversed.
Mr. Snagsby's deference to his wife remains within the bounds
of conventional Dickensian social comedy and by itself is
neither morbid nor especially significant:

> Mr. Snagsby refers everything not in the practical mysteries of
> the business to Mrs. Snagsby. She manages the money, reproaches
> the Tax-gatherers, appoints the time and places of devotion on
> Sundays, licenses Mr. Snagsby's entertainments, and acknowledges
> no responsibility as to what she thinks fit to provide for dinner;
> insomuch that she is the high standard of comparison among the
> neighboring wives, a long way down Chancery Lane on both
> sides, and even out in Holborn. [ch. 10]

But, as in the case of Skimpole, what begins in the light-
hearted vein of comedy quickly darkens, and the relation assumes an unhealthy taint. Mrs. Snagsby, who enters as the
conventional loud-voiced shrew, becomes, before her final
exit, a shrinking paranoiac, "a woman overwhelmed with in-
juries and wrongs, whom Mr. Snagsby has habitually deceived,
abandoned, and sought to keep in darkness. . . . Everybody
it appears . . . has plotted against Mrs. Snagsby's peace" (ch.
54). And the Snagsby menage is further significant in that it

provides a pattern of the marriage relation that is disturbingly common. Mr. Bayham Badger's uxoriousness far surpasses Mr. Snagsby's. It extends so far, in fact, that he is willing to suffer total eclipse in favor of his predecessors, Mrs. Badger's former husbands. And even the happy and amiable Bagnets display a domestic arrangement which, in spite of Matthew's stoutly (though not very convincingly) maintained fiction that "discipline must be preserved," places Mrs. Bagnet firmly in command of the family fortunes and policy. There is special meaning and pathos, however, in the union of Rick Carstone and Ada Clare, perhaps the only truly romantic pairing in the whole story (for, it must be noted in passing, some of the most admirable characters either are denied or deliberately evade the responsibilities of marriage—Mr. Jarndyce, Captain Hawdon, Boythorn, and Trooper George). This couple, the epitome of youth and hope and beauty, is doomed to frustration and tragedy because they take the contagion of Chancery, but that infection is itself made possible by the fact that the moral resources in their marriage, the courage, strength, and devotion, all belong to Ada. The corruption that marks the society of *Bleak House* may find its center and aptest symbol in Lincoln's Inn Hall, but its true origin is in the decay of the most fundamental social institution, the family. When parents will not or cannot take care of their children, when husbands refuse to be masters in their own houses, above all when these relations are not illuminated and softened by love, it is useless to expect those public institutions in which the relations of the family are mirrored to supply their defects.

But Dickens does not limit himself to the family. His novel is an intricate, if not always very systematic, study of the bonds which link human beings together. The very shape of his imaginative vision is perhaps given by the invariability with which people are seen as demonstrating potential or actual relations of responsibility or dependency toward one another.

Here are masters and servants, landlords and tenants, employers
and employees, professional men and clients, officers and men,
all enforcing the inescapable truth that men and women share
a common destiny. I do not propose to examine these various
relations in detail; examples will suggest themselves to every
reader of *Bleak House*. I believe that the breadth and the closeness of Dickens's analysis of society imply both his conviction
that man cannot evade the consequences of his brotherhood
with every other man, and his belief that human brotherhood
can never be adequately affirmed or practiced through agencies
which are the product of the intellect alone.

II

Edmund Wilson long ago hailed *Bleak House* as inaugurating
a new genre, the novel of the "social group." [6] The term is
both apt and suggestive, but it defines the inner form of the
novel without explaining how Dickens imposed structural form
upon it. The tendency of recent criticism has been to seek
the novel's main structural principle in patterns of diction,
imagery, or symbolism which are essentially verbal. This
approach has led to some interesting and valuable insights,[7]
but they have sometimes been achieved at the expense of ig-
noring other, more obvious and palpable features. The art of
the novel, as Dickens conceived and practiced it, was still a
story-telling art, and though it is certainly true that his language, especially in the mature works, is richly charged and
implicative, I do not believe that we can understand the structure of *Bleak House* without reference to those ingredients
which are constituted by its participation in a story-telling
tradition—I mean, specifically, plot and the closely related
layers of character and point of view.

First the plot. "Plot" here means the record of events, organized according to some intelligible principle of selection
and arrangement. The narration of unrelated (even though

sequential) events does not give rise to plot; time sequence alone does not organize experience in any meaningful way. The loosest kind of organization is supplied by character; events may be related in that they happen to the same person, whether or not they reveal any growth, either in the character himself, or in our understanding of him. A somewhat more complicated structure arises when events are related to each other by their common illustration of a single idea or of several related ideas. Finally, events may be organized according to a causal sequence in which each successive event is in some way caused by the one which precedes it. Now only in the last sense does plot function as the unifying element in a story, for though it is possible for a story to have a plot in either of the first two senses, we would, in those cases, probably refer the story's unity to, respectively, character or theme.

It is virtually impossible to put all the events of *Bleak House* into a single causal sequence, or even into several, as long as we understand by "events" what that word normally signifies, that is, births, deaths, betrothals, marriages, whatever, in short, is likely to be entered in the family Bible, and perhaps also such other occurrences (of a less public and ceremonial nature) as quarreling, making love, eating, drinking, working, etc., which may have an interest of their own. *Bleak House* is full enough of "events" in this sense; I count nine deaths, four marriages, and four births. The difficulty is in assigning their causes or their consequences. What are we to make of the death of Krook for example? The question is not one of physiology; I don't propose to reopen the question of spontaneous combustion. The question is properly one of psychology: how is Krook's death related to the play of human motives and purposes? The answer, of course, is that it is not so related at all; it is a simple *deus ex machina* whose only artistic justification is to be sought at the level of symbolism. Rick Carstone's death, by contrast, is integrated with plot, for though its physiological causes may be as obscure as those of Krook's death, its psychological causes are palpable and satisfying. Or take Esther's marriage to Allan Woodcourt. Is it the inevitable culmination of a pattern of events or merely a concession to popular sentiment, like the second ending of *Great Expectations?* A great many, perhaps most, of the "events" of *Bleak House* consist of such hard and stubborn facts—stubborn in that they are not amenable to the construction of any intelligible law; they exist virtually uncaused, and they beget effects which are quite disproportionate to their own nature or importance. Events have a way of taking us by surprise, for even though Dickens is careful to create an appropriate atmosphere whenever he is about to take someone off, the time and manner of death are generally unpredictable.

The artistic center of the novel is generally taken to be Chancery, but if so it seems to me that Chancery functions as a symbol, not as a device of plot. We are permitted glimpses from time to time of what "happens" in Chancery, but Jarndyce and Jarndyce obviously follows no intelligible law of development, and so it is meaningless to talk about a Chancery plot or subplot. Furthermore, though Chancery affects the lives of many, perhaps all, of the characters in *Bleak House,* it does not do so in the sense that significant events take place there. The only event in the Court of Chancery that proves to have significant consequences for the people outside is the cessation of Jarndyce and Jarndyce when the whole property in dispute has been consumed in legal costs. But this is itself a conclusion reached by the stern requirements of economics rather than by the arcane logic of the law. Chancery affects men's lives the way God does, not by direct intervention in human affairs, but by commanding belief or disbelief.

In a few instances events align themselves in something approaching a genuine causal sequence. The story of Rick Carstone, for example, who undergoes a slow moral deterioration because he is gradually seduced into believing in Chancery, provides an example of a meaningful pattern of events. But Rick's story is neither central, nor altogether satisfying, principally, I believe, because it is observed only at intervals, and from without.[8] It remains true that it is all but impossible to describe what happens in *Bleak House* by constructing a causal sequence of events.

The difficulty largely disappears, however, when we stop trying to discover a more or less systematic pattern of events, and try instead to define the organization of the book in terms of discovery, the Aristotelian anagnorisis. The plot, in this case, is still woven of "events," but the word now signifies some determinate stage in the growth of awareness of truths which are in existence, potentially knowable, before the novel opens. Events, in the original sense of that term, become important chiefly as the instrumentalities of discovery. Krook's death, for example, leads to the unearthing of an important document in Jarndyce and Jarndyce, and incidentally to the disclosure of a complex web of relations involving the Smallweed, Snagsby, and Chadband families. The murder of Tulkinghorn and the arrest of Trooper George are red herrings, designed to confuse the issue, but ultimately they make possible the complete unveiling of the pattern of human relations that it is the chief business of the novel to disclose. The progressive discovery of that pattern is, then, the "plot" of the novel, and it constitutes a causal sequence, not in that each discovery brings about the next, but in that each discovery presupposes the one before. We need to know that Lady Dedlock harbors a secret which she regards as shameful before we can discover the existence of some former connection between her and Nemo, and we need to be aware of that connection before we can add to it the more important discovery that Esther is the daughter of Nemo and Lady Dedlock. And so on, until the whole complicated web stands clearly revealed.

This kind of structure is, as everyone knows, the typical pattern of the detective story. Such fundamentally human concerns as crime and punishment lie outside the scope of detective fiction, in which the murder may take place before the story begins, and the retribution may finally catch up with the murderer after it ends. The plot of the detective story consists simply in the discovery—withheld, of course, as long as possible—of the one hypothesis which will account for all the disparate facts or "events" that make up the story. The interest is centered, in classical specimens of the genre, not in the events, but in the process by which the events are rendered meaningful, ordinarily in the activity of the detective as he proceeds toward a solution. *Bleak House*, of course, has many detectives. Not counting the unforgettable Inspector Bucket "of the Detective," a great many characters are at work throughout the novel at unraveling some private and vexing problem of their own: Mr. Tulkinghorn, stalking Lady Dedlock's secret with fearful persistency, or Mr. Guppy, approaching the same mystery from Esther's side, or Mrs. Snagsby, endeavoring to surprise her husband's guilty connections, or even Esther herself, troubled by the riddle of her own mysterious origin and still more mysterious participation in the guilt of her unknown mother. But the presence or activity of a detective is incidental to the main scheme of such fiction, from *Oedipus Tyrannus* onward, to present a mystery and then solve it. The beginning, middle, and end of such an action can be described only in terms of the reader's awareness; the beginning consists of the exposition in which the reader is made aware of the mystery, that is of the facts that require explanation; the end consists of his reaching a full understanding of the mystery which confronted him, for when all is known the story must come to an end. The middle, then, is comprised of his successive states of partial or incorrect knowledge.

The mystery presents itself, in the typical detective novel, with crystalline purity. Someone has been murdered; the problem is to discover, in the graphic but ungrammatical language of the usual cognomen, Who done it? In *Bleak House* the problem is somewhat different. It is true that there is a murder, and that the murderer must subsequently be picked out of three likely suspects, but the main mystery, the one that sustains the motion of the whole book and gives it a unity of plot, is not a question of determining the agent of some past action (though the mystery may be formulated in these terms) so much as it is a question of establishing the identity of all the characters involved, and in the world of *Bleak House* one's identity is defined according to his relations to other people. Two recent writers, James H. Broderick and John E. Grant, consider that the novel is given its shape by Esther's successful quest for identity, or place, in the society of the book,[9] and I see no reason why the establishment of identity, not merely for Esther, but for all or most of the characters may not provide a workable principle of structure. Esther's identity is secure when she discovers who her parents are, and this is certainly the heart of *Bleak House*'s mystery, but that discovery comes shortly after the middle of the book, when Lady Dedlock discloses herself to Esther. The novel is not complete until all the relations of its various characters are recognized and established (or re-established) on some stable footing. Sir Leicester Dedlock must adjust his whole view of the world to conform to the discovery he makes about his wife; harmony must be restored between Mr. Jarndyce and Rick; Esther must discover her true relation to Mr. Jarndyce—and to Allan Woodcourt. Even the minor characters must be accounted for: Trooper George must become once again the son of Sir Leicester's housekeeper and the brother of the ironmaster; Mr. and Mrs. Snagsby must be reconciled as man and wife; all misunderstandings, in short, must be cleared away.

One of the most curious features of *Bleak House*, one of the attributes which is most likely to obtrude itself and bring down the charge of staginess is Dickens's careful husbandry of characters. That he disposes of so many may perhaps be worthy of remark, but still more remarkable is the fact that he makes them all, even the most obscure, serve double and triple functions. Mr. Boythorn, for example, the friend of Mr. Jarndyce who is always at law with his next-door neighbor, Sir Leicester Dedlock, doubles as the rejected suitor of Miss Barbary, Esther's aunt. And it is surely a curious coincidence which sends Rick, when he is in need of a fencing teacher, to Trooper George, who is not only related to the Chesney Wold household through his mother, but also deeply in debt to Grandfather Smallweed (Krook's brother-in-law), and of course he has served under Captain Hawdon, Esther's father. Mrs. Rachael, Miss Barbary's servant, turns up again as the wife of the oily Mr. Chadband, and even Jenny, the brickmaker's wife, appears fortuitously to change clothes with Lady Dedlock. These examples, which might easily be multiplied, irresistibly create the impression, not of a vast, chaotic, utterly disorganized world, but of a small, tightly ordered one. That the novel thus smacks of theatrical artifice constitutes a threat to the "bleakness" of *Bleak House,* for we are never confronted, in this world, by the blank and featureless faces of total strangers, the heart-rending indifference of the nameless mob; all the evils of this world are the work of men whose names and domestic habits we know, and for that reason, it would appear, are deprived of most of their terrors.

Perhaps the most serious charge that can be brought against the artistry of *Bleak House* grows out of some of the characteristic features which I have been discussing. How can the discerning reader avoid being offended, it will be argued, by a novel which obviously wants to say something serious and important about society, but at the same time contrives to say it in the most elaborately artificial way possible? How can we be serious about social criticisms which come to us through the medium of the most sensational literary genre, and are obscured by every artifice of melodrama? The objection seems to be a damaging one, but I wonder if Dickens's employment of the techniques of the detective story and of melodrama may not enforce, rather than weaken, his rhetorical strategy. The plot, as I conceive it, consists of the progressive and relentless revelation of an intricate web of relations uniting all the characters of the novel, by ties of blood or feeling or contract. And Dickens's assignment of multiple functions to the minor characters is merely a means of reinforcing and underscoring our sense that human beings are bound to each other in countless, often unpredictable ways. It is difficult to see how Dickens could have found a clearer, more emphatic way of drawing up his indictment against society for its failure to exercise responsibility than by his elaborate demonstration of human brotherhood.

The bleakness of *Bleak House* is the sense of hopelessness inspired by the knowledge that men and women, subjected to the common shocks of mortality, will nevertheless consistently repudiate the claims which other people have on them. The sense of hopelessness is intensified and made ironic by the closeness, figuratively speaking, of their relations to other people (sometimes, of course, the closeness is literal, as in the hermetic little community of Cook's Court, Cursitor Street). It is appropriate that the novel should be shaped by discoveries rather than by events, for the sense of hopelessness, or bleakness, can hardly be sustained in a world that can be shaped to human ends by human will. The events of this novel are accidental in a double sense; most of them are unplanned and unpredictable, and they are moreover nonessential to the view of human experience that Dickens is concerned to present. Human relations, the ones that are important, are not constituted by events (though they may be revealed by events—

Esther's smallpox, for example), because events just happen, they follow no intelligible law either of God or man. Human relations are inherent in the nature of society, and the duty of man is therefore not something arbitrary and intrinsically meaningless which can be prescribed and handed down to him by some external authority (like law); it is discoverable in, and inferable from, his social condition and only needs to be seen to command allegiance. The tragedy of *Bleak House* is that awareness of human responsibility invariably comes too late for it to be of any use. Nemo's, or Coavinses's, or Jo's membership in the human race is discovered only after his death, and Sir Leicester Dedlock awakens to recognition of the true nature of the marriage bond only when his wife has gone forth to die. Still, it is important to have that awareness, and the most effective way to produce it, surely, is to make its slow growth the animating principle of the novel.

III

If we choose to talk about the plot of *Bleak House* as constituted by a growing awareness of human relations and human responsibilities, sooner or later we must raise the question, *Whose* awareness? The problem of point of view is so important in the detective story, in fact, that it is most often met by the creation of a special point-of-view character. The classical instance, of course, is Dr. Watson, but Dr. Watson has had countless avatars. *Bleak House* is enough of a detective story so that it must reckon with some, at least, of the problems that Dr. Watson was invented to solve. The mystery must be preserved, so the narrator's perspicacity must have rather clearly defined limits, but at the same time the mystery must take hold of the reader, so the narrator must possess lively human sympathies and be capable of moral insights which are as just and true as his practical judgments are absurd. Such considerations impose limits on the choice of a narrative perspective for

Bleak House, but there are other considerations which affect that choice too. The mystery whose solution dominates the novel is not such a simple, or at any rate such a limited problem as identifying a particular character as the criminal; Dickens's villain is a whole society, and its guilt cannot be disclosed by a sudden dramatic unveiling. Furthermore Dickens is only partly concerned with the disclosure of the truth to the reader; a more fundamental matter is the discovery by the agents themselves of the relations in which they stand toward all the other members of society. It is the story of Oedipus on a large scale.

Because of the staggering breadth of Dickens's design the selection of a narrative point of view is extraordinarily difficult. If he chooses an omniscient, third person point of view a good deal of the emotional charge is lost, particularly if the narrator remains (as he must) sufficiently aloof from the actions and events he describes to avoid premature disclosures. On the other hand, a first person narrator suffers equally important disabilities. The most immediately obtrusive of these is physical and practical. How can a single character be expected to participate directly in all the relations the novel is about? How can one character contribute evidence (as opposed to hearsay) of events which take place in London, in Lincolnshire, and in Hertfordshire, sometimes simultaneously? The difficulty could be partly met by the selection of one of those numerous characters like Tulkinghorn or Mr. Guppy or young Bart Smallweed who seem to be always on the "inside," in control of events simply because they know about them, yet one difficulty yields only to be replaced by another. Characters like Tulkinghorn obviously lack the "lively human sympathies" which give to the first person point of view its special value, and as narrator Tulkinghorn (who is in any case disqualified on the more fundamental ground that he is killed) would offer no advantage over the omniscient point of view. The obvious solution to this dilemma is to have both points of view, alternating the narration between them.

The dual point of view in *Bleak House* has always served as a speck of grit around which the commentators have secreted their critical pearls. E. M. Forster regards it as a blemish, though he thinks Dickens's talent can make us forget it: "Logically, *Bleak House* is all to pieces, but Dickens bounces us, so that we do not mind the shiftings of the view point."[10] Others defend the double point of view as artistically appropriate.[11] I regard the device as a concession to a necessity that I can see no other way of circumventing, but there are perhaps one or two things to be said about it.

Bleak House is a novel without a center. There is no single character to whom the events of the story happen, or with reference to whom those events are significant. It is not even possible (as I have already argued) to understand the novel as a unified system of coordinate plots or of plot and subplots. Except for this want of a center the novel might be compared to a spider web in which each intersection represents a character, connected by almost invisible but nonetheless tenacious filaments to a circle of characters immediately surrounding him and ultimately, of course, to all the other characters. But the spider web has a center (and a villain), so a more appropriate comparison might be made to a continuous section of netting, or better still, to the system of galaxies which make up the universe. It appears to a terrestrial observer that all the other galaxies are receding from him at an unthinkable rate of speed, implying that his own post of observation constitutes the center of things. Yet the centrality of his own position is merely a function of his special point of view. So with *Bleak House*. Esther is, in this special sense, the "center" of the novel, not because she so regards herself, but because she supplies the central observation point, because relations are measured according to their nearness or farness from her just as astronomical distances are measured in parsecs—heliocentric parallax (in seconds of arc) as recorded for a terrestrial observer. To pass, for example, from Esther to Nemo (or some other intermediate character) to George to Matthew Bagnet is to move, so to speak, from the center outward. But Esther is not really the center of the novel. To think of her as such is to destroy or at least to do serious violence to Dickens's view of the world and transform his indictment of society into a sentimental fable. To deprive the novel of its specious center, to provide it with a new perspective which, like stereoscopic vision, adds depth, is an important function of the omniscient point of view.

Dickens's handling of that portion of the narrative which is related by the omniscient observer (roughly half of the novel) is, on the whole, masterly. I do not know that any critic denies the full measure of praise for things like the opening paragraph or two of the novel, that magnificent evocation of the London fog which has been quoted so often that I may be excused from doing so here. The laconic, unemotional style, with its sentence fragments and present participles in place of finite verbs, the roving eye, which, like the movie camera mounted on an overhead crane, can follow the action at will, are brilliantly conceived and deftly executed. It is a descriptive style emancipated from the limitations of time and space, and accordingly well-suited to its special role in the novel. But Dickens's control of this narrator is uneven. Superbly fitted for the descriptive passages of the novel, his tight-lipped manner must give way to something else in passages of narration, or, still more conspicuously, in those purple rhetorical passages that Dickens loves to indulge in. As a narrator, the omniscient persona (now speaking in finite verbs in the present tense) suffers somewhat from a hollow portentousness, a lack of flexibility, and a rather pointless reticence which can become annoying, as in the narration of Tulkinghorn's death (though here again the descriptive powers get full play). The requirements of consistency do not seem to trouble Dickens when it is time to step forward and point the finger at the object of his satire. The narrative persona is dropped completely when Dickens speaks of Buffy and company, or apostrophizes the "right" and "wrong" reverends whom he holds responsible for the death of Jo. But these passages win us by their obvious sincerity, and we need not trouble ourselves over the fact that the mask has been inadvertently dropped. To insist on a rigorous consistency here is to quibble over trifles, for generally speaking the third person narration is adroit and effective.

The focus of discontent with the manipulation of point of view in *Bleak House* is Esther Summerson. Fred W. Boege writes: "There is nothing necessarily wrong with the idea of alternating between the first and third persons. The fault lies rather with Dickens' choice of a medium for the first-person passages. *David Copperfield* demonstrates that the conventional Victorian hero is not a commanding figure in the center of a novel. Esther Summerson proves that the conventional heroine is worse; for the hero is hardly more than colorless, whereas she has positive bad qualities, such as the simpering affectation of innocence." [12] I think it is essential to distinguish carefully between Esther's qualities as "heroine" and Esther's qualities as narrator, for though the two functions are not wholly separate, it ought to be possible to have a bad heroine who is a good narrator and vice versa. As a heroine she clearly belongs to a tradition that we tend to regard as hopelessly sentimental and out-of-date. She is sweet-tempered and affectionate, and she is also capable and strong and self-denying. The first two qualities almost invariably (at least within the conventions of Victorian fiction) render their possessor both unsympathetic and unreal. One thinks of Amelia Sedley or Dinah Morris or Dickens's own Agnes Wickfield, and prefers, usually, the society of such demireps as Becky Sharp or Lizzie Eustace. Still, Esther's strength of character ought to save her and give her a genuine hold on our regard, except for the fact that as narrator she is faced with the necessity of talking about herself, and her modest disclaimers ring false. When she tells us that she is neither good, nor clever, nor beautiful, she forfeits a good deal of the regard that her genuinely attractive and admirable qualities demand. Esther the heroine is in a sense betrayed by Esther the narrator into assuming a posture that cannot be honestly maintained.

Whatever one thinks of Esther as a person, the important question at the moment is her discharge of the narrator's responsibility. The sensibility which is revealed by her attributes as a character (the term "heroine" is somewhat misleading) is of course the same one which will determine the quality of her perceptions and insights as narrator, and it is here, I think, that some confusion arises, for it is generally assumed that Esther's simplicity, her want of what might be called "diffractive" vision, the power of subjecting every experience to the play of different lights and colors, is held to undermine or even destroy her value as narrator. We have become so used to accepting the Jamesian canons of art and experience that we refuse validity to any others. The attitude is unfortunate, not to say parochial. For James "experience" (the only kind of experience that concerned the artist) was constituted by the perception of it. "Experience," he writes in "The Art of Fiction," "is never limited, and it is never complete; it is an immense sensibility, a kind of huge spider-web of the finest silken threads suspended in the chamber of consciousness, and catching every air-borne particle in its tissue. It is the very atmosphere of the mind; and when the mind is imaginative . . . it takes to itself the faintest hints of life, it converts the very pulses of the air into revelations." [13] This conception of experience is at the root of James's conception of the art of the novel, for it prescribes that the simplest kind of happening may be converted to the stuff of art by a sufficiently vibrant and sensitive point of view character. To a Lambert Strether the relations of Chad Newsome and Mme. de Vionnet are subtle, complex, and beautiful, because he is; but to another observer the same liaison is common and vulgar. Strether possesses what I have chosen to call diffractive vision, the ability to see a whole spectrum where the vulgar can see only the light of common day.

How can poor little Esther Summerson manage to perform the same function as a character with the depth and resonance of Lambert Strether? The answer, obviously, is that she can't. But I must hasten to add that she doesn't have to. The ontological basis of James's fiction is radically different from that of Dickens's; for in James what seems is more important than what is, and he accordingly requires a perceiving intelligence of the highest order. In Dickens, on the other hand, though he too is concerned with the characters' awareness, the relations which they are to perceive have a "real" existence which is not contingent on their being seen in a certain way. For this reason Esther does not have to serve as the instrument of diffraction; the light is colored at its source. To the sensitive Jamesian observer a single human relation appears in almost an infinite number of lights, and a single act may be interpreted in many ways. But Dickens does not work that way, at least not in *Bleak House*. Here the richness and infinite variety of human experience are suggested by the sheer weight of example, by the incredible multiplication of instances, and the narrator's chief function is simply to record them.

When Socrates and his friends Glaucon and Adeimantus differed over the nature of justice and injustice, Socrates proposed to settle the dispute, in the passage of the *Republic* from which my epigraph is taken, by constructing an imaginary and ideal state in order to see how justice originates. The method is not at all unlike that of Dickens, who proposes to investigate the abstraction "injustice" by seeing how it arises in an imaginary replica of the real world. Both methods assume that what is universal and abstract is rendered most readily intelligible by what is particular and concrete, and furthermore that the particular and concrete establish a firmer hold on our feelings than the universal and abstract. For both Plato and Dickens are concerned, not only with making justice and injustice understood, but with making them loved and hated, respectively. The method is perhaps suggestive of allegory, but it differs in important ways from any technique of symbolic representation. It is a species of definition which proceeds by attempting to specify the complete denotation of the thing to be defined. To the question, "What is Justice?" Plato replies by showing us his republic, perfect in all its details, and saying, "Justice is here." To a similar question about injustice Dickens need only reply by unfolding the world of *Bleak House*.

Let me particularize briefly. One of the important ethical abstractions the novel deals with is charity (a useful check list of such abstractions might be derived from the names of Miss Flite's birds). Dickens nowhere provides a statement of the meaning of this concept except by supplying a wide range of instances from which the concept may be inferred. Mrs. Jellyby (for example), Mrs. Pardiggle, Mr. Quale, and Mr. Chadband demonstrate various specious modes of the principal Christian virtue, and Captain Hawdon, Mr. Snagsby, Mr. Jarndyce, and Esther provide glimpses of the genuine article. None of these characters, and none of the acts by which they reveal their nature can be said to *stand for* the general idea, charity; collectively they *are* charity, which is thus defined by representing, on as ample a scale as possible, its denotation. So with the whole spectrum of moral ideas and human relations in *Bleak House;* Dickens offers his main commentary, not by names or labels, certainly not by analysis, and not even by symbolic analogues (though he uses them). His principal technique is the multiplication of instances. To say that in a novel which is as richly and palpably symbolic as *Bleak House* symbolism is unimportant would be absurd, and I have no intention of going so far. I wish only to direct attention toward a narrative method which seems to me to have been strangely neglected by comparison with the symbolism which has proved so fruitful of insight.

At any rate, I think Esther is vindicated as narrator. The narrative design of the novel really requires only two qualities of her, both of which she exemplifies perfectly. In the first place, she should be as transparent as glass. The complex sensibility which is a characteristic feature of the Jamesian observer would be in Esther not simply no advantage, it would interfere with the plain and limpid narration she is charged with. We must never be allowed to feel that the impressions of characters and events which we derive from her are significantly colored by her own personality, that the light from them (to revert to my optical figure) is diffracted by anything in her so as to distort the image she projects. One partial exception to this generalization implies the second of the two characteristics I have imputed to her. In the second place, then, we require of Esther sufficient integrity, in a literal sense, to draw together the manifold observations she sets down. The most complex and elaborate act of synthesis is reserved for the reader, but to Esther falls the important choric function of suggesting the lines along which that synthesis should take place by drawing her observations together under a simple, traditional, and predictable system of moral values. If Esther occasionally strikes us as a little goody-goody, we must recall her function to provide a sane and wholesome standard of morality in a topsy-turvy world.

No critic, surely, can remain unimpressed by the richness of *Bleak House*, a quality which is both admirable in itself and characteristically Dickensian. But the quality which raises the novel to a class by itself among Dickens's works is its integrity, a product of the perfect harmony of structure and idea. Edmund Wilson located the peculiar achievement of *Bleak House* in its establishment of a new literary form, "the detective story which is also a social fable," but he provided no real insight into the method by which these radically unlike forms were made to coalesce. The secret, I believe, is partly in that instinctive and unfathomable resourcefulness of the artist, which enables him to convert his liabilities into assets, to make, for example, out of such an unpromising figure as Esther Summerson, just the right point of view character for the first-person portion of the novel. But the real greatness of *Bleak House* lies in the happy accident of Dickens's hitting upon a structural form (the mystery story) and a system of symbols (Chancery) which could hold, for once, the richness of the Dickensian matter without allowing characters and incidents to distract the reader from the total design. The mysterious and sensational elements of the plot are not superimposed on the social fable; they are part of its substance. The slow but relentless disclosure of the web of human relations which constitutes the novel's inner form makes a superb mystery, but what makes it a monumental artistic achievement is that it is also and simultaneously one of the most powerful indictments of a heartless and irresponsible society ever written. *Bleak House* is the greatest of Dickens's novels because it represents the most fertile, as well as the most perfectly annealed, union of subject and technique he was ever to achieve.

‡ CHAPTER X ‡

Afterword

> Instead of a continuous, endless scene, in which
> the eye is caught in a thousand directions at
> once, with nothing to hold it to a fixed centre,
> the landscape that opens before the critic is
> whole and single; it has passed through an im-
> agination, it has shed its irrelevancy and is
> compact with its own meaning.
> —Percy Lubbock, *The Craft of Fiction*

Of all the questions which literary historians have pro-
pounded to themselves, the most difficult, and at the same time
the most fruitless, is probably "When did the novel begin?"
Nashe, Sidney, Mrs. Behn, Bunyan, Defoe, Richardson, Fielding, and even Addison and Steele have all found champions to
put forward their claims to having originated the English
novel, and it is still difficult, or impossible, to find any clearly
marked concurrence. The question is a bad one, not because
the experts fail to agree, but because all the answers are correct. The novel is the invention of critics (or of authors qua
critics), not of novelists, and insofar as the word "novel"
means anything it designates the critic's abstraction from existent literary works. Nevertheless, the author qua author must
have some notion of the kind of thing he is writing, and if

there is no clear-cut idea of outer form ready to his hand, he will have to borrow, perhaps unconsciously, from some existent genre. Defoe's elaborate pretense of manuscript sources is less a device to secure the reader's credence than it is a means of providing Defoe himself with a workable model of outer form. Until the novel came into its own more or less recognizable outer form novelists had to rely on external models, and the novel might be said to have begun afresh with each new production, or with each new set of models. Not until the middle of the nineteenth century could the novel be said to constitute a self-perpetuating tradition.

To talk about the history of the novel is to be led almost irresistibly into generalizations about outer form. My own interest, in the preceding chapters, has been less in outer form than in the relation of inner form to structure, but it may nevertheless be possible to adopt a historical perspective, even though inner form, being the product of a unique vision, resists generalization. Though it will be impossible to discuss, in the terms I have proposed, the origin and development of such an abstraction as "the novel," it may be possible and fruitful to talk about some characteristic likenesses and differences in the imaginative vision of the English novelists from Defoe to Dickens to establish their qualities of uniqueness, and beyond this, to say something of the growing complexity and sophistication of the structural forms developed to contain and display that imaginative vision.

From the point of view of outer form Defoe's novels are casual and amorphous. The autobiographical matrix is liberating rather than confining, for it frees Defoe from the necessity of constructing a plot; he can always appeal from the criterion of probability to that of actuality. But as soon as the reader feels that a novel is written the way it is because of its need to be faithful to external fact, he stops looking at it as a novel at all, that is, as a literary work with an intrinsic formal principle, and dismisses it as pseudo-autobiography. It is not really accurate, I think, to regard Defoe's novels as without form or structure, but the compelling form is implicit in the processes of Defoe's imagination, not in the outer or conventional form.

One characteristic which Defoe shares with other eighteenth-century novelists, and which indeed has often been taken to differentiate the eighteenth-century novel from earlier modes of prose fiction, is what Ian Watt refers to as the "minutely discriminated time-scale." [1] *Robinson Crusoe* gives us a minute-by-minute chronicle of events quite unlike the narrative method of, say, Sidney's *Arcadia*. One might generalize this difference by saying (as Watt in effect does) that the novel is distinguished from what is generally called the romance by being more detailed and particularized. The tendency to particularize, however, does not by itself yield a formal principle, and it is, moreover, too widespread a phenomenon to characterize Defoe alone. It should be asked, not how detailed a picture he gives, but what details he offers, and by implication which ones he regards as non-essential or unimportant. I have no intention of recapitulating my earlier discussion here, but it might be convenient to mention one or two leading principles which control Defoe's narrative texture. One explanation for the apparent randomness of the information Defoe thinks it necessary to include in a typical narrative specimen is that the very formlessness or artlessness of the narration guarantees its authenticity, but I have already suggested that I do not believe that the reader's credulity is a main objective; Defoe is not offering a literary equivalent of *trompe-l'oeil*. A closer look at nearly any of Defoe's novels reveals a more or less clear-cut pattern of selection and therefore a characteristic inner form.[2] I can best indicate the configuration of this pattern by suggesting that its center is the area of practical choice (why else should Defoe include, verbatim, three prospectuses for Moll Flanders's lying-in?) and that the degree of specificity immediately falls off when Defoe approaches the areas of moral choice, aesthetic response, or speculative thought.

In *Crusoe* Defoe found the specific subject matter which was most nearly consonant with the shape of his novelistic imagination, for Crusoe is removed effectively from the area of moral choice and confronted irresistibly with the necessity of continuous practical decision. *Moll Flanders*, though psychologically more interesting than *Crusoe* because of the dramatic tension between Moll's two selves, is perhaps less faithful to Defoe's vision as a novelist, and the scenes of self-recrimination and moral anguish are patently less convincing than the accounts of Moll's exploits as whore and thief, less because they are insincere, than because they lack solidity of specification. It would be wrong, however, to say that because there are areas of human experience that Defoe's vision cannot reach he is a failure as a novelist. It would not even be true to say that as a novelist he is immature; whatever his imagination is equal to is constituted, made real, with a vividness and power that Dickens himself could not surpass. Consider, for example, the Newgate scenes, or any of Moll's thieving forays in *Moll Flanders*. What does limit Defoe's artistic success, even within the confines of his special vision, is the lack of a viable outer form, of a convention that he could use.

Comparison between Defoe and Richardson immediately reveals some rather striking similarities, although this is not to argue either direct influence or a simple, linear course of development. Like Defoe's, Richardson's imagination is fine-grained, and the area of greatest specificity is that of practical choice, though there is once again an effort to disguise this fact by reference to specious moral issues. Pamela's moralizing is as tiresome (and ineffectual) as Moll's; what constitutes the vitality of both stories is the way in which the respective heroines confront exigent practical choices.

Nevertheless, in spite of apparent similarities, Richardson's vision is different from Defoe's, and the differences are even more important and suggestive than the similarities. While it may be said that the choice which confronts Pamela is a practical—as distinct from a moral—one, the nature of the choice is dictated by the social conditions of the world in which she lives, and those conditions are in turn a function of the novelist's imaginative vision. The world of Defoe's imagination is a projection of economic society, and the practical choices thrust upon his characters are dictated by economic necessities.[3] Crusoe's problem is the economic problem of human society reduced to its simplest and crudest form, but Moll Flanders, too, is haunted by the necessity of procuring enough to eat and a place to sleep. Richardson's characters are clearly beyond the need of such elemental sustenance, but the world they live in, a projection of the highly structured class society of the eighteenth century, also makes practical demands upon them, most importantly the achievement or maintenance of a clear-cut class identity and the strict observance of the forms of behavior without which a rigid class structure is unthinkable. If the center of Defoe's imaginative vision is occupied by human experience conceived as economic struggle, Richardson's is occupied by human experience conceived as social behavior. Try to imagine Pamela on a desert island.

The principal difference in the imaginative vision of Defoe and Richardson is typified by their handling of sex. Considering that he deals with sexual looseness and promiscuity in most of his novels, Defoe is singularly flat and unconvincing when he has to talk about sex, and will certainly prove a disappointment to those who purchase modern editions because of their lurid dust covers or suggestive illustrations. The reason is not that Defoe is excessively prudish, but that his interest as a novelist centers, so to speak, on the economics of sex—the monetary returns of prostitution or the cost of bearing and disposing of an illegitimate child. On the other hand, Richardson, whose novels enforce the most stringent code of sexual morality, is curiously detailed and pungent in his description of sexual encounters. He seems, in fact, to be obsessed with sex, but his obsession is naturally explicable, I believe, in terms of his interest in the proprieties of social behavior, which are most severely threatened by, at the same time that they most closely regulate, the sexual appetites. For neither one is the handling of sex consistent with the ostensible moral purpose of his work.

The real moralist among the early English novelists is Fielding. Unlike Defoe and Richardson he does not attempt to impose a moral lesson on a fragment of human experience which has been imagined in other terms; his imagination represents human experience as constituted by the necessity for difficult moral choices. Moll Flanders he could not have understood, for however much Moll may talk about conscience, it is clear that she hasn't any, and we cannot be moved by penitence which does not recognize the true nature of guilt. Moll's acknowledgment of lechery may in fact be a maneuver to conceal from herself her inability to love, and her confessed avarice may disguise her real venality. Pamela, we know, Fielding detested, either because her "virtue" was an out-and-out sham (the assumption of *Shamela*), or because she assigned to continence the importance that belonged to charity (the assumption of *Joseph Andrews*). In neither case could Fielding approach Richardson's novel on other than moral grounds, in which predilection, it must be observed, he is at one with most subsequent critics of *Pamela*.

In his own novels the moralizing tendency is unmistakable, but even more important, the moralizing tendency is inherent in Fielding's imaginative vision. *Joseph Andrews*, as I have already argued in more detail, is animated throughout, as well as given form, by Fielding's indignant response to Richardson's morality; even the most apparently autonomous elements of the book—like the quixotic Parson Adams—are conceived as offering the lie to Richardson's comfortable moral assumptions. But since *Joseph Andrews* is ostensibly a parody of *Pamela*, more interesting evidence is offered by the apparently self-sufficient *Tom Jones*. At first sight the picaresque saga of its sanguine hero is a story without a moral, in which indeed we take our most intense pleasure because the necessity of moral valuation is temporarily suspended, but such a judgment can survive only the most casual and superficial of readings. The very names of the characters—Allworthy, Thwackum, Square —suggest the possibility that the book is dealing in moral allegory, and even more conclusively the introduction of young Blifil makes it clear that Fielding is presenting a story not so much of interlocking destinies as of contrasting moral types. Tom Jones, in fact, is a kind of anti-Pamela, impulsive, warm-blooded, and generous, who is to be contrasted to the abstemious, but self-centered Blifil to the disadvantage of the latter. Tom's sins against prudence, thrift, continence, in a word against all the self-regarding virtues, serve chiefly to make clear the moral superiority of generosity and love. The essential conflict is no longer between individual desire and physical environment, as it was in *Crusoe*, or between individual desire and public opinion, as it was in *Pamela*, but between two contrasting moral ideals, one of which must be vindicated by trial. *Tom Jones* is as legitimate a descendant of *Pilgrim's Progress* as it is of *Gil Blas*.

But to argue that *Tom Jones* (or any other Fielding novel) is a moral allegory is to fly in the face of the tradition of Fielding's realism, so it might be prudent to offer some qualification. Insofar as it suggests giving names to moral abstractions, allegory is no doubt an inaccurate term, for Tom Jones is clearly as vivid and full-blooded a character as any of Defoe's or Richardson's, but it is still necessary to acknowledge in some way that the moral questions raised by Fielding's novel are somehow more immediate than they are in either Defoe's or

Richardson's works. Tom's moral qualities are not, that is to say, something which is added to him, but integral to Fielding's conception of him. It would be as well, however, to point out immediately that Fielding's realism is of another kind than either Defoe's or Richardson's. Realism, in the last-named novelist's work, is partly a matter of immediacy, of the spontaneity and power of the experience being rendered. We are made to feel, in reading *Pamela* or *Clarissa*, that we are confronting events as they happen. And in both Defoe and Richardson we are impressed by the apparent lack of selectivity in the recording consciousness, so that we are made to respond to their works, not as tales being told, but as life unfolding in its random and erratic way. Fielding's realism, on the other hand, is of a more conventional, literary type, which is never achieved by a surrender—not even an apparent surrender—of authorial control. It is a consequence of an accumulation of specific details which are both concrete and selective. Realism of the type of Defoe's or Richardson's, because it must be autonomous to exist at all, resists the kind of ordering which Fielding's imaginative vision automatically supplies. Fielding's realism, however, is perfectly consistent with, and indeed inseparable from, the necessity of seeing life as morally significant.

This difference in kinds of realism may, it is true, be thought of as entirely a matter of technique. The realistic effect I have attributed to Richardson is plainly to be related to his selection of a first person, epistolary point of view, which in turn derives from his selection of an appropriate literary model, the book of letters. Both Defoe and Richardson, however, are less concerned with the imitation of literary models than they are with the imitation of actuality, so that they evade the technical clichés of epic, romance, or drama. Fielding, on the contrary, characteristically writes his narratives from the outside (in which respect he differs from all the other major eighteenth-

century masters), frequently intrudes in his own person to
remind us that we are reading a work of literary artifice,
proudly lays claim to respectable literary antecedents, and ex-
uberantly laces his work with all the conventional devices he
can lay hands on—invocations, similes, peripeties, and so on.
Nevertheless, though the difference in kinds of realism that
I am here concerned to trace is manifested at the level of technique, I am bound by my earlier assumption to regard technique as a means to some more or less consciously selected end.
However skillful or unskillful he may be, however conscious
or unconscious his craftsmanship, the novelist uses technique
to give expression to his peculiar vision, and the technical differences between Fielding and his predecessors ultimately reflect the more fundamental difference, that he sees life as
morally ordered, and they do not.

The foregoing discussion will perhaps adequately illustrate
the comparative judgments which seem to me possible and
useful, so that I may be permitted, in what follows, a sharp
reduction in scale. My purpose here is not to summarize the
arguments of earlier chapters, but to suggest the kinds of conclusions which my critical assumptions and methods lead to.

By the middle of the eighteenth century the novel was sufficiently well established as an outer form that writers no longer
needed either to pretend that they were writing history, or to
seek out recondite pedigrees in order to establish the legitimacy
of the fictional form they were using. Experimentation was by
no means at an end, but writers could experiment within a
more or less clearly recognized convention, and no longer
needed to discover new outer forms to embody or contain
their imaginative vision. The two chief masters of the second
half of the century both extended the possibilities of the form.

Sterne's antinovel, *Tristram Shandy*, of course depends for
many of its effects on our instant recognition of the conventions it violates, and is thus a relatively sophisticated *jeu*

d'esprit. But it is much more than that at the same time, for Sterne is quite serious in his probing of the possible relations between the object and means of imitation. No other novelist of the century, surely, held such subtle or penetrating ideas on the powers and limitations of language. It might even be said that Sterne recognized language—viewed not as malleable and perfectly expressive, but as highly structured, bound by conventions and prejudices, wholly inadequate as an instrument of communication—as itself the inner form which determined the kinds of things he as a novelist could write about. His failure to enclose his vision of life within a clearly definable structural form is, I think, deliberate. *Tristram Shandy* illustrates the quality of "openness" which Robert Adams predicates of works containing "a major unresolved conflict," though whether Sterne's irresolution serves "to express a philosophy, to gain a perspective, or to fulfill the requirements of a style" remains in doubt.[4] Probably all three. Sterne's other "contributions"—the idea of fictional time and the technique of the stream of consciousness—seem to me less important; the former, in particular, is nothing more than a sly Shandean joke. Still, *Tristram Shandy* continues to serve as a storehouse of innovations and experiments which help to reveal the limits of the solidifying conventions of the novel.

Smollett, after an apprenticeship in the well-understood convention of the picaresque tale, broke new ground with *Humphry Clinker* by experimenting with a multiple point of view, a novelty which is less striking for the ironies it permits than for the perspective it gives to human experience as rendered by the novel. The method and its implications are subtle enough, and new enough, so that it is easy to miss the novel's formal center, as many of Smollett's commentators have, by seeking that center outside the novel altogether. They have paid attention, as Browning would say, to the ring metal, and not to the shape of the ring, for the crude fact is important in

Humphry Clinker chiefly for the light it can be made to throw on the characters themselves and the developing relations among them.

The beginning of the nineteenth century brought fundamental changes of direction to most literary currents in England, but curiously left untouched the tradition of the novel. Scott and Jane Austen are doubtless just what they would have been had the Preface to *Lyrical Ballads* not been written, and neither one gives any apparent indication of belonging to the same century as Byron, Delacroix, and Berlioz. As nearly all historians of the novel agree, they are much more closely related to Richardson and Fielding than they are to George Eliot or Conrad. Jane Austen is squarely in the tradition of Fielding, not, as Leavis seems to think, because she drew on him for techniques of plotting and construction, but because her imagination reveals the same strong moralizing tendency. Her novels appear intricately wrought, particularly when we think of the level of technical competence achieved by Defoe or Richardson, but her extraordinary craftsmanship is in the service of an imaginative vision which is startlingly simple and direct. I am not speaking of her so-called "narrowness," which has been made the target of some generally unconvincing attacks, but of the moral attributes of the world she has imagined for us. As complicated as her heroines often seem, as intricate as their adjustment often must be to the world they inhabit, they invariably remain faithful to the inner laws of their being, and these laws are surprisingly simple and uniform. Elizabeth and Emma, for all their cleverness, for all their quickness and subtlety of perception, are finally impelled to decisive action by qualities of character which undergo no real or significant change. Unlike Moll Flanders, Jane Austen's heroines are "inner-directed," which means, in effect, that they have their being in a world governed by a kind of moral determinism, according to which the characters—both good and bad—are predestined to find a means of expression for their moral natures. The richness and interest of this world reside in the complications which temporarily impede the operation of its inexorable laws.

Writers have never been noted for perceptive comments about their own work, but I think few judgments are so wholly mistaken as Scott's characterization of his own style in the well-known journal entry on Jane Austen: "The Big Bow-wow strain I can do myself like any now going; but the exquisite touch, which renders ordinary commonplace things and characters interesting, from the truth of the description and the sentiment, is denied to me." [5] Though his novels differ widely and in many respects from Jane Austen's, his imagination is as fine-grained as her own, and no phrase could miss the texture of his prose more widely than "the Big Bow-wow strain." Scott's main concern is with the way in which private experience is embedded in public events, both because the juxtaposition affords a unique perspective on public places, characters, and events (in which respect he resembles Smollett), and because (as David Daiches has rightly shown) it engenders a thematic contrast between the romantic past and the prosaic present. But Scott develops his typical contrasts—to which the story conflicts are often secondary—not with the broad brushstrokes that "the Big Bow-wow strain" implies, but with the endless minutiae of the patient antiquarian. These remarks, it need hardly be said, apply only, or pre-eminently, to the Scottish novels, which represent the crown of Scott's achievement, and which seem to me to deserve more serious critical attention than they have been getting.

The two principal novelists of the mid-century, Thackeray and Dickens, display a somewhat belated romanticism—or what might be interpreted as a revival of Richardsonian sentimentality—but in most respects they are content to follow where their predecessors led, without significant technical innovations. They are, however, widely different from their predecessors and from each other in the qualities of their imaginative vision. Thackeray's interests often run close to Scott's, but where Scott seeks to magnify public events by comparing them with private, Thackeray brings everything down to a common level of cynical sentimentality, in which the cynicism may be suspect, but the sentimentality is real enough. "I would have history familiar rather than heroic," he announces at the beginning of *Esmond*. No one can see more clearly the lurking meannesses in most "heroic" characters, but Thackeray's clairvoyance in this respect is achieved at the cost of being morbidly suspicious of authentic heroism when he encounters it. Ironically, he is easily deceived by cant of selflessness and devotion; he can see through Marlborough, but not Helen Pendennis, and he is wrong about both. He has a breadth of vision which makes him extraordinarily sensitive to the ironies of civilized life, and which is engaged most fully and effectively in his masterpiece, *Vanity Fair*, but in spite of the historical format of most of his novels he has no really imaginative grasp of history. If Arnold's line, "Not deep the poet sees, but wide," has any relevance for the novelist, it admirably describes Thackeray's strength—and his limitations.

Dickens is a much more commanding figure and deserves to stand as the culminating point in the first phase of the novel's development. His own long career serves as a recapitulation of the English novel's first hundred years. In *Pickwick Papers* we can watch the author of *Sketches by Boz* seize the idea of a novel, as distinct from a series of vignettes, and even more to the point, we can observe the products of the shaping vision tumbling out without any structural form prepared to receive them, so that Dickens is constrained to invent one as he goes along. The result may not be entirely satisfying artistically, but to the student of the novel it is engrossing. Here is the stuff of Dickens's creative imagination, unconstrained and unmodified by the artificial patterns he was later to impose on it, but already bearing unmistakably the unique lineaments, the inner form, of his own vision.

Whether or not Dickens began *Pickwick* with Seymour's plates before him, there can be no doubt of the pre-eminently visual quality of his imagination, a quality which induces realism, but a realism different from either Richardson's or Fielding's. There is nothing literary or derivative in the scenes Dickens offers us (in spite of the fact that such scenes were more or less commonplace in the era of Surtees), but neither do they depend for their effect on the psychological immediacy that Richardson relied on. On the contrary, Dickens seems to insist on a certain amount of distance, precisely as though he were afraid the audience might confuse his creatures with real people, and we observe the spectacle he offers as though in a mirror, sometimes, perhaps, a distorting mirror. Readers often dismiss Dickens's creations as caricatures, and there is an element of truth in the indictment, though we ought certainly to preserve the distinction between deliberate distortion of reality as a kind of mannerism, and the eccentricities of the genuinely original artist (like El Greco or Modigliani) who distorts because that is the way he sees. Dickens's "realism" is a question of his constituting power; he does not fashion a world like the real one, but his world is made real by its own inner coherence as well as by its almost surrealistic vividness and clarity.

Dickens shares with Richardson the disposition to see life as social activity, but he is less concerned with the problems of social mobility than he is with the individual's relation to the concentric circles of social organizations he must inhabit in an urban and industrial world. In *Pickwick* Dickens suddenly speaks with new authority and dignity when Mr. Pickwick's allegiance to the Pickwick Club is transcended and superseded by an allegiance to society at large which he is first made conscious of in the Fleet Prison. Dickens could be called a moralist, but no abstract system holds his allegiance, and unlike Fielding and Jane Austen he does not view life as the dialectic of good and evil, as a moral process. Life is organized for him, in fact, not temporally, as a cause and effect sequence, but spatially, as an intricate set of potential and actual human relations, ruled ideally by human benevolence. From *Pickwick* to *Our Mutual Friend* and *Edwin Drood*, Dickens matured in craftsmanship and structural skill, but his imaginative vision did not change its essential character; it merely grew darker and more intense.

With Dickens's arrival at maturity a new chapter in the history of the English novel begins. The novel enters what might be called its classical period; the writer no longer has to improvise his outer form or to apologize for not writing biography or history or travelogue. He can adopt the fictive premise with confidence that his reader will share it, and he has a richly varied tradition to draw on. Henry James declared that the only legitimate expectation one can bring to a novel is that it be "interesting," [6] which is to deny all prescriptive notions of form, and it is certain that the outer form of the novel has never become rigidly fixed. But this looseness of form is only relative. Though the structural possibilities of the novel seem inexhaustible compared with those of (for example) neoclassic verse, most novels in fact belong to one of a limited number of easily recognizable formal types, and even the most consciously eccentric novel, like *Tristram Shandy*, owes its value and effect to the existence of a tradition which if not prescriptive is nevertheless authoritative. The tradition of any art form is both confining and liberating, and no doubt the absence—or simply the meagerness—of a tradition has both advantages and disadvantages. Among its disadvantages might be reckoned the expenditure of creative energy to devise an appropriate outer form to receive the matter. On the other hand, the writer who must invent or improvise his own outer form is less likely to betray his vision by stuffing it into a prefabricated mold; the inner form of what he has to say will be displayed with greater vigor, freshness, and spontaneity. It has always seemed to me, in fact, that the English novel before 1850 offers a unique opportunity for studying, not, perhaps, the *art* of the novel, but the creative imagination itself as it shapes the materials of art.

Notes

Chapter I: Vision and Form

1. F. R. Leavis, *The Great Tradition* (Garden City, N.Y., 1954). "All that need be said about [Defoe] as a novelist was said by Leslie Stephen" (p. 10, n.); "It's no use pretending that Richardson can ever be made a current classic again" (p. 13); "[Fielding] is important . . . because he leads to Jane Austen, to appreciate whose distinction is to feel that life isn't long enough to permit of one's giving much time to Fielding" (p. 12). Leavis dismisses Sterne's work as "irresponsible (and nasty) trifling" (p. 11, n.). I cannot find that he mentions Smollett at all. Leavis regards Scott's influence as pernicious because it "imposed on the novelist a romantic resolution of his themes" (p. 41); and he firmly repudiates Thackeray's pretensions by reversing a cliché: "Thackeray is a greater Trollope" (p. 34). He does, however, grant distinction to Emily Brontë's *Wuthering Heights* (1847), though by calling the novel a "sport" he implies that it lies outside of any pre-existing tradition and that its greatness is therefore in defiance of ordinary expectation (p. 41).

2. Wayne Booth, in *The Rhetoric of Fiction* (Chicago, 1961), is similarly concerned with the limiting effects on criticism of certain modern critical dogmas about novel form. He seeks, for example, to cast doubt on such truisms as that showing is necessarily superior to telling, or that art ought to be pure (that is, innocent of rhetoric). This may be the place to acknowledge the considerable help I have received from Booth's pioneering study, though that help has been rather indirect and general, because we are interested in the problems of literary form for different ends. He looks at form as a reflection of the rhetorical necessity of communicating with an audience; I look at form as an expression of the imaginative processes of the artist. Still, I am indebted to Booth's work in many ways that will never, or rarely, find acknowledgment in footnotes.

3. Dorothy Van Ghent's treatment of *Moll Flanders* in *The English Novel: Form and Function* (New York, 1959) provides an example of the danger of approaching a relatively primitive work of art with a highly sophisticated set of critical values. She says: "Either *Moll Flanders* is a collection of scandal-sheet anecdotes naïvely patched together with the platitudes that form the morality of an impoverished soul (Defoe's), a 'sincere' soul but a confused and degraded one; or *Moll Flanders* is a great novel, coherent in structure, unified and given its shape and significance by a complex system of ironies" (p. 42). This permits the demonstration to proceed something like this: *Moll Flanders* is obviously *not* a collection of scandal-sheet anecdotes, etc. Therefore it is a great novel . . . unified . . . coherent . . . complex. Q.E.D. The difficulty, of course, is that such conclusions are not to be reached deductively, and (more important for my present purpose) that the major premise does not acknowledge the possibility of other literary values or other modes of coherence than the ones it specifies.

4. I shall have more to say about this bewildering variety in Chapter VI.

5. Frederick Lawrence, *The Life of Henry Fielding* (London, 1855), p. 160; Lord David Cecil, *Jane Austen* (The Leslie Stephen Lecture; Cambridge, 1935), p. 19; Wayne C. Booth, "Did Sterne Complete *Tristram Shandy?*," *Modern Philology*, XLVIII (1951), 172–83.

6. Martin Battestin, *The Moral Basis of Fielding's Art: A Study of "Joseph Andrews"* (Middletown, Conn., 1959); John Butt and Kathleen Tillotson, "The Topicality of *Bleak House*," *Dickens at Work* (London, 1957), pp. 177–200.

7. T. S. Eliot, "Tradition and the Individual Talent," *Selected Essays* (New York, 1950), pp. 3–11. Eliot is of course relatively unconcerned with distinctions of genre, and would therefore seem to offer little help in approaching the concept of outer form, but in his attention to the complex relations between the individual work and the tradition which in a sense "contains" it, he does deal with those external relations of the work of art which collectively determine its outer form.

8. I use these terms in the sense given them by Northrop Frye, *The Anatomy of Criticism* (Princeton, 1957), pp. 52–53.

9. I am aware that organic or holistic theories of literature do more than acknowledge the inseparability of form and matter; they insist on it. See, for example, Cleanth Brooks's essay, "The Formalist Critic," *The Modern Critical Spectrum*, ed. Gerald J. Goldberg and Nancy M. Goldberg (Englewood Cliffs, N.J., 1962), p. 1. My own conception is not really holistic, however, for I do not maintain that the whole is greater than the parts. If one wants to call my position "organic," I have no objection, but as I shall shortly explain, I prefer to draw my

key metaphor from chemistry rather than from biology. In any case I am less interested in the relation of form and matter than I am in the nature of form and the ways in which we apprehend it, and here I have little in common with the New Critics.

10. Ian Watt, *The Rise of the Novel* (Berkeley and Los Angeles, 1957), pp. 9–34.

11. Frye, p. 77.

12. Donald Francis Tovey, "Sonata Forms," *The Forms of Music* (New York, 1959), pp. 208–32.

13. *The Arabian Nights' Entertainment,* trans. Edward W. Lane (New York, n.d.), I, 62.

14. Samuel Taylor Coleridge, *Table Talk,* May 31, 1830, *The Complete Works,* ed. W. G. T. Shedd (New York, 1853), VI, 324. Humphry House takes issue with Coleridge on the question of whether the tale contains a moral. Although he concedes that there is no "detachable maxim," he concludes that "one cannot possibly read the story without being very aware of moral issues in it" (*Coleridge: The Clark Lectures* [London, 1953], p. 91). I wonder whether the moral issues are in fact "in it," or whether they are supplied by the reader.

15. *The Novels of Jane Austen,* ed. R. W. Chapman (Oxford, 1923), II, 3–4.

Chapter II: The Two Heroines of *Moll Flanders*

1. Shakespeare Head Edition; Oxford, 1927. All references are to this edition, except as noted.

2. "Defoe had such an uncanny way of getting inside the skin of the people he was imagining himself to be, that one asks whether, while writing, he ever stopped to consider at all, or ever thought in terms of 'presenting' anything or anyone" (Bonamy Dobrée, "Some Aspects of Defoe's Prose," *Pope and His Contemporaries: Essays Presented to George Sherburn,* ed. James L. Clifford and Louis A. Landa [Oxford, 1949], p. 175).

3. Defoe declares that as editor he has had to temper the vulgarity and coarseness of Moll's language, but I can only account for this statement by assuming that it is one of those rare lapses in Defoe's imaginative sympathy with Moll. She is capable of almost any enormity of conduct but I cannot believe that she would ever abandon propriety of language.

4. Dorothy Van Ghent notes the absence of sensuousness in the language, but argues that Moll's nature is nonetheless a strongly sensual one, and that the discrepancy functions as one of the novel's structural

ironies (*The English Novel: Form and Function* [New York, 1959],
pp. 35–36).

5. *Moll Flanders* ("The World's Classics"; London, 1961), p. 67.
The phrase was deleted from the second and subsequent editions (The
Shakespeare Head text follows the third edition) and is to be found
only in those modern reprints which are based on the first edition.

6. Ian Watt has remarked that many of the characters seem more
devoted to Moll than a purely objective appraisal of her character
warrants, a fact which he interprets as evidence of a "paranoid delusion" on Moll's part (*The Rise of the Novel* [Berkeley and Los Angeles, 1957], p. 112).

7. H. L. Koonce advances the interesting hypothesis that the incongruity between Moll's actions and her moral principles is to be
taken as "the consistent, lifelike muddle of a woman with a powerful,
unmotivated sense of manifest destiny which she is in the act of re-
conciling with an equally powerful, if conveniently underdeveloped,
sense of morality" ("Moll's Muddle: Defoe's Use of Irony in *Moll
Flanders*," *ELH*, XXX [1963], 380). The point at which I must dis-
agree is in the assumption that Moll's moral sentiments are genuine.

8. It will not do to say that Moll's self-contempt is consistent with
her presumed motive in writing her account—to expose her own conduct to opprobrium—because her moral valuations are usually made
at the time, not in retrospect (see Watt, pp. 116–17). In any case
Moll's "repentence" is suspect, if only because she makes no sacrifice
for it. The truth is that Moll undergoes no real change at all.

9. "Whatever disagreement there may be about particular instances,
it is surely certain that there is no consistently ironical attitude present in *Moll Flanders*. Irony in its extended sense expresses a deep
awareness of the contradictions and incongruities that beset man in
this vale of tears, an awareness which is manifested in the text's pur-
poseful susceptibility to contradictory interpretations. . . . It is, as we
have seen, very unlikely that Defoe wrote in this way" (Watt, p. 126).

10. Mark Schorer, Introduction to the Modern Library edition of
Moll Flanders (New York, 1950), p. xiii.

11. I doubt whether this ambiguity will lend any support to Watt's
contention that "the essence of her character and actions is . . . masculine" (p. 113). In view of her lack of tenderness, Moll cannot very
well be called *womanly*, but in her practical common sense, in her
placing of expedience above principle, and in her unself-conscious
vanity she seems to me quintessentially *feminine*.

12. Robert Alter argues that Moll is too unimaginative and literal-
minded to be comfortable in any disguise (*Rogue's Progress* [Cam-
bridge, Mass., 1964], p. 42). Disguise certainly may (and in the present

instance actually does) threaten Moll's sense of self. What I do not think Alter reckons with is the zest with which Moll nevertheless enters into her impersonations. I shall take up immediately what seems to me the most convincing evidence.

Chapter III: The Problem of Pamela

1. Aaron Hill, *Works* (1753), II 240–41.
2. The most recent account of the anti-Pamela literature is Bernard Kreissman's *Pamela-Shamela* (Lincoln, Neb., 1960). Kreissman carries the story down to 1950 with Upton Sinclair's *Another Pamela; or Virtue Still Rewarded.* Still authoritative is Alan D. McKillop's *Samuel Richardson* (Chapel Hill, 1936). See the long first chapter, "The Story of *Pamela.*"
3. J. W. Krutch, *Five Masters* (New York, 1930), p. 131.
4. B. L. Reid, "Justice to *Pamela,*" *Hudson Review,* IX (1956–57), 527–28.
5. *An Apology for the Life of Mrs. Shamela Andrews,* ed. Sheridan Baker, Jr. (Berkeley and Los Angeles, 1953), p. 53.
6. W. M. Sale, Jr., "From *Pamela* to *Clarissa,*" *The Age of Johnson: Essays Presented to Chauncey Brewster Tinker* (New Haven, 1949), pp. 127–38.
7. W. Allen, *The English Novel* (London [1954]), p. 41.
8. For the effect of the epistolary method see A. D. McKillop, "Epistolary Technique in Richardson's Novels," *Rice Institute Pamphlet,* XXXVIII (April 1951), 36–54. For the effects of Richardson's "minutely discriminated time-scale" see Ian Watt, *The Rise of the Novel* (Berkeley and Los Angeles, 1957), particularly the chapters entitled "Realism and the Novel Form" and "Private Experience and the Novel."
9. *Pamela* (Shakespeare Head Edition; Oxford, 1929), I, 6–7. All references are to this edition.
10. See, for example, Clara L. Thompson, *Samuel Richardson* (London, 1900), p. 162. Also Watt, p. 149.
11. The full title was *Letters Written to and for Particular Friends on the Most Important Occasions, Directing Not Only the Requisite Style and Forms to be Observed in Writing Familiar Letters; but How to Think and Act Justly and Prudently, in the Common Concerns of Human Life* (ed. Brian Downs [London, 1928]).

Chapter IV: *Joseph Andrews* as Parody

1. Irvin Ehrenpreis, "Fielding's Use of Fiction: The Autonomy of *Joseph Andrews*," *Twelve Original Essays on Great English Novels*, ed. Charles Shapiro (Detroit, 1960), pp. 23–41.

2. This view of the novel has been so often repeated that I shall not attempt to record all the statements of it. The earliest formulation I have found is by Frederick Lawrence: "It is very evident that, as Fielding proceeded, he thought less of his original design, as he became more attached to those excellent beings whom his fancy had called into existence—good Parson Adams, honest Joseph Andrews, and beautiful, tender-hearted Fanny. As it has been said of Cervantes, so it may be said of his English follower, that he came 'at last to love the creations of his marvellous power, as if they were real familiar personages'; and if at the outset he thought only of ridiculing Richardson, and throwing in a sly sarcasm at Cibber, as he advanced in his narrative he ceased to think of those personages or their works" (*The Life of Henry Fielding* [London, 1855], p. 160). That this view, or one very like it, is still current is suggested by Ehrenpreis and by Maurice Johnson in *Fielding's Art of Fiction* (Philadelphia, 1961), pp. 47–48. Martin Battestin, on the other hand, takes a quite different position, but one equally removed from my own. He argues, in his introduction to the Riverside edition of *Joseph Andrews and Shamela*, that Fielding did not change his mind, but that parody was never a significant part of his intention (*Joseph Andrews and Shamela*, ed. Martin Battestin [Boston, 1961], p. xviii).

3. "Ce qui est irritant et parfois exaspérant, ce n'est point l'héroïne, mais c'est l'admiration béate de l'auteur pour elle" (Aurélien Digeon, *Les Romans de Fielding* [Paris, 1923], p. 71). And later: "On le sent clairement en lisant Fielding, c'est contre l'état d'esprit de l'auteur, contre son affectation constante de vertu qu'il s'insurge, beaucoup plus que contre le roman lui-même" (Digeon, p. 72).

4. *An Apology for the Life of Mrs. Shamela Andrews* (Augustan Reprint Society Publication No. 57; Los Angeles, 1956), p. 16.

5. Dick Taylor, Jr., argues that Joseph is the real hero of the novel, but he seems to me to press the point too hard. Joseph undoubtedly becomes much more than the pasteboard simulacrum of his sister he seems at the beginning, but it is Adams who is not only the center of interest, but also, according to the view advanced here, the thematic center of the novel ("Joseph as Hero in *Joseph Andrews*," *Tulane Studies in English*, VII [1957], 91–109).

6. *The History of the Adventures of Joseph Andrews* (Shakespeare Head Edition; Oxford, 1926), Bk. I, ch. 8. All quotations follow the text of this edition.

7. This highly significant shift of tone was noticed and explained by Digeon, p. 73.

8. See, for example, Wilbur L. Cross, *The History of Henry Fielding* (New Haven, 1918), I, 322–24.

9. The dualism of Abraham Adams's nature is implicit, of course, in his name, which combines connotations of patriarch and *ingénu* (Johnson, p. 81).

10. *Pamela or, Virtue Rewarded* (Shakespeare Head Edition; Oxford, 1929), I, 235–36.

11. I. B. Cauthen, Jr., accounts for the four principal "digressions" in very much these terms ("Fielding's Digressions in *Joseph Andrews*," *College English*, XVII [1956], 372–82).

12. It is true, of course, that at the end of the novel Adams is presented by Mr. Booby with a living of the value of one hundred thirty pounds per annum, but as I shall presently attempt to demonstrate, the distribution of rewards in the final chapter must be taken as ironic.

13. Mark Spilka finds a deeper significance in this chapter of accidents ("Comic Resolution in Fielding's 'Joseph Andrews,'" *College English*, XV [1953], 11–19).

14. "En Fanny sa fiancée Fielding a peut-être déjà voulu opposer à la fausse ingénue Pamela la peinture d'une jeune fille authentiquement chaste. . . . C'est une belle campagnarde bien en chair, qui aime assez goulûment son Joseph. Elle ignore les raffinements de Pamela et ses 'vapeurs d'honneur'" (Digeon, p. 77).

15. "The denouement . . . is in gay imitation of a common type of the drama known since Aristotle's time as that of 'discovery and revolution'" (Cross, I, 319. Cf. Ehrenpreis, p. 35).

16. Ehrenpreis, pp. 35–36.

17. See especially James A. Work,"Henry Fielding, Christian Censor," *The Age of Johnson: Essays Presented to Chauncey Brewster Tinker* (New Haven, 1949), pp. 139–48; and George Sherburn, "Fielding's Social Outlook," *Philological Quarterly*, XXXV (1956), 1–23. The most specific and exhaustive account of the moral assumptions of *Joseph Andrews* is in Martin Battestin, *The Moral Basis of Fielding's Art: A Study of "Joseph Andrews"* (Middletown, Conn., 1959).

Chapter V: Sterne and the Logos

1. As Work points out, Sterne even plagiarizes Burton in the process of inveighing against plagiarism (*The Life and Opinions of Tristram Shandy, Gentleman*, ed. James A. Work [New York, 1940], V, 1, n.). All quotations from *Tristram Shandy* follow the text of this edition (though I have dropped the italics which Sterne regularly uses for proper names). The literature on *Tristram Shandy* is so rich

that my notes can acknowledge only a small part of my debt to other writers. I should like to record my appreciation of several essays which I have found illuminating, but which, so far as I am aware, I have not followed on any specific points: W. C. B. Watkins, "Yorick Revisited," *Perilous Balance* (Princeton, 1939), pp. 99–156; Rufus D. S. Putney, "Laurence Sterne, Apostle of Laughter," *The Age of Johnson: Essays Presented to Chauncey Brewster Tinker* (New Haven, 1949), pp. 159–70; Alan D. McKillop, "The Reinterpretation of Laurence Sterne," *Etudes Anglaises*, VII (1954), 36–47; A. E. Dyson, "Sterne: The Novelist as Jester" *Critical Quarterly*, IV (1962), 309–20.

2. J. M. Stedmond finds that Sterne's "coinages are mainly playful, they are never exploratory thrusts into the unknown" ("Style and *Tristram Shandy*," *Modern Language Quarterly*, XX [1959], 248).

3. That language, or an attitude toward language, is at the center of the novel is a common enough idea. It is the fundamental assumption of John Traugott's study, *Tristram Shandy's World: Sterne's Philosophic Rhetoric* (Berkeley and Los Angeles, 1954), though Traugott is concerned primarily with language as *rhetoric* (that is, as involving the reader in a process of persuasion). Much closer to my own view is the position taken by Sigurd Burckhardt in a splendid Shandean essay which concludes that the novel is itself "a universe of language which reveals the nature of its medium by that medium's motions" ("*Tristram Shandy's* Law of Gravity," *ELH*, XXVIII [1961], 87).

4. *Gargantua and Pantagruel*, trans. Urquhart and Le Motteux (London, 1900), Bk. I, ch. 14.

5. Of course no one who believes that *Tristram Shandy* has any sort of coherent organization will regard the progression as really erratic. The point is ably argued by William B. Piper ("Tristram Shandy's Digressive Artistry," *Studies in English Literature*, I [1961], 65–76).

6. See Wayne C. Booth, "Did Sterne Complete *Tristram Shandy?*," *Modern Philology*, XLVIII (1951), 172–83.

7. A useful chronology is provided by Theodore Baird, "The Time Scheme of *Tristram Shandy* and a Source," *PMLA*, LI (1936), 803–20.

8. Melvin Friedman claims Sterne as a significant predecessor of Joyce (*Stream of Consciousness: A Study in Literary Method* [New Haven, 1955], pp. 28–31).

Chapter VI: *Humphry Clinker* and the Novelist's Imagination

1. The only clear exception I am aware of is supplied by Sheridan Baker, "*Humphry Clinker* as Comic Romance," *Papers of the Michigan Academy of Science, Arts, and Letters*, XLVI (1961), 645–54.

2. Not of course original in itself, for Smollett followed the example of Christopher Anstey's *New Bath Guide* (1766), a series of humorous letters in verse, but Smollett's use of the device in the novel, for reasons that I hope to make clear, is far more flexible and subtle than Anstey's.

3. *The Expedition of Humphry Clinker* (Shakespeare Head Edition; Oxford, 1925), I, 7. All references are to this edition.

4. For an account of some of Mr. Bramble's antecedents in this tradition, see Thomas R. Preston, "Smollett and the Benevolent Misanthrope Type," *PMLA*, LXXIX (1964), 51–57.

5. *The Works of Tobias Smollett*, ed. George Saintsbury (London and Philadelphia, 1903), XI, xiii.

6. Horace Walpole referred to *Humphry Clinker* as "a party novel, written by the profligate hireling Smollett, to vindicate the Scots and cry down juries" (*Memoirs of the Reign of King George the Third* [London, 1894], IV, 218). Martz's thesis is that *Humphry Clinker* grew out of an essentially polemic impulse, to correct and strengthen the pro-Scottish, anti-English bias of *The Present State of All Nations* (*The Later Career of Tobias Smollett* [New Haven, 1942], pp. 124–93).

7. Milton A. Goldberg, *Smollett and the Scottish School* (Albuquerque, 1959), pp. 143–81.

8. William Hazlitt, "Lectures on the English Comic Writers," *The Collected Works of William Hazlitt*, ed. A. R. Waller and Arnold Glover (London, 1902–1906), VIII, 117; Saintsbury, XI, viii.

Chapter VII: *Mansfield Park* and Jane Austen's Moral Universe

1. Barbara Bail Collins does in fact regard *Mansfield Park* as a Victorian sport, blooming before its time ("Jane Austen's Victorian Novel," *Nineteenth-Century Fiction*, IV [1949], 175–85).

2. Marvin Mudrick defines the atypical quality of *Mansfield Park* by arguing the failure of the ironic vision that shapes the other novels ("The Triumph of Gentility: *Mansfield Park*," *Jane Austen: Irony as Defense and Discovery* [Princeton, 1952], pp. 155–80). Lionel Trilling regards *Mansfield Park* as offering a necessary antithesis to the view of human personality central to *Pride and Prejudice* ("*Mansfield Park*," *The Opposing Self* [New York, 1955], pp. 206–30).

3. Of the many who have done so, one of the most vigorous and eloquent is Reginald Farrer, who calls her "the most persistently brilliant of Jane Austen's heroines." His opinion of Fanny is correspond-

ingly low ("Jane Austen," *Quarterly Review*, CCXXVIII [1917], 1–
30). For a concurring view, see Kingsley Amis, "What Became of
Jane Austen?" *Spectator*, CXCIX (1957), 439–40.

4. *Mansfield Park*, ch. 47. Quotations will follow the text of R. W.
Chapman's edition, *The Novels of Jane Austen* (Oxford, 1923), but
will be identified parenthetically by reference to the chapter number
in modern one-volume editions.

5. I am not going to suggest that authorial comment is inadmissible
or inartistic. My intention is to dispose of what I consider specious
judgments about Jane Austen's use of commentary and to establish
what I take to be the real (and valid) use of that commentary. Wayne
Booth's discussion of the general question of the author's voice in
fiction is relevant and illuminating (*The Rhetoric of Fiction* [Chicago,
1961]).

6. Joseph M. Duffy, Jr., "Moral Integrity and Moral Anarchy in
Mansfield Park," ELH, XXIII (1956), 71–91.

7. *The Novels of Jane Austen*, ed. Chapman, V, 8.

8. D. W. Harding, "Regulated Hatred: An Aspect of the Work of
Jane Austen," *Scrutiny*, VIII (1940), 346–62.

9. See especially Edd Winfield Parks, "Exegesis in Austen's Works,"
South Atlantic Quarterly, LI (1952), 103–19.

10. Mrs. Leavis accounts for the second-hand quality of the novel
by its presumed origin in an epistolary form: "The dimmed and distant
effect of much of this novel, the impression it gives of low spirits in
its presentation, is due, I suggest, to its being retold from letters. A
good deal of *Mansfield Park* reads like paraphrases of letters, and,
once the action is launched with the young people grown up, a very
great deal actually is letters or summaries of these, and bridge passages
between letters or summaries of letters" (Q. D. Leavis, "A Critical
Theory of Jane Austen's Writings [II] 'Lady Susan' into 'Mansfield
Park,' " *Scrutiny*, X [1941], 122).

11. Lord David Cecil, *Jane Austen* (The Leslie Stephen Lecture;
Cambridge, 1935), p. 19.

12. This suggestion was strikingly anticipated a generation ago by
Edwin Muir. Speaking of *Pride and Prejudice*, he says, "The action is
created . . . by those characters who remain true to themselves; it is
their constancy which, like a law of necessity, sets the events moving"
(*The Structure of the Novel* [London, 1928], p. 45).

13. Charles Murrah offers the most systematic discussion of the setting ("The Background of *Mansfield Park*," *From Jane Austen to
Joseph Conrad*, ed. R. C. Rathburn and M. Steinmann, Jr. [Minne-
apolis, 1958], pp. 23–34).

14. Duffy, p. 73.

Chapter VIII: *Redgauntlet, Henry Esmond,* and the Modes of Historical Fiction

1. Georg Lukács, in his monumental treatise on the historical novel, maintains exactly the contrary, but it must be remembered that in a discussion controlled by Marxist assumptions *epic* means a work which reflects the class struggle, or the dialectic of quite impersonal historic forces, and by no means requires a hero of "epic" stature (*The Historical Novel,* trans. H. and S. Mitchell [Boston, 1963], p. 35).

2. *Redgauntlet,* ed. Andrew Lang (Border Edition; London, 1894), I, 3–4. All references are to this edition.

3. My account of Daiches's position is based on three sources: Introduction to the Rinehart Edition, *The Heart of Midlothian* (New York, 1948), pp. v–xxii; "Scott's Achievement as a Novelist," *Nineteenth-Century Fiction,* VI (1951), 81–95, 153–73, reprinted in *Literary Essays* (Edinburgh, 1956), pp. 88–121; "Scott's *Redgauntlet,*" *From Jane Austen to Joseph Conrad,* ed. R. C. Rathburn and M. Steinmann, Jr. (Minneapolis, 1958), pp. 46–59.

4. Daiches offers this date somewhat tentatively, and commentators are by no means in agreement. Andrew Lang says "about 1767" (I, xix); D. D. Devlin puts the action in 1763 or 1764 ("Scott and *Redgauntlet,*" *Review of English Studies,* IV, i [1963], 92); and Alexander Welsh says 1770 (*The Hero of the Waverley Novels* [New Haven, 1963], p. 70). I think the date can be established on internal evidence with reasonable precision. Darsie Latimer, who is just twenty-one as the novel opens, is the elder of two children born to a father executed in 1746. Since he could not have been born later than 1745, the latest possible date of the action is 1766, but this is also the earliest possible date, because Charles Edward Stuart is addressed as "your majesty," a style to which he could have no claim before the death of his father in 1766.

5. D. D. Devlin sees Peter Peebles as a grotesque parody of Redgauntlet himself: "Both of them have been ruined by the Law; and both of them spend their time and energy obsessively trying to resuscitate a lost and hopeless cause" (p. 94).

6. *The History of Henry Esmond,* ed. George Saintsbury (London, New York, and Toronto [1908]), Bk. II, ch. 9. All quotations follow the text of this edition.

7. Charles Whibley's perceptive comment is relevant: "Thackeray's characters are never further from reality than when they bear real names" (*William Makepeace Thackeray* [New York, 1903], p. 176).

8. Gordon N. Ray, *Thackeray: The Age of Wisdom* (New York, 1955), p. 178.

9. The same effect is served by the publisher's use of eighteenth-century details of typography and format in the first edition (Ray, p. 461, n.).

10. Geoffrey Tillotson, *Thackeray the Novelist* (Cambridge, 1954), pp. 1–4.

11. Ray, pp. 180–88.

12. Edwin Muir makes the same point about *Vanity Fair;* indeed it is the most important and conspicuous ingredient of Thackeray's art which leads Muir to classify *Vanity Fair* as what he calls a "novel of character" (*The Structure of the Novel* [London, 1928], p. 24. See also pp. 68, 84, 86, 124). In *Vanity Fair* the restriction to a spatial dimension is not so much a defect as a defining limit, but in *Esmond,* in which the historical dimension is insisted upon, it seems to me a serious limitation.

13. Charles Dickens, *Great Expectations* (The Nonesuch Dickens; Bloomsbury, 1937), p. 10.

14. Henri-A Talon, "Time and Memory in Thackeray's *Henry Esmond*," *Review of English Studies,* n.s. XIII (1962), 156.

Chapter IX: Structure and Idea in *Bleak House*

1. Edinburgh, 1937. Reprinted in *Majority, 1931–52,* ed. Hamish Hamilton (London, 1952).

2. Thomas A. Jackson, *Charles Dickens* (New York, 1938); Jack Lindsay, *Charles Dickens* (New York, 1950).

3. *Bleak House* (The Nonesuch Dickens; Bloomsbury, 1938), ch. 3. All quotations follow the text of this edition.

4. William S. Holdsworth, *Dickens as a Legal Historian* (New Haven, 1929), p. 91.

5. Sir William Blackstone, *Commentaries on the Laws of England* (London, 1800), III, 50–51.

6. Edmund Wilson, "Dickens: The Two Scrooges," *The Wound and the Bow* (Boston, 1941), p. 34.

7. See, for example, Norman Friedman, "The Shadow and the Sun: Notes toward a Reading of *Bleak House*," *Boston University Studies in English,* III (1957), 147–66; J. Hillis Miller, *Charles Dickens: The World of His Novels* (Cambridge, Mass., 1958), pp. 160–224; Louis Crompton, "Satire and Symbolism in *Bleak House*," *Nineteenth-Century Fiction,* XII (1957–58), 284–303.

8. As Edgar Johnson has argued, Dickens was not to do justice to the theme of the moral deterioration of the hero until *Great Expecta-*

tions (*Charles Dickens: His Tragedy and Triumph* [New York, 1952], p. 767).

9. "The Identity of Esther Summerson," *Modern Philology*, LV (1958), 252–58.

10. *Aspects of the Novel* (London, 1927), p. 108.

11. For example, M. E. Grenander, "The Mystery and the Moral: Point of View in Dickens's 'Bleak House,'" *Nineteenth-Century Fiction*, X (1955–56), 301–305.

12. "Point of View in Dickens," *PMLA*, LXV (1950), 94.

13. *Partial Portraits* (London, 1888), p. 388.

Chapter X: Afterword

1. Ian Watt, *The Rise of the Novel* (Berkeley and Los Angeles, 1957), p. 22.

2. I do not think it necessary to quibble about *whose* selection of detail we are concerned with in any given case. If we choose to think of the vision displayed and the consciousness recorded as belonging to Moll Flanders or Robinson Crusoe or Colonel Jack rather than to Defoe himself, we are merely asserting tacitly that the novel is to be read as a study of character, a kind of extended dramatic monologue.

3. Watt, p. 63.

4. Robert M. Adams, *Strains of Discord: Studies in Literary Openness* (Ithaca, N.Y., 1958), pp. 13, 206.

5. *The Journal of Sir Walter Scott* (New York, 1891), pp. 99–100 (entry dated March 14, 1826).

6. Henry James, "The Art of Fiction," *Partial Portraits* (London, 1888), p. 384.

Index